DISCOVERING DIFFERENCE

DISCOVERING DIFFERENCE

Contemporary Essays in American Culture

EDITED BY

CHRISTOPH K. LOHMANN

INDIANA UNIVERSITY PRESS

Bloomington & Indianapolis

94-562

Manufactured in the United States of America

Library of Congress Cataloging-in-Publication Data

Discovering difference : contemporary essays in American culture /
edited by Christoph K. Lohmann.
    p.   cm.
    Includes bibliographical references.
    ISBN 0-253-33607-4 (cloth). — ISBN 0-253-20815-7 (paper)
    1. American literature—History and criticism—Theory, etc.
2. United States—Civilization.   3. Pluralism (Social sciences)
I. Lohmann, Christoph K.
PS25.D56 1993
810.9'355—dc20   92-41566
        1 2 3 4 5   97 96 95 94 93

There can *be* no difference anywhere that doesn't *make* a difference elsewhere—no difference in abstract truth that doesn't express itself in a difference in concrete fact and in conduct consequent upon that fact. . . .

William James, *Essays in Pragmatism*

CONTENTS

INTRODUCTION   ix
Christoph K. Lohmann

Why Did the European Cross the Ocean?
A Seventeenth-Century Riddle   1
Myra Jehlen

American Literature Discovers Columbus   16
Terence Martin

Charlotte Temple's Remains   35
Eva Cherniavsky

The Underheard Reader in the Writing of the Old Southwest   48
James H. Justus

Poe, Plagiarism, and the Prescriptive Right of the Mob   65
Jonathan Elmer

Hawthorne and the Making of the Middle Class   88
Michael T. Gilmore

"Margaret Garner": A Cincinnati Story   105
Cynthia Griffin Wolff

Antinomies of Liberalism: The Politics of "Belief" and
the Project of Americanist Criticism   123
Cary Wolfe

**The Great Mother Domesticated: Sexual Difference and
Sexual Indifference in D. W. Griffith's *Intolerance***   148
  Michael Rogin

**Choicelessness as Choice: The Conflation of Racism
and Sexism**   189
  Carolyn A. Mitchell

CONTRIBUTORS   202

Introduction
Christoph K. Lohmann

The current state of literary and cultural studies in the humanities—especially English—makes the publication of a volume of diverse essays such as this a somewhat problematic venture. Both inside and outside academia, literature departments are seen as divided between two warring factions: the "traditionalists" and the "poststructuralists" or "multiculturalists." This perception has its origins in discussions and debates about new directions in scholarship and new curricular developments that have been carried on in colleges and universities—with much vigor and sometimes rancor—for well over a decade. Such discussions, especially when they are intended to lead to changes in course offerings, degree requirements, and tenure and promotion criteria, often have a polarizing effect. The differences in ideology or educational philosophy may be far more complex than a simple conservative/radical opposition, but the chief result may still be polarization.

When these issues of "campus politics" enter the larger political arena and therefore catch the attention of the electronic media, a kind of cops-and-robbers polarization is all but inevitable. It is one thing to *read* Allan Bloom's *The Closing of the American Mind* (1987) and Gerald Graff's *Professing Literature* (1987); but it is an altogether different experience to *see* these two authors on the *Oprah Winfrey Show*.[1] The image of Bloom's deliberately conservative three-piece-suit respectability opposite Graff's studied blue-jeans-and-open-collar insurgency reduces the complexity of issues to the point where viewers can make gratifyingly easy—because culturally conditioned—choices between "good guy" and "bad guy." Even attempts at providing more incisive television coverage—such as the twenty-minute appearances on the *MacNeil/Lehrer News Hour* by Dinesh D'Souza and Stanley Fish, Lynne Cheney and Catherine Stimpson—turn out to be debating contests in which image and soundbite determine "winners" and "losers."[2] Given the nature of the media and the political interests at stake after a dozen years of ascendant conservatism, there is little room for nuance in discussing what students should read or write in introductory literature courses; what are intellectually and socially significant topics for scholarly research or graduate seminars; and whether literary texts (if indeed there is such a distinct category) should be read for their universal artistic and humanistic value or for what they say about the social context (class, race, gender) that has produced them. The public clash between the leadership of the Modern Language Association and the head of the National Endowment for the Humanities over a particular candidate's nomination for appointment to the NEH, with all its preposterous charges and countercharges, was the most visible recent public staging of this reductive contest for media advantage between "traditionalists" representing the agenda of a conservative Republican administration and "radicals" profoundly opposed to that agenda.[3]

In this climate, most prospective readers are probably conditioned to expect some kind of clear ideological alignment in such a volume of essays as this.

Those outside the academy who are aware only of the sketchy outlines of the controversy presented in the press and on television will want to know on which side of the great political divide the following essays array themselves. And those who have themselves taken positions in academic debates among a wide range of views within the profession—deconstructionism, feminism, Marxism, psychoanalysis, neo-historicism, cultural studies, multiculturalism, and all their many overlaps and subdivisions—are also likely to look for a definite theoretical alignment among the essays, though probably preferring it to be congruent with their own particular intellectual (and political) interests and commitments. In other words, in a highly charged political context and an environment of strongly contested methodological and theoretical positions, a deliberately eclectic collection of essays may please neither the outside observer of the academic scene nor the specialist within the academy.

As my colleagues and I were planning the lecture series on which most of these essays are based, we naturally thought about this problem of focus. We soon came to the conclusion, however, that in keeping with the general ethos of our department as well as with the interests and needs of our students we should offer a wide variety of genuinely stimulating lectures rather than insist either on some sort of conservative/radical alignment or on any particular theoretical orthodoxy.[4] We wanted to gain new impulses for our own widely diverse teaching and writing by bringing to campus colleagues from other universities whose interests and scholarship were different from ours yet equally varied, and by joining them in this public discourse with contributions from our own ranks. We also intended to combine in this series presentations by mature scholars with distinguished reputations and papers by a group of younger colleagues, most of whom had recently completed their graduate work. In other words, we were—and remain—convinced that the variety of a lecture series featuring women and men, African Americans and European Americans, older and younger scholars, more traditional criticism and more theory-based analyses would not only be in keeping with what really goes on—or should go on—in English departments across the country but present a singular occasion for the discovery of difference.

Discovering difference is, of course, what literary and cultural studies have been all about for the last two decades. Derrida's elaboration of the notion of "différance"—that famous neologism indicating the way language (hence all conceptual, social, and subjective identity) differs from itself—has had a well-documented impact on the American academy. Moreover, in tandem with the influence of continental philosophical thought, the more immediately political pressures of a heterogeneous society have added new and urgent resonance to the question of cultural, racial, and gender differences. Yet for many, Derrida's understanding of difference has remained suspiciously unspecific, and the very concept of what counts as difference—socially, culturally, intellectually—has had no stable identity, but has been and remains contested terrain.[5]

In a quite different sense, the discovery of difference has had an equally profound and perhaps even more far-reaching effect on literary studies since the late 1960s: the discovery—in some instances the rediscovery—of texts different from those admitted to the traditional canon of "masterworks." These are texts that had been there all along but remained un(re)discovered or were deliberately ignored or dismissed as long as aestheticism and formalism had been the dominant modes of critical inquiry. Texts by women, people of color, and other marginalized groups have not only been made available for study and teaching, but have forced the profession both to redefine the term "text" itself and to develop new ways of reading and discussing them. This in turn has brought with it new approaches and provocatively different assessments of the literature constituting the traditional canon.

Moreover, the title of this collection of essays also refers to the experience we had in listening to the original lectures, an experience we hope readers of this volume will share with us: listening to different voices speaking to each other in open dialogue rather than for the purpose of waging intellectual turf battles. If close observers of the most recent developments in English departments are correct, it is the speaking and listening to each other — dialogic engagement rather than rhetorical aggression — that seems gradually to (re)emerge as the mode of discourse among ourselves. As David Laurence, who has his ear perhaps closer to the ground than anyone else in the profession, put it recently: "faculty members are thinking about new styles of disagreement — for argument conducted in other than combative tones. An effort, however tentative, is underway to reinvent collegial conversation or perhaps to transpose it into a different key."[6] One may dismiss this observation as mere wishful thinking, but if these essays can contribute even a little to a realization of such a wish, they will have served an excellent purpose.

Finally, as Myra Jehlen in her opening essay demonstrates, the discovery of difference has a particularly relevant meaning in 1992, the year in which the entire problematic of Columbus' "discovery" of the Western hemisphere is played out in events ranging from flag-waving celebrations and touristic extravaganzas to angry arguments and demonstrations by those who have been the victims of imperialism, exploitation, geno- and ecocide. There has been a flood of books and articles, magazine cover stories, and television programs on the quincentennial of this historic event, and this volume of essays is not intended to swell it. Yet we hope that reading these essays on a broad range of topics and a wide variety of texts and listening to the different voices of their authors imaginatively and attentively may be a step toward (re)discovering not only our diverse academic enterprise but America and its essential, constituent differences.

The ten essays that make up this volume are arranged in roughly chronological order of subject matter rather than in a distinct order of methodologies. However, Myra Jehlen's "Why Did the European Cross the Ocean?" opens the series not only because it deals with sixteenth-century French, Spanish, and Aztec writings related to the European conquest of the Americas, but because her essay analyzes the central issue of cultural "difference" and "otherness." Considering efforts to establish anti-imperialist definitions of cultural alterity by writers as diverse in purpose and historical time as Montaigne and Tzvetan

Todorov, Jehlen shows that the concept of "difference" tends to slide off into either "otherness" (which is based on taking one's own culture as the universal standard) or a "universalism" that is rooted in a well-meaning but vague sense of a shared fundamental humanity. In the important concluding section of her essay, she proposes to move the focus of this discussion away from an increasingly futile and problematic definition of cultural groups to a consideration of "zones of contest"—the areas and occasions where cultures encounter each other and, through such encounters, "seek to define each its own way."

Terence Martin's essay is immediately connected to these more theoretical considerations in its focus on the varying perceptions and encodings of the figure of Christopher Columbus in historical, literary, and popular texts from the eighteenth century to the present. American writers, he argues, have shaped Columbus to the "needs of the nation," or at least to those needs these writers perceived. Thus, a history of the representations of Columbus—as a hero with divine powers and qualities, who is given credit for establishing a "New World Eden"; as an agent of European imperialism, who bears the burden of exploitation and destruction—amounts to a history of conflicting and changing definitions of cultural and national identity. Martin's essay explores the range of representations that lies at and between those extremes and in so doing suggests the constructions of different national identities through the process of mythicizing a historical figure, rendering it in its full range from hero to villain.

Turning from the dominant male figure of Columbus to the heroine of popular eighteenth-century fiction, Eva Cherniavsky's essay on Susanna Rowson's *Charlotte Temple* focuses on issues of gender differences rather than on the problematic encounters between cultures. She argues that the emerging sentimental novel both assumed and contested a republican ideology that, while appearing in the rhetoric of "the general interest," reflected the logic of women's exclusion from the emerging political order. Rowson, in this analysis, uses the sentimental mode, the appeal to the affective sympathies of a middle-class female readership, to develop not only a critical distance from their culture's placement of women but a sense of "collective identity." Cherniavsky shows that Rowson undermines the ideal of republican motherhood, which was defined in terms of a domesticated, interiorized moral influence severely circumscribed in its relations to the economic and political institutions of society. *Charlotte Temple*, instead, "reveals a maternal succession that operates independently of republican standards of social legitimation" and thus prepares the way for many of the major American women authors of the nineteenth century.

Shifting from the American women writers of the Northeast to the intensely male humorists of the Old Southwest, James Justus' essay concentrates on the fictional constructions resulting from the encounter between regional folk culture and the standards of literary culture accepted by the authors of popular humorous sketches in the 1830s and 1840s. Justus shows that the Southwestern sketch, primarily written for an emerging mass readership, was largely shaped by well-established literary conventions of form and language rather than by the raw vernacular of the marginalized social groups from which the characters that populate the sketch were drawn. The enduring power of literary conventions is particularly noted in stories in which an educated traveler from the city meets a crude backwoodsman who talks of his exploits and adventures. The authors of such sketches faced the task of giving an amusing written account of a distinctly oral tradition for middle-class readers who shared the authors' assertion of cultural order rather than their characters' deviant language of cultural primitivism. While Justus recognizes the authors' participation in the hegemony of social power through their use of literary conventions of form and language, he demonstrates that that language is also modulated by the vernacular. Thus, he concludes, the language of the humorous sketch does not function "as a blatant rhetoric of difference"; rather, it suggests "a difference without grotesquerie," a difference that reflects the flexible class relationships of the Old Southwest.

Jonathan Elmer's essay on "William Wilson," Poe's most complex treatment of the double, can be said to deal with difference by looking at its inverted mirror image. Instead of developing his analysis of the double by maintaining such conventional opposites as identity and shadow, self (ego) and conscience (superego), originality and plagiarism, beginnings and endings, he presents what could be called "the discovery of nondifference" and the intense anxiety attending such a discovery in the age of emerging mass culture. Anxiety in regard to the originality of writing permeates Poe's preoccupation with plagiarism, just as "William Wilson" enacts an "agonized drama of self-writing" that probes the fantasy of the self's originality and the nightmarish recognition of its lack of identity because of its "origination from without, in others, by others." In showing that Poe's tale "tells the story of the origin's repetition of an always already misrecognized, and hence effaced, aboriginality," Elmer implicitly challenges some of the assumptions of social heterogeneity on which the other essays in this volume are based, not by denying difference as a constitutive principle of society but by unraveling Poe's paradoxial and perplexing treatment of questions of subjective identity, property, and textuality.

Michael Gilmore challenges much of contemporary literary and cultural criticism in his essay on *The Scarlet Letter* by arguing that the important new conceptual triad of race, gender, and class—which has largely defined the discovery of difference over the past two decades—has in fact neglected class as an analytical category. Taking, in this sense, a revisionist neo-historical approach, he focuses on the novel's representation of the emergence of middle-class culture. However, rather than rehearsing the argument of recent critics who have traced direct correspondences between Hawthorne's fiction and its social context, Gilmore emphasizes "the highly ambiguous character of that construction" and the instability of class loyalties in *The Scarlet Letter*. Partly because the definition of social class is closely linked to the considerable problems of gender in this novel—such as the inversion of Hester's and Dimmesdale's social attributions of gender characteristics—and partly because of Hawthorne's own uncertain class status, this instability is so great, Gilmore suggests, that the emerging middle class "threatens to come apart even as it comes into being."

Considerations of gender and race, rather than class, are at the center of Cynthia Griffin Wolff's telling of the "Margaret Garner" story, which she sees as representative of the story of the slave mother both in its harrowing content and in the silencing that has been enforced on it through the social and cultural conditions that make such stories "untellable." Wolff's telling performance itself, then, rather than being a theoretical and analytical engagement with the conditions that have stifled the voices of women in general and of women of color in particular, becomes the critical act, one that she sees as placing her narrative in a tradition of women writers extending from Harriet Beecher Stowe to Toni Morrison. In this sense, her contribution to this volume is in a somewhat different register from the other essays (one could say that it is more directly "historical"), yet the difference is more a matter of mode than substance. The author's concluding comments about the "community of women . . . united in . . . *making the 'story,'* " clearly suggest connections—albeit in newly configured circumstances that focus on race as much as on gender—to Eva Cherniavsky's discussion of the contesting strategies of earlier fictions by women. They also look forward to Carolyn Mitchell's analysis, at the end of this volume, of the recent silencing of Anita Hill's "untellable story" by the combined power of history, politics, and the media.

The preoccupation with difference takes a considerably more theoretical and philosophical turn with Cary Wolfe's critical assessment of the pervasiveness of liberal thought in Americanist scholarship, even in some recent manifestations of it that present themselves under the banner of a critique of liberalism. His exemplum is the recent work of Walter Benn Michaels, which he analyzes in terms of its indebtedness to principles of individual autonomy that are symptomatic of much of the enterprise of American cultural studies. The fundamental problem with liberalism, according to Wolfe, "is not that it cannot think difference . . . but rather that the difference it thinks is always reified"; in other words, its problem is its firm belief in an individual "freedom in which we are all 'the same' in spite of . . . our differences." Wolfe challenges Michaels' use of the concepts of "exchange" and "the market," which together provide the cornerstone of his economic interpretation in *The Gold Standard and the Logic of Naturalism* (1987). Michaels' liberal contention that our actions, choices, and beliefs are *either* completely constituted by the market *or* wholly free, needs to be abandoned, Wolfe concludes, if one is to give an adequate economic analysis of the social conditions and historical changes that have brought about the constitutive differences of American culture.

If Marxism provides the theoretical base for Wolfe's essay, it is a kind of neo-Freudian theory that is at the core of Michael Rogin's discussion of the social and cultural implications of D. W. Griffith's film *Intolerance.* Rogin's essay begins and ends with psychoanalytic observations on the projections of Griffith's sexual fantasies in his rendition of the Babylonian goddess Ishtar, thereby setting a frame for a wide-ranging, detailed, and richly suggestive analysis of the importance of Griffith's film(s) in a culture in which major problems of race, gender, and class intersected in the cinematic mass medium. Frequently connecting his discussion to his earlier essay on *Birth of a Nation* and, hence, to the inextricable link between race and sexuality, Rogin concentrates here both on Griffith's conscious intentions in his treatment of "the New Woman" in a modern, urban America and on the ways in which unconscious cultural and psychological factors undermined these intentions. While "Griffith wanted to bring female sexuality, public pleasure, and the family together, . . . he could not do so," and the result is a technically brilliant and innovative film that offers a bifurcated stereotype of women: the glorified sexual libertine and the vilified spinster/lesbian. Thus, *Intolerance,* while representing "Griffith's last stand for the modern metropolis and the New Woman, shows the sources and the limits of his modernism."

Rogin's discussion of the matrix of racial and sexual taboos and fantasies, Wolff's concern with "untellable stories," and Cherniavsky's interest in contesting the role of women as defined by a male political hegemony—are all motifs implicitly revisited and reconsidered in the very contemporary context on which Carolyn Mitchell focuses in her concluding essay. If popular fiction, newspaper accounts, and film supplied the cultural texts subjected to critical analysis in the preceding essays, it is television and the American mass audience that Mitchell scrutinizes here. Using concepts of modern film theory, she "reads" both the visible and the "unseen" images of the Senate hearings featuring Clarence Thomas, Anita Hill, Virginia Thomas, and John Danforth, and she argues that it is the "subliminal history" of slavery, miscegenation, and lynching that the televised hearings invoked and that the television cameras manipulated. The victims of this "politics of the camera," she concludes, were not only Hill (primarily) and Thomas, but the viewing public, for whom the only available choice is the choicelessness of the manipulated and manipulating camera.

In suggesting some of the connections among the essays in this volume and in pointing out that there is a certain formalistic shapeliness in the movement from the early literature of European conquest to the dominant patriarchal figure of Senator Danforth on American TV screens in 1991, I do not wish to countermand the argument for diversity and difference with which this introduction began. The differences of subject matter and the differences in theoretical assumptions and methodologies remain the chief characteristic—and, I hope, value—of this collection. They reflect, moreover, the realities of our lives as scholars, teachers, students, and participants in the dynamics of American culture.[7] They are also an expression of our hope—if I may for once speak collectively and with William James—that "There can *be* no difference anywhere that doesn't *make* a difference elsewhere—no difference in abstract truth that doesn't express itself in a difference in concrete fact and in conduct consequent upon that fact. . . ." It is conduct, scholarly and civil, rather than mere theory, that we hope will increasingly be shaped by a discovery of difference.

NOTES

1. "How Dumb Are We" was aired on the *Oprah Winfrey Show,* on November 2,

1988. It dealt with the problem of "cultural illiteracy" and the question whether college humanities courses have contributed to what Bloom calls "the closing of the American mind," or—as Graff argued—whether they have been too traditional and Eurocentric to meet the interests and needs of an increasingly multicultural population.

2. MacNeil/Lehrer featured three segments devoted to a discussion of multiculturalism and "political correctness" in June 1991. D'Souza, former editor of the *Dartmouth Review* and author of *Illiberal Education: The Politics of Race and Sex on Campus* (1991), appeared on June 18; Stanley Fish, Chair and Professor of English at Duke University, on June 19; and Lynne Cheney, Bush-appointed Chairman of the National Endowment for the Humanities, and Catharine Stimpson, Professor of English and Dean of the Graduate School at Rutgers University, as well as the 1990 president of the Modern Language Association, appeared together on June 21. For the transcript of the D'Souza interview and for statements by others involved in the debate of these issues (including Fish and Stimpson), see *Debating P. C.: The Controversy Over Political Correctness on College Campuses,* ed. Paul Berman (New York: Dell, 1992).

3. The controversy over the nomination of Professor Carol Iannone of New York University for membership on the board of the NEH raged for months. Several scholarly organizations, including the Modern Language Association, opposed her nomination on the grounds that she did not meet the standards of academic distinction that the enabling legislation for the NEH called for. Her supporters, on the other hand, argued that her academic credentials were superior. Each side, naturally, accused the other of hiding a political agenda behind the smokescreen of a supposedly objective evaluation of her scholarship. See "Iannone Smoke, N. E. H. Fire," *New York Times* (July 14, 1991), Sect. 4: 18, and the debate between Lynne Cheney and Catharine Stimpson on the MacNeil/Lehrer program, June 21, 1991. Later that year, Iannone's nomination was defeated.

4. As Gerald Graff recently argued in an excellent short essay, "the way to turn an ugly scene of anger and recrimination into a useful and productive debate is to bring our present disagreements into our classrooms. The way to protect students from intimidation by dogmatists of the left, the right, and the center is to expose them to the debates among these factions." "What Has Literary Theory Wrought?" *The Chronicle of Higher Education* (12 February, 1992): A48.

5. I want to thank Jonathan Elmer for his help in defining "différance." He would have added to this definition the point that the lack of specificity in Derrida's understanding of difference is "in ironic conformity to the logic of his notion, which would insist that 'différance,' too, differ from itself."

6. David Laurence, "From the Editor," *ADE Bulletin* 100 (1991): 1.

7. While I do not agree with Frederick Crews's most recent caricaturization of "the New Americanists" and their recent ascendency in English departments ("these young academics [who] launch their arguments from a base of egalitarian pieties about race, class, and gender as routinely as the cold war liberals started from formalist aesthetics"), I share with him an "unshaken allegiance to liberalism in the broadest meaning of that term"—a liberalism that values and encourages diversity not only as a subject of inquiry but as a shared practice in our professional lives. Contrary to Crews's description of the current state of affairs, my own experience suggests that this standard of liberalism still prevails far more than has been acknowledged in recent discussions. See Crews, "The New Americanists," *New York Review of Books* (September 24, 1992), 32-34; this essay will appear as the Introduction to his forthcoming collection of essays, *The Critics Bear It Away: American Fiction and the Academy.*

DISCOVERING DIFFERENCE

Why Did the European Cross the Ocean? A Seventeenth-Century Riddle

Myra Jehlen

Flaubert's *Dictionary of Received Ideas* offers, for the entry "Colonies (our),"
a cautionary definition: "Register sadness in speaking of them." With this recommendation, the author, as is his wont, mocks his compatriots of good conscience, ridiculing hypocrisies that mask horrors. The empire here joins romance, bourgeois marriage, and the excellence of provincial virtue in
Flaubert's catalogue of foundational falsehoods of the nineteenth century. In
his time, the creed of empire was as basic to French and European right-think-
ing as that of domesticity, was indeed the complement of domesticity since the
common wisdom held until well into this century that an imperial impulse was
the very pulse of Western man and colonies the natural fruit of his overflowing
virility. Though the West's civilizing mission might occasionally lapse and was
often disappointed (inducing sadness), colonizing lay in the order of things and
those who questioned that order were alienated souls who probably also had
doubts about conjugal love.

Now, however, at the close of the millennium and concurrently nightfall in
the empire whose day began five centuries ago, most Westerners living through
the end of their era have taken skepticism for their familiar. If the empire
seemed to rest on a natural foundation when it encircled the globe, for us who
mainly fear having made the whole world unnatural, history is too clearly of
human provenance. Even the annexation of the American continents, where
Europeans made themselves so thoroughly at home they considered removing
the former inhabitants just housekeeping, no longer seems so self-evident. It is
not obvious anymore that the Spanish, the French, and the English would naturally impose their civilizations upon two continents on the other side of the
world. The conquest of America suddenly needs explaining.

At the same time, out of the empire's penumbra, the civilizations it long
shadowed are emerging with renewed clarity. Indeed these formerly eclipsed
civilizations themselves, particularly through the narrative of their colonization, seem to be coining the dominant idiom—as one would have said, the
King's English—of the current international conversation. Postcolonial recu-
perations and reconstructions are providing the organizing terms of an increas-

ingly influential revisionary history that attempts to turn the analytical tables on Europe itself (and as well on Europe-in-America). Such a refraction of Europe through the colonies is perfectly in line, of course, since European civilization is inconceivable without its empire. Equally, the experience of colonization fundamentally reshaped the colonized; so we ought not to be surprised if, even as it dissolves, the empire proves as adhesive as ever, conquest and colonization remaining central issues of national self-definition for former imperialists and imperialized alike. But though unsurprising, this adhesiveness needs noting, both in itself as a political and cultural phenomenon and because it glosses one of the key-words of the current analytical discourse, the word "difference."

In turn, "difference" glosses another key-word, "other," glosses it by attempting to replace it as oppressive to those so designated.[1] Naming them "other" seems to cast the speaker's cultural interlocutors in an inferior position by rendering them mere negative quantities defined by an opposition to which they do not contribute. The term "different" proposes to right this imbalance by granting others identities of their own. With the substitution of difference for otherness, it is hoped that the imperial monologue becomes a two-sided exchange. Describing oneself or one's kind as "other," one would not only represent the very meaning of alienation but be incapable of further self-definition and even speech; while to declare oneself "different" leads logically to self-description, even to monologue. Let's just say "Rousseau" and move on.

Derridean deconstruction lends a certain formulaic rigor to the notion of difference as part of the neologism "différance." Différance, gerundial and antinomian, combines two verbs, to differ and to defer, to explain how (also why) no definition can ever attain a definitive authority. In time, difference is the stuff of Zeno's paradox, preventing any account from reaching a final truth. The race that never ends cannot go to the swift. In space, difference denies the centrality of any point of view and the all-encompassingness of any horizon. All this amounts to denying the ground for the transcending self-sufficiency that authorizes designating the Emersonian "Not-Me" as "the other." To return to our original vocabulary, difference is the anti-colonial response to the imperial history of otherness.

Students of difference might be said to be the reluctant heirs of Europe's late empire, dismantling its house and marking for return piles of looted goods. Edward Said's analysis of "orientalism" suggests why the metaphysical goods have been especially difficult to catalogue. In the American colonies, a mass of European presumption overwhelmed Amerindian cultures, perhaps beyond extricating. The arriving Europeans were so intent on taking over that few even registered the indigenous cultures. The Discoverer himself began his first letter home not with what he found but what he did to it. "I reached the Indian sea," Columbus reported, "where I discovered many islands, thickly peopled, of which I took possession without resistance in the name of our most illustrious Monarch, by public proclamation and with unfurled banners."[2] (Proving, in this invocation of sonorous Spanish and snappy standards deployed on an innocent beach, that when you have the upper hand you can afford to look ridiculous.) Columbus' admirably succinct account of his landfall would do as the first example in a primer of imperial prose. "I reached . . . I discovered . . . I took," he writes; the objects of my actions were both abundant and anonymous, "many islands, thickly peopled," an indefinite, possibly infinite plenitude lacking only the agency to resist. Therefore imposing my will, which is the will of white civilization, was only natural and right. "I took possession" of this latent world and named it: in making it mine I made *it*, imparting to it political capability, bringing it into the Law. I baptized it in the name of "our most illustrious Monarch" with the ceremonies and symbols in which civilization inheres, with rhetoric and flags. I acted as a prime mover, creating order and meaning, making objects into subjects; or rather subjects into objects and thus subjects of the Spanish Crown.

An accounting follows: "The inhabitants of both sexes in this island . . .," Columbus notes, "go always naked as they were born, with the exception of some of the women. . . . None of them . . . are possessed of any iron, neither have they weapons, being unacquainted with, and indeed incompetent to use them, not from any deformity of body (for they are well-formed), but because they are timid and full of fear." The lineaments of the benign savage emerge, his simplicity, honesty, and rather foolish generosity. Withal he is not stupid "but of very clear understanding" demonstrated in one or two "admirable descriptions" local informants have contributed to Columbus' report. So far so good; the expropriation of the New World—which Columbus will never quite recognize as such—is progressing unproblematically through the arrogation not only of the Indians' land but of their intellectual resources which, in these first passages describing their cooperative quiescence, is simply another piece of the local treasure. Thus far too the difference between Indians and Spanish is both absolute and inert, that is, without implications beyond those that pertain to the New World generally as a place of yet untapped resources. At this point the relations between conqueror and conquered are still not political. One does not have political relations with a beach or a tree; in Columbus' first *Letter*, the inhabitants of San Salvador are not even properly other, do not quite yet comprise a negative term.

But when subsequent explorations discover a second and much different group of islanders, the bloodthirsty Caribs who will shortly lend their name to coin the appalling "cannibal," the process of mastering foreign peoples reveals itself more complicated than just taking over their land. The Arawaks are morally uninflected, benign like the local climate but not actually "good," until they come to contrast with the "bad" Caribs. This moral differentiation entails more than a refinement, a transformation of categories: the bad Caribs reveal the Indians as human beings not fruit-trees. The rhetoric of oppression often characterizes victims as in- or sub-human but the meaning of that accusation is worth investigating further. "Inhuman" may not be meant literally but, like "unthinkable," as judgment rather than fact. Were inhumanity a fact it would preclude a self-justifying condemnation. The enemy on the battlefield arouses not only repugnance but anger, resentment, indignation, rage. These emotions directed at inanimate objects or animals involve an ancillary anthropomorphism. In the same way, the Caribs/cannibals need to be granted a portion of humanity before they can be seen worthy of annihilation for their inhumanity.[3] Thus it is their categorical humanity that places them beyond the pale; savagery has its ethics just like civilization. Discovering the humanity of the New World savages when he finds that some are actively evil, Columbus tells a story ironically paralleling that of the Fall in which being bad similarly achieves a distinct human status defined basically as the capacity to choose between good and evil. The irony, of course, lies in acknowledging that the Indians are categorically people as a step toward enslaving them; down that road, the vision of the New World as potentially a second Eden will inspire the genocide of its first inhabitants whose difference from the Europeans is now qualified (limited), in that they *are* human, but insuperable and fraught with implications for their violent suppression. To kill Indians with conviction, Columbus had to attribute to them a mode of life whose very evil made it basically commensurate with his own.

That is a sword that cuts both ways. With the edge sharpened by a view of the savages as unworthy of humane treatment, it kills them with moral impunity. But Flaubert's ancestor, Montaigne, honed its other edge in an essay entitled "Of Cannibals" (1578-80) which argues that bad as New World anthropophagites may be, we (sixteenth-century Frenchmen) are worse, more deeply fallen and farther alienated from our common human nature. Like us but unlike us, the cannibals deserve freedom for their, not otherness (since they are comparable), but difference. Human like us and therefore deserving humane treatment, they have an entirely different civilization which, to behave humanely, we ought to respect.

The concept of cultural difference as an autonomous, self-generated mode appears new to us, even post-new, but it dates back at least to Montaigne's response to what he too saw as a lethal notion of otherness. The response was not entirely successful, however, for a closer look will reveal that Montaigne's anti-colonial notion of difference remains tied to an irresistibly emerging sense of European centrality; that indeed, for all he resists, "difference" tends perhaps irresistibly to slide toward "otherness."[4]

Yet, in "Of Cannibals," Montaigne sets out precisely to separate difference and otherness, explicitly rejecting the attitude that makes one's kind the universal standard. A returning colonizer's tales of the wild men of Brazil have had a contrary effect on Montaigne. "I think," he muses, "there is nothing barbarous and savage in that nation, from what I have been told, except that each man calls barbarism whatever is not his own practice; for indeed it seems we have no other test of truth and reason than the example and pattern of the opinions and customs of the country we live in." Hopelessly provincial, we are convinced that where we are is the epitome of all good things. "*There* is always the perfect religion, the perfect government, the perfect and accomplished manners in all things" (152).[5]

Recent discoveries of alien peoples leading vastly different lives ought to be teaching us that other ways can also make sense, even better sense. A Brazilian

tribe of cannibals surely represents the epitome of difference,[6] yet these prover-
bial pariahs of civilized society nonetheless have their virtues. Montaigne finds
much about them to admire, like their honesty and generosity, their innocence
of any lust for riches. Comparison does not flatter Europe, for doing their
worst, the cannibals still appear better people than the French. "I think there is
more of barbarity," Montaigne observes, referring to certain contemporary
practices, "in eating a man alive than in eating him dead; and in tearing by
tortures and the rack a body still full of feeling, in roasting a man bit by bit, in
having him bitten and mangled by dogs and swine . . . than in roasting and
eating him after he is dead" (155). "We surpass them in every kind of barbarity" (156). Instead of their masters, we ought to be the cannibals' pupils. But
we are too parochial to learn from others; all that Montaigne's compatriots
seem capable of recognizing in the cannibal culture is that "They don't wear
breeches" (159).

Five years later, when Montaigne again took up the theme of cultural
difference, it was not to mock but to mourn. "Of Coaches" (1585-88) denounces the Spanish slaughter of the Incas in terms at first familiar from the
cannibals essay. Children in an infant world, the Incas differ from us by their
proximity to nature. They are innocent of our civilized perversions, simple
and direct where we lie and cheat, loyal and true where we will resort to any
guile to satisfy our bloated greed. Beyond this precocious projection of the concept of the noble savage—it will be another century before Rousseau codifies
him—Montaigne moves in this essay toward a still more precocious anti-colonialism. True, he does not formulate this opposition to the conquest of America
as an absolute principle, since he can imagine a worthy and even improving
colonization by the ancient Greeks and Romans (694-95). But these benign tu-
tors, far from scorning the Incas as other, would have actually helped difference unfold, "strengthened and fostered the good seeds that nature had produced in them . . ." (694).

The Spanish, on the other hand, are nowhere more vile than in their insistence that the humiliated Incas abandon their gods along with their goods and
lands. Having used every form of treachery to defeat the Peruvian king, his
ignoble captors "permitted [him] to buy his way out of the torment of being
burned alive by submitting to baptism at the moment of execution" (696).
Montaigne opposed conversion at a time when it was the empire's major ethical justification. Even Bartolomé de Las Casas did not abandon the missionary
pursuit when he saw where it could lead; but Las Casas, for all his outrage
at the brutality of Spanish exploitation, disputed the administration of the
empire, not its existence. More radically, for Montaigne the Incas' "indomita-
ble ardor" in "the defense of their gods" represents an equal capacity for
autonomy.

In fact the Incas are generally not at all inferior to their invaders, even on
the battlefield where, Montaigne speculates, "if anyone had attacked them on
equal terms, with equal arms, experience and numbers, it would have been just
as dangerous for him as in any other war we know of, and more so." Unequal
odds decided the outcome of the battle, not unequal opponents. "Eliminate

[the] disparity, I say, and you take from the conquerors the whole basis of many victories" (694). Military disparity is not to be taken as a sign of the sort of cultural/racial inferiority that Europeans invoked to justify colonization; disparity does not imply a disparaging difference. The problem, however, lies in the converse, that difference does seem to engender a disparaging disparity. Over the course of the narrative of the Indian defeat, the notion of difference as the ground for arguing against colonization develops complications that were not evident in the mere statement of the principle. Never a *justification* for the subjection of the Incas, difference in "Of Coaches" does tend to become an *explanation*.

Montaigne's essays are typically labyrinthine and "Of Coaches" especially so. Tracing the singular path of the idea of Indian difference requires a plan of the whole. The essay, then, starts with the observation that the classics are not always reliable; even Aristotle and Plutarch were capable of reporting legend as truth. This bringing to mind that not only the figurative but the actual ground under one's feet is not always entirely firm reminds Montaigne that he is phobically afraid of falling which can make his travels unpleasant, particularly in swaying vehicles like boats and coaches. We have arrived at our coaches. These come in many varieties including war-coaches drawn in ancient times by all sorts of odd beasts—stags, dogs, naked women, ostriches. To be sure, it was the plebes who paid for such princely displays, but still, they were magnificent in those days and Montaigne doubts we will see their like again.

On the other hand history can take unexpected turns. Here, for example, it has just revealed a whole new world. With this Montaigne enters on the account of the Incas as above and the essay ends with an anecdote proving the Incas' moral excellence in their devotion to their king. As Montaigne tells it, the Inca monarch rode to his last battle on a golden litter borne by trusted warriors. As fast as the Spaniards killed these bearers others took their places so that the king would never have fallen had not a Spanish soldier, raised astride his horse to the height of the litter, seized the king bodily and dashed him to the ground. Montaigne's fear of falling makes this episode especially dramatic and, recalling his earlier discussion of various means of conveyance, not an absolutely incoherent conclusion to an essay about coaches.

One may ask what coaches have to do with Peru in the first place? A Montaigne scholar, Marcel Gutwirth, has proposed a link whereby coaches represent a crucial difference between Spaniard and Inca: coaches, that is, wheels. The Spanish have wheels and the Incas don't.[7] To be sure, Montaigne hastens to acknowledge, the Incas have accomplished amazing things without the wheel, notably a magnificent road from Quito to Cuzco that is easily the match of any in Europe. Roads being the trademark of the Roman empire, this is a most telling example of Inca achievement. Wheel-less, therefore, the Incas are different but not lesser. Indeed in another sense, they are different and therefore greater, since it takes a greater effort to build roads without pulleys or carts.

Exactly here, however, even as Montaigne directly affirms the equal worth of Inca civilization, the ambiguity of that affirmation begins to emerge. This ambiguity lies in the blurred status of wheel-lessness—an *occasion* for Inca virtue that is sliding toward becoming its *condition*. Does the lack of wheels merely provide an occasion for demonstrating Inca virtue (which exists independently of such occasions)? or does the need to overcome their wheel-less-ness generate a special virtue not extant among those possessed of wheels? The problem with that question, of course, lies in the very asking, for the Incas, lacking the concept of the wheel, cannot query that lack themselves. Only Montaigne can pose that question and, to make things worse, by posing it, he demonstrates not only the epistemological ascendancy of having wheels but the additional power that accrues to those who know that others don't.

In other words, while Montaigne insists on the fundamental equality of all human beings (and proves that conviction when he shudders in identification with the Inca king's fall), this equality turns out to be limited to the fundamentally human. The Incas are only *fundamentally* human: the technology of the litter only extends the body. But the Spanish control, in addition to their fundamental humanity, a technology that transforms their bodily energy into something of which bodies on their own are incapable. Montaigne may be terrified when he imagines himself falling from a litter but, thank Heaven, litters are not his problem which is, fearsome enough but not fatal, coaches: witness the title of his essay. The Indian litter-bearers are exceedingly brave, as the workers who build the Mexican road are surpassingly skilled, but all in vain. From being the *occasion* for virtue, then its *condition,* lacking the wheel has become the sign of its *futility.* Tragically and to its shame, the modern world has rendered certain virtues futile. But inasmuch as these virtues are associated with the technology of litters, it is difficult to regret them in the sense of wanting them back for ourselves.

While coaches embody the corruption of Europe, they also carry the weight of a history that has traded innocence for knowledge. Cowering in his coach, Montaigne dreads the wheels that the Incas lack; dreads as well the technology that will destroy the Incas. But since fear is here the measure of knowledge, he can hardly wish himself ignorantly fearless, however brave. As "Of Coaches" develops the concept of difference beyond "Of Cannibals," it now figures as the remainder in a subtraction problem, so that the difference between the Spanish and the Incas equals the reason for the latters' defeat, a difference that, as the ground for anti-colonialism, is as shaky as a coach.

In the twentieth century, Europe's former colonies being at least nominally independent, anti-colonialism means cultural liberation. And since this new definition makes the recognition of difference central, what we might call the problem of the wheel becomes commensurately greater. Almost four hundred years after Montaigne, Tzvetan Todorov subtitled his book on *The Conquest of America, The Question of the Other* and defined its subject as "the discovery *self* makes of the *other.*"[8] Todorov's purpose is the same as Montaigne's, to denounce the concept of the other as a chief weapon of colonial outrage, and, revisiting essentially the same site, he writes about the fall of the Aztec empire a decade before the Inca. But to explain the defeat of a civilization in many respects easily Europe's match, the late twentieth-century Todorov is unimpressed by technology and seeks the determining force of history rather in culture, specifically in a profound difference (as he sees it) in the Aztec and Spanish conceptions of language and communication.

In brief, his thesis is that the Aztecs could not counter the alien assault for lack of a concept of the other; while the Spanish in their encounter with the New World discovered otherness and how to manipulate it. Unlike the Spanish who, for all their religiosity, saw themselves first as men among men, the Aztecs located themselves first in relation to a sacred plan whose laws they were to implement. This precedence of universal over human order was expressed with special force in their conception of language as the articulation of a world order. For the Spanish, language functioned instead as an instrument of human relations and a means of reordering things to their liking. In a word, the Spanish knew how to lie. Lying is language taking power by overthrowing rightful meanings, and lying won the Spanish their empire. In control of communication, Cortes plunged his prey into fatal confusion. Control of communication, in Todorov's account, is a second Spanish wheel.

As appalled as Montaigne by the ravages of colonization and more knowing, Todorov regrets the epistemological imbalance that gave the conquistadors their bloody victory. But to understand this unhappy event, he has had himself to know something of which the vanquished were ignorant, and this imbalance he can hardly regret. For while knowing is associated with the guilt of the conquest, ignorance was and remains annihilative. Remains so because Todorov could not write his book nor we read it without knowing (indeed taking as fact) what the Spanish knew.

Is Todorov then doing what he denounces, rendering the Aztecs as Europe's negatives? This is certainly not what he intends. Indeed, some time after *The Conquest of America*, he took up the issue explicitly, arguing in response to an essay by Abdul R. JanMohamed[9] that we should be careful not to exaggerate differences. Todorov finds JanMohamed's stipulation that understanding the other required " 'negating one's very being' " "excessively pessimistic." Even if " 'one's culture is what formed that being,'. . . human beings are not trees, and they can be uprooted without provoking such dramatic consequences," he insists. For "We are not only separated by cultural differences; we are also united by a common human identity, and it is this which renders possible communication, dialogue, and, in the final analysis, the comprehension of Otherness — it is possible precisely because Otherness is never radical."[10]

In this concern that difference when it is cast as absolute precludes precisely the interactions it is intended to engender, Todorov joins a growing number of scholars, many themselves descended from or representing the peoples Europe designated "Other," who are dissatisfied with studies that discover only divergence and distinctiveness.[11] Though these scholars are presumably the beneficiaries of a concept of difference that returns to them the agency of their own interpretation, they have been finding that what is represented as autonomy often turns out to be exclusion: that difference too easily reverses into otherness. The Native-American writer Michael Dorris has complained that "the paradigm of European confusion"[12] which renders Indians "objects of mystery and speculation, not people" still organizes a current scholarship willy-nilly producing images that are the complementary opposites of the old myths. We need to "stipulate only a few givens," he writes with some impatience. "That human beings *qua* human beings, where and whenever they may live, share some traits; that Indians were and are human beings—then we have at least a start." And Dorris concludes his essay by urging that we "begin the hard, terribly difficult and unpredictable quest of regarding [Indians] as human beings."[13]

It is hard to disagree with such a program, but even harder to carry it out. The principle that one should explicate people's differences (in Dorris' words) "within the configurations of their own cultures," while at the same time "regarding [others] as human beings," seems clear enough stated abstractly, but its practice is another matter. Unfortunately, Todorov does not reflect upon his *Conquest of America* in relation to his later postulate that "Otherness is never radical." But the otherness of the Aztecs, defined as their inability to comprehend otherness, constitutes the very definition of "radical." At the same time, what content can one imagine imparting to the universal term "human being" that would render its universality genuinely multiform? If in the past the notion of the universal human being served the colonizing enterprise, as the anti-colonial scholarship has been arguing for the last two decades, what is now going to make universality useful on the other side? What is a "human being" when he's at home? how do we keep him civil when he goes visiting?

In short, the universalities upon which Todorov falls back in order to temper radical otherness and transform it into relative difference are both vague with regard to future incarnations and discouraging in their past. Moreover, the logic that invokes universality as the counter to difference is the logic of otherness which reduces differences to an abstract negativity; and it is difficult to see how the same logic can organize an account of others that makes them *more* autonomously substantial. In that difference *is* substance or it collapses into otherness, resorting to universalities in order to correct extreme difference seems inauspicious, methodologically as well as politically. To qualify difference we need to know more about its content, not less. More content, in other words more history. Let's go back then and look more substantively at the history of the Aztecs.

As it happens, it is possible to reconstruct the Aztecs' own sense of their place in the history of American colonization with relative conviction in that, exceptionally among New World cultures at the time of the discovery, they had a written language in which they produced a conquest literature of their own.[14] The earliest of these Nahuatl writings by Aztec priests and wise men date from only seven years after the fall of Mexico. Their complicated account of the two-year war preceding the fall offers some unexpected perspectives.

For one thing, it comes as a surprise to find that, contrary to the European tradition of the first encounters, the Aztecs are not unambiguously impressed. Though amazed, as who would not have been, by their first sightings of the bedecked and bemetaled Spanish, they retain some critical distance from which they find the response to their welcoming gifts of gold and precious feathers less than inspiring. "They picked up the gold and fingered it like monkeys," recalls an Aztec observer. "Their bodies swelled with greed, and their hunger was ravenous; they hungered like pigs for that gold. They snatched at the golden ensigns, waved them from side to side and examined every inch of them." In this depiction the Spanish are flatly bestial, not super- but sub-human. Repugnantly different, others outside the pale: "They were like one who speaks a barbarous tongue," the writer continues: "everything they said was in a barbarous tongue."[15] In other words, they were of the category of person with whom by definition it is impossible to communicate. From the Aztec point of view, not surprisingly, it is the Spanish who cannot communicate.

At other times recounted in other passages, it seems true, as tradition has it, that the Aztecs greeted the Spanish like gods, and overall the Mexicans perhaps understood their enemy less well than the reverse. But passages like the one just cited suggest that the Aztecs' perceptions were not entirely clouded, indicating that we might usefully look for other explanations besides cultural incapacity even for their misunderstandings. Explanations, for instance, like the fact that the invaders knew whence they came and to what end; while for the invaded the sudden irruption of strange peoples from unknown lands was an impenetrable mystery. The Aztecs' epistemological passivity seems a not unlikely response to impenetrable mysteries. Beyond this, granting that control of communication was a decisive factor in the Spanish victory, it seems well to note that Cortes controlled communication in large part through his control of a translator/interpreter, a slave woman whom he acquired upon landing on the Mexican coast and who then accompanied him on his progress to the capital city. Motecuhzoma not only did not have a translator of his own, he depended on Cortes': by this alone the Mexicans lost linguistic control to the point that they heard their own language speaking an enemy meaning. In the process of making available the world of the Mexicans along with their language, La Malinche, who is still referred to in Mexico as "the traitor" (and more ambiguously the "fucked one"), at several critical junctures in the campaign took the lead in manipulating the Indians, if not into submission, certainly into confusion. Alterity was not a mystery at least for her.[16]

Politics and biology can provide two other reasons for the Mexican defeat. The Aztecs were nomadic intruders who arrived in the region and established their city only around 1325. Thus the Aztec empire which at its height ruled several million people was rising, ironically, at the same time as the European. The opponents at the siege of Mexico City were politically more alike than either realized; and their resemblance may have worked as much as their difference to the advantage of the Spanish who were able to forge alliances with those the Aztecs had recently vanquished. By the end of the war the situation looked little like the puzzling story of a few hundred Spaniards in alien territory conquering hundreds of thousands of Indians on their home ground. The sides were probably roughly balanced, Cortes commanding, against no more than 300,000 Aztecs, at least 200,000 (some suggest 225,000) Indians in addition to his own men with their far more destructive arms.[17]

Finally, Alfred Crosby has argued that biology was the decisive factor, devastating the Mexican society so quickly that the role of technology and politics was essentially moot.[18] The Aztecs repelled the first Spanish assault on the city causing such losses among the attackers that their defeat became legend as "la triste noche." Upon his return, Cortes was reinforced not only by new Indian recruits but, within the walls, by the plague which, according to accounts on both sides, had heaped rotting corpses in all the streets of the city and left virtually none to defend it.

The factors suggested by Aztec documents as equally important in the conquest of Mexico as cultural difference are not inconsiderable: the possession of specific knowledge of the origins, the purposes, and the motives of the enemy; the balance of military force measured both in arms and men; the natural imbalance derived from the Aztecs' lack of biological immunity. Todorov stipulates all these, but seems not to consider them decisive in that they do not figure in his explanation of the final outcome. On the other hand, figuring them in profoundly changes the entire picture; though the Aztec defeat seems no less historically likely, it no longer appears inherently inevitable. Neither passive nor helpless, the Aztecs represent themselves in their own writings acting, in relation to overwhelming odds, but with reason (with their own reasons) and will.

In traditional accounts of the Aztecs as helpless before the Spanish, one of the pieces of evidence is an account to be found in their conquest literature of omens said ten years before to have predicted the coming apocalypse. Of course the omens could be just that, in which case fate rules the world and there's nothing further to say about it. If, however, the omens are the creature of the conquest, there is another way to read them than as evidence of helplessness. For while they prophesy doom, they also hold out a certain hope. George Orwell wrote that who controls the past controls the future.[19] The catastrophic future predicted in the Aztec omens takes place, in relation to the invention of the omens themselves, in the present. The effect is to release the future—even if only for oppression—by restoring purposeful direction to a present that would otherwise appear to be the end of the world. If the present has grown out of the past, the future can be expected to grow out of the present, to *have* a future. In the omens, therefore, the Aztecs can be seen demonstrating instead of epistemological passivity, something like an opposite historical capability, one that is more congruent with the picture of interactions that emerges from their own accounts than with the view that they were culturally paralyzed.[20]

All these ways in which Aztecs and Spanish were not only unlike but also like, both relations, moreover, evolving over the course of their conflict,[21] seriously complicate notions of both difference and universality. Colonizer and colonized emerge as similar as they are different in that they profit and lose in the same ways from common situations: the imperialist Aztecs, for instance, lose out when their history in the region makes willing allies for Cortes who, when he wins, will kill and exploit like the Aztecs before him. On the other hand, it is difficult to talk of the Aztecs and the Spanish as simply universally "human" and let it go at that in the presence of their fundamentally different visions of the universe and of humanity's place in it. In that context, the term "universally human" just does not seem very useful.

This said, however, a solution or more modestly a strategy may be emerging out of these very difficulties. Dubbing them different, one reflects that they came together in related ways; dubbing them all human beings, one contrarily wants to point to the basic issues on which they oppose one another. In both cases, however, there is a common denominator which is precisely the commonality of their encounter, the common ground they construct, new to both, and on which they are neither the same nor different but only inextricably related; indeed neither the same nor different *through* their relation.

I would suggest that the encounter of Aztecs and Spanish offers the terms for avoiding, as the orientalist, exoticist tendencies of the concept of the other (the different) emerge, falling back into an equally worrisome universalism. From focusing on the history of the conquest—from locating oneself on the site of the encounter rather than attempting to project oneself simultaneously on both sides of it—a concept of commonality or common ground[22] emerges that is not a compromise between the universal and the different, but a distinct third term. This third term indeed stands opposed to both "human being" and "other/different." The shortcomings of "other" even when it is chastened into "different" we have already examined. As for "human being" shorn of its covert content—when it really means white man, Prince of Denmark, or President of the United States—one is hard put to say what it is. Besides mortality, the urge to satisfy three or four physical needs, a proneness to foregather, which human traits can be considered universal? On the contrary, commonalities abound being continuously generated by precisely the historical process that works to limit the realm of the universal.

One term that recurs in histories of difference is "contested zone," meaning cultural areas and social regions that different groups seek to define each its own way. The notion of "commonality" or common ground implies a reversal of that term, thus "zone of contest": a territory whose contours are sketched as overlappings rather than boundaries, a terrain of mediations and equally of confrontations. The history of the European empire seems exactly such a terrain upon which peoples define themselves as modalities of shared experience. The moment Columbus landed in San Salvador, as soon as the home of the Arawaks became San Salvador, the reason the European crossed the ocean became inextricable from what he found when he got to the other side. A passionate traveler, Montaigne sought, in difficult journeys he made more difficult by refusing an orderly itinerary, the same process of becoming he recorded in his essays. He understood that what he found upon his travels was inextricable from the finding, and that he himself would be transformed by both.

Put another way, all this has been to suggest that a difference so distinct as to constitute the opposite of universality, cannot be. As vehicles of meaning, the ships that discovered America exploded on impact. After the landfall, all there was on the beach was a confusion of European timber and American sand. Difference being an analytical concept, its objective reality lies only in its construction of subjective realities. Thus while the Aztecs and the Spanish certainly existed before their encounter, the difference between them did not. *That* was the creature of the conquest. The children of difference as well as its students, we find ourselves, therefore, fulfilling the eighth and last Aztec omen, the appearance of "monstrous beings . . .: deformed men with two heads but only one body." Monstrous, deformed, two- and many-headed, "human beings" and "others" in post-colonial America have one body divisible only by its own parts.

NOTES

1. I am grateful to Rick Livingston for an illuminating discussion of the dynamic between the concepts of "difference" and of the "other."

2. Christopher Columbus, *Four Voyages to the New World*, ed. and trans. R. H. Major (Gloucester MA: Peter Smith, 1978), 1-2.

3. Arkady Plotnitsky has brought to my attention in connection with this Marlowe's account of the horrifying Africans in *Heart of Darkness*. The landscape, Marlowe recalls shuddering, "was unearthly, and the men were—No, they were not inhuman. Well, you know, that was the worst of it—this suspicion of their not being inhuman." *Youth, Heart of Darkness, The End of the Tether* (New York: Oxford UP, 1984), 96-97.

4. One kind of scholarly essay is inspired by worry. The worry from which this essay has grown is that the current concept of difference may not be as cleanly liberatory as hoped. To identify its political concern is also to locate this essay in an ongoing discussion. Worrying about the shortcomings of the concept of difference can only arise as the continuation of a search for non-oppressive representation that the assertion of difference has already carried a long way. I stipulate this context here not out of filiopiety but to say quite clearly, in this period when "multiculturalism" names a growing controversy, that nothing herein implies otherwise than that it is intellectually as well as politically desirable for different cultural constituencies to represent themselves in the national conversation in their own terms.

5. Page references in the text are to "Of Cannibals" and "Of Coaches," *Complete Works: Essays, Travel Journal, Letters,* trans. Donald M. Frame (Stanford: Stanford UP, 1957), 150-59, 685-99.

6. It should be noted that there is no unimpeachable evidence for the existence of cannibals in the New World. For a particularly illuminating analysis of the evidence, see David Beers Quinn, "The New Geographical Literature," *First Images of America: The Impact of the New World on the Old*, ed. Fredi Chiappelli (Berkeley: U of California P, 1976), 635-57. A more recent instance of this ongoing controversy is in Peter Hulme, *Caribbean Encounters: Europe and the Native Caribbean, 1492-1797* (London: Methuen, 1986). This noted, we might go on nonetheless to ask why, as in Hulme's case, Western scholars have shown such fervor in denying this particular attribution? What if there were cannibals? Would that change the terms of our analysis or alter our judgment of the political morality of colonialism? A text to ponder in this regard is Ishmael's reflection just before he meets Queequeg whom he already suspects of being a cannibal but whom he is trying not to prejudge: "Not ignoring what is good," Ishmael muses, "I am quick to perceive a horror, and could still be social with it—would they let me—since it is but well to be on friendly terms with all the inmates of the place one lodges in." A collector of shrunken human heads, Queequeg may not be an actual consumer of bodies but then again he might be. He's still a nice guy and an excellent friend.

7. "Des coches, ou la structuration d'une absence," *L'Esprit Créateur* 15 (1975): 8-20. Since Montaigne's time, anthropologists have determined that the Incas did make

wheels, but only on toys. Of course this only deepens the distinction between Europeans and Americans being projected here. I am indebted to Rolph Trouillot for this correction.

8. Tzvetan Todorov, *The Conquest of America: The Question of the Other,* trans. Richard Howard (New York: Harper, 1987), 3. Originally published as *La conquête de l'Amérique* (Paris: Editions du Seuil, 1982).

9. Tzvetan Todorov, " 'Race,' Writing and Culture," *"Race," Writing and Difference,* ed. Henry Louis Gates, Jr. (Chicago: U of Chicago P, 1986), 370-80. Todorov's essay responds to one published earlier in a special issue of *Critical Inquiry,* edited by Henry Louis Gates, Jr., which was the first version of this book: Abdul R. JanMohamed, "The Economy of Manichean Allegory: The Function of Racial Difference in Colonialist Literature," *Critical Inquiry* 12 (1985): 59-87. The passage which Todorov cites is on page 65. To clarify JanMohamed's part in this argument, I should say that Todorov seems to me to misrepresent it a little. JanMohamed also seeks a way out of the predicament of absolute alterity and, as I read him, only stresses the difficulties it entails on the way to proposing a way of overcoming them.

10. Todorov, " 'Race,' Writing and Culture," 374.

11. An interesting version of this argument is made in Rey Chow's " 'It's you, and not me': Domination and 'Othering' in Theorizing the 'Third World,' " *Coming to Terms: Feminism, Theory, Politics,* ed. Elizabeth Weed (New York: Routledge, 1989), 152-61. Rey Chow uses a short story by the twentieth-century Chinese writer Lu Xun to criticize current Western projections of an absolutely other Third World. Lu Xun's story, according to her, "foretells much that is happening in the contemporary 'Western' theoretical scene." This foretelling, of course, demonstrates a shared universe of concerns. An equally telling discussion occurs in V. Y. Mudimbe's *Invention of Africa: Gnosis, Philosophy, and the Order of Knowledge* (Bloomington: Indiana UP, 1988) in a section of chapter III, "The Power of Speech," entitled "The Panacea of Otherness: J.-P. Sartre as an African Philosopher." Mudimbe here analyzes the effect of the theory of "Négritude" set forth in Sartre's essay *Black Orpheus,* which attempts precisely to identify a different culture without rendering it in any way inferior. On the contrary, Sartre is prepared to find in the values and energies of Négritude the next world-important culture to take over in the twilight of European culture. Without attempting to rehearse an exceptionally complex and dense argument, I want to invoke it here as a particularly penetrating treatment of the contradictions of the concept of difference and particularly of its fatal tendency to move toward an obliterating otherness.

12. Michael Dorris, "Indians on the Shelf," *The American Indian and the Problem of History,* ed. Calvin Martin (New York: Oxford UP, 1987), 98-105. Interestingly, Martin himself argues the opposite in his introduction. Attempts to write Indian history in the conventional Western terms so distort its fundamental structures of meaning, Martin claims, as to render the results either meaningless or, worse, new instances of ethnic and racial suppression. A recent theoretical study of Indian literature urges on the contrary that the same models of interpretation be applied to it as to any literature, and that not to do so is to continue excluding this literature from United States culture. See Arnold Krupat, *The Voice in the Margin: Native American Literature and the Canon* (Berkeley: U of California P, 1989).

13. Dorris, 104-5.

14. A selection from these writings is available in a paperback collection, *The Broken Spears: The Aztec Account of the Conquest of Mexico,* ed. Miguel Leon-Portilla (Boston: Beacon, 1966).

15. *The Broken Spears,* 51-52.

16. La Malinche is a figure of enormous interest who would repay more attention from historians. A woman and a slave, Mexican and woman, she was at once helpless and decisively powerful, victim of an oppressive gender and class system, yet also a significant agent in the defeat of her people. Her subsequent reputation, moreover, is still another part of the complexity of the problem she represents, in that when they make a

woman the symbol of national failure, Mexican Indians invoke more than the circumstances of their own history.

17. These are Indian figures (*The Broken Spears*, 124). They also estimate that of the 300,000 on the Aztec side, 240,000 were killed by the end of the final siege.

18. Alfred Crosby, *The Columbian Exchange: Biological and Cultural Consequences of 1492* (Westport, CT: Greenwood, 1972). Within five years of the arrival of Europeans, nine out of ten Americans were dead of diseases ranging from the common cold to smallpox. A contemporary account of the North American part of the holocaust, which puzzled the whites almost as much as it terrified the Indians, is in Thomas Harriot's *Briefe and True Report of the New Found Land of Virginia* (1588).

19. The full citation, from *1984*, is "who controls the past controls the future; who controls the present controls the past." This is the Party's slogan.

20. Todorov interprets the same phenomenon differently, suggesting that what the Aztecs preserve through the invention of the omens is a meaningful past, demonstrating the orderliness of their universe by having it forecast its own end. I am suggesting on the contrary that what is safeguarded in the omens is the future; after the end of their universe, the possibility of an ongoing orderliness however horrific the order.

21. One of the most problematical aspects of the Todorov account is its failure to incorporate any effects from the historical process itself of the conquest. The Spanish learn to see others as others, but this is already implicit or anyway potential in Spanish culture; the Aztecs don't learn about otherness and that is also implicit in their culture. The events and experiences of the conquest itself dramatize and illustrate but they don't really inform, let alone form.

22. By "common ground" here I intend something quite different from "bridge." Bridging two cultures emphasizes their distinctness while on the contrary I want to sketch their interactions. I am once again grateful to Arkady Plotnitsky for suggesting this distinction.

American Literature Discovers Columbus

Terence Martin

PROLOGUE

As most people are aware, the quincentennial of Christopher Columbus' arrival in the Western hemisphere has generated a substantial amount of comment and controversy. From Edward T. Stone's portrait of an explorer who attacked "defenseless Indians" to the plans of the 1992 Alliance to hold "a mock trial of Columbus for war crimes against Indigenous Americans," the Admiral himself has come under attack for the consequences of colonization and exploitation.[1] As the historian Garry Wills has observed, "If any historical figure can appropriately be loaded up with all the heresies of our time — Eurocentrism, phallocentrism, imperialism, eliteism, and all-bad-things-generally-ism — Columbus is the man."[2]

In the context of this revisionism (perhaps as a context *for* this revisionism) celebratory plans are of course underway — with parades, commemorative speeches, replicas of the Admiral's ships sailing from Spain, and praise for the admittedly imperfect civilization we have fashioned. One of the most unconventional tributes will feature "an international fleet of solar powered ships" racing to Mars to demonstrate "the benefits of solar power and symbolically re-enact the search for a New World."[3]

But the national mood incorporates a generous serving of concern and guilt. Out of a perception that the consequences of Columbus' journey brought "oppression, degradation, and genocide" to an indigenous population, the Council of the American Churches of Christ has declared 1992 "a year of reflection and repentance."[4] The city council of Berkeley, California, has proclaimed October 12, 1992, "Indigenous People's Day," wiping Columbus off the calendar in a demonstration of cultural awareness or historical correctness (depending on your point of view). In many communities, including the academic, the traditional language of the age of exploration has been assailed, with the word "encounter" replacing "discovery" and the term "New World" disparaged because the inhabited continents of North and South America existed long before the arrival of Europeans. The very titles of Francis Jennings' *The Invasion of America* (1975) and Russell Thornton's *American Indian Holocaust and Survival* (1987) imply a perspective inimical to celebration and a disposition that, at its most savage, brought the *New York Times* to remind us editorially (on 17 June 1991) that Columbus was "no Eichmann." Alert to the commercial possibilities of a warming dialogue, *Newsweek* entitled its "Historic Special Issue" of October 14, 1991, "When Worlds Collide" (the title appropriated from a 1951 film in which Manhattan was inundated), and announced it as "an exceptional opportunity for advertisers."

I have no inclination to jump into the eddies of an either/or debate—any more than does the General Secretariat of the Organization of American States, which calls its current newsletter *Quincentennial of the Discovery of America: Encounter of Two Worlds*. Rather, I wish to suggest how, at various stages in our history, American writers have adapted the figure of Columbus to the needs of the nation—have made him, as it were, an image of what we like, and dislike, about ourselves. For with all the shapings and reshapings of our national story, it is ultimately ourselves as we have been in our history that we measure with our attitudes toward the quincentennial.

I. NEW WORLD, EMPTY WORLD

Not until the first years of independence did American writers look to Christopher Columbus as a figure of significance. Indentured to matters of religion and politics, the poetry and prose of the early and middle eighteenth century had little concern for heroes of exploration. Histories, it is true, sought out founders to establish points of departure for their narratives and perforce mentioned the journeys of Columbus. But because pre-Revolutionary histories focused on the settlement of individual colonies, they subordinated the Admiral to local, more proximate figures who could provide a sense of continuity and purpose. In his *History of the Colony and Province of Massachusetts-Bay* (1764), for example, Thomas Hutchinson states explicitly that he will not consider "the discovery of America by Columbus" but will begin with the voyage of Bartholomew Gosnold, "an Englishman," to New England. As late as 1804 John Daly Burk adopted a similar perspective for his *History of Virginia*: pleased at the prospect of writing about founders who "are scarcely out of sight," Burk makes the "discovery of a new world" an insignificant detail, virtually unrelated to his account of the first settlers.[5]

Whether or not Columbus is mentioned, the initial act in such histories and in literary works of the early Republic is regarded as one of "discovery." And what is discovered is the "New World." No matter that two formidable continents had existed for uncounted centuries before the arrival of European explorers; no matter that generations of human beings had lived and died and fashioned complex societies on those continents. "Discovery" (then as now) was in the eye of the discoverer. And the enabling perception of those who had named territories New England, New France, and New Spain (or New Amsterdam, New Jersey, and New Orleans) was that they had come to a New World. From this manifestly European perspective on where they, the early colonists, lived, where they were situated, came the opposing term, "Old World," and the powerful dialectic that went into the making of a national identity during the first half century of independence. From the Old World came a conception of the New, from the New a conception of the Old by means of which Americans could announce what they were not and thereby proclaim their superiority.

An often-remarked passage in Crèvecoeur's *Letters from an American Farmer* (1782) distinguishes between Old World and New in terms that became virtually a refrain in the years after the American Revolution: "Here," he writes, "are no aristocratical families, no courts, no kings, no bishops, no ec-clesiastical dominion, no invisible power giving to the few a very visible one; no great manufacturers employing thousands, no great refinements of luxury." Thomas Cooper, later president of the College of South Carolina, explained in 1794 that he and other Englishmen came to America because it had "no tythes nor game laws . . . , no men of great rank, nor many of great riches." And Noah Webster found the United States uniquely blessed because it had "no beg-garly monks and fryars, no princely ecclesiastes and titled mendicants."[6] Such statements mark the difference between an old world and a new by enumerat-ing what is missing in the new. Their manner is festive, insistently so; for their intent is to negate Europe in order to define and possess America.

Although lists of this sort might seem home-grown with their unrelenting patriotism, they take form and impulse from early European conceptions of the New World. The letters of Amerigo Vespucci provide an example of how nega-tion conveyed to Europeans a sense of a continent (actually two) that had come upon them by surprise. Extremely popular with a population hungry for infor-mation about the new lands, Vespucci's letters describe such things as herbs and fruits, local customs and sexual practices, in fascinating detail. A letter of 1502 adds the following significant passage: the inhabitants, Vespucci writes, have "no religious belief, but live according to the dictates of nature alone. They know nothing of the immortality of the soul; they have no private prop-erty; they have no boundaries of kingdom or province; they obey no king or lord . . . , they have no laws," and no master.[7]

By using negatives to characterize beliefs and customs in a place not yet named, Vespucci adopts a manner of speaking that became a habit in Europe before it evolved into an American formula. Montaigne uses similar language when he praises the natural purity of the world "we have just discovered." He wishes he could tell Plato of this utopia in which "there is no sort of traffic, no knowledge of letters, no science of numbers, no name for a magistrate or for political superiority, no custom of servitude, no riches or poverty, no contracts, no successions, no partitions, no occupations but leisure ones, no care for any but common kinship, no clothes, no agriculture, no metal, no use of wine or wheat."[8] By way of John Florio's translation of Montaigne, these same nega-tives found their way into the different context of Gonzalo's speech about gov-erning the island with no name in Shakespeare's *The Tempest*: "Had I planta-tion of this isle," Gonzalo says,

> no kind of traffic
> Would I admit; no name of magistrate;
> Letters should not be known; riches, poverty,

And use of service, none; contract, succession,
Bourn, bound of land, tilth, vineyard, none;
No use of metal, corn, or wine, or oil;
No occupation . . . ;
No sovereignty. . . . (II,i,148-56)

Having found what was to them a New World, Europeans endowed it with the simplicity and fundamental purity of paradise (invented it, as Edmundo O'Gorman said some years ago), even as they exploited its resources and its inhabitants. Indeed, the conception of paradise, fundamentally and always negative, made exploitation all the more predictable; for, as an idealization of what the Old World no longer (or never) was, the New World became a negative construct, not only pristine but empty, unnamed—and therefore vulnerable. Had Columbus sailed to Cathay, as he intended, the terms "discovery" and "New World" would not have come into being. But he did not, and the consequences of Europe "finding this thumping bantling laid at its door" (as James Kirke Paulding put it) are the stuff of our history.

Patricia Caldwell has pointed out that the experience of crossing the Atlantic forced colonists to reappraise the self in a world bereft of familiar surroundings (dramatizing the move from something to nothing in personal terms).[9] Yet the stripping away involved in such a crossing could be seen retrospectively as a happy first step in making American citizens. The most extravagant of the negative catalogues, that of Mr. Evelyn in Sylvester Judd's *Margaret: A Tale of the Real and the Ideal* (1845), comes acrobatically out of such a perspective—with a regional bias thrown in for good measure. New England, Mr. Evelyn tells the young Margaret, is an "unencumbered region" superior to "all other nations" precisely because much of "the Old World on its passage to the New was lost overboard." "Our ancestors," he asserts, "were very considerably cleansed by the dashing waters of the Atlantic." Then follows his account of all that is missing from the soil of New England. A slender example will serve to suggest the way it converts absence to identity:

We have no monarchical supremacy, no hereditary prerogatives, no patent nobility, no Kings. . . . We have no traditions, legends, fables, and scarcely a history. All these things our fathers left behind in England, or they were brushed away by contact with the thick, spiny forests of America. Our atmosphere is transparent, unoccupied, empty from the bottom of our wells to the zenith. . . .[10]

Mr. Evelyn's controlling metaphors are those of cleansing, of things being brushed away—his tone that of a joyous iconoclast. He negates out of a preference for simplicity of belief, each declaration cancelling European fullness in favor of an American emptiness. To the exuberant Mr. Evelyn (as to Crèvecoeur, Thomas Cooper, and Noah Webster), what Americans lack is what they are. The blessings of an empty world deliver them from the past and open up unparalleled opportunities. "No country has ever had such a good future," wrote Margaret Fuller in 1849; "the vast prospects of our country" make it a "blessing to be born an American."[11]

2. IMAGE AND NAME:
COLUMBUS AND VESPUCCI

While historians gradually domesticated 1492 as a date of national significance, orators and poets of the new republic began to fashion the image of the
Admiral according to American specifications. Among the most notable expressions of praise that clustered in the late years of the eighteenth and the early
years of the nineteenth century were the ceremonies at the first Columbus Day
festivities in Boston in 1792, Philip Freneau's speculative "Pictures of Columbus, the Genoese" (1788), and Joel Barlow's *The Columbiad* (1807), first written as *The Vision of Columbus* in 1787. Alive with the buzz of implication in
their culture, functioning parts of what Claude Lévi-Strauss would call a "hot"
or "dense" period of history, these statements created a dual image of the navigator that proclaimed a durable American faith in progress and rebirth.

On the tricentennial of his landing at San Salvador, the Admiral first received official public attention. In New York (on October 12), the Tammany
Society, or Columbian Order, sponsored a celebration that featured an oration
on Columbus by John Barent Johnson: the spirit of the courageous navigator,
Johnson explained, lived on in the New World he had discovered. In Boston (on
October 23), the newly formed Massachusetts Historical Society conducted
elaborate festivities praising both Columbus and Columbia, one a symbol of
expansive destiny, the other of nurturing and regeneration. Jeremy Belknap
(founder of the Society) began the ceremonies by characterizing the voyage of
1492 as "a splendid instance of that remarkable prediction of the prophet
Daniel, chap. xii, ver. 4. '*Many shall run to and fro and knowledge shall be
increased.*' " Then, in an ode written for the occasion, a choir sang of the advent of freedom in the Western World. According to Belknap, Columbus discovered America and "opened to the Europeans a new world." According to
the choir, Columbus uncovered a "Western World" that had been formed at
creation and hidden "from European eyes" during centuries of discord. Until
the appointed moment "Fair Columbia lay conceal'd"; then "Her friendly
arms extended wide" to embrace "Freedom" and "pure religion." Whereas
Belknap puts his emphasis on a skillful and daring Columbus who kindled "the
spirit of enterprise and commerce" (including the "detestable" practice of slavery), the ode attends to an unspoiled Columbia ready to welcome "her
adopted children."[12] Ideas of rebirth and regeneration thus join with those of
courage and destiny to define a nation that embraced the past with clear designs on the future: while Columbia could nourish and harbor, Columbus
could serve as a symbol of ongoing expansion.

In "The Pictures of Columbus" (1788) Freneau presents a visionary with
pragmatic resolve who sails on a voyage of discovery because he sees "blun-
ders" on the maps, an arrangement of land he cannot accept as reality. As he
studies his maps (in the first picture), Columbus is troubled with the "disproportion" sketched out before him. "Nature," he thinks, would not have positioned the land in "one poor corner" of the world; there must be land else-

where to balance "Asia's vast extent." Perhaps, he continues with prophetic instinct, in these unknown "regions dwell / Forms wrought like man, and lov'd as well." Putting aside the existing maps, he draws "a new world" far to the west—and wonders if

> God who hung this globe
> In the clear void, and governs all,
> On those dread scenes, remote from view,
> Has trac'd his great idea too.

Finally, Columbus the designer of "a new world" becomes Columbus the explorer, who declares "O'er real seas I mean to sail." If fortune will assist him in his "grand design," he adds with a surge of hope (and a curious possessiveness), "Worlds yet unthought of shall be mine."[13]

Practical dreamer that he is, Freneau's Columbus rejects the "disproportion" of European maps by invoking (for his own purposes) a medieval conception that God would have put more land than water on the globe because land was destined for the creation of human souls. Jeremy Belknap secularizes the same idea both in his Columbus Day address and in his *Biographies of the Early Discoverers of America* (1798) to make Columbus a man of keen intelligence who argued for the probability of land in the Atlantic Ocean from his knowledge of enlightened opinion in Europe and "from the necessity of a counterpoise in the west, for the immense quantity of land which was known to be in the east."[14]

Because it presented a rational (and more Americanized) Columbus, this was the kind of explanation frequently adopted in the colonies and in the early United States to give evidence of the Admiral's bold powers of mind. As early as 1736 Thomas Prince had Columbus envisioning the westward lands as a "mighty Continent" in the final section of his ambitious *Chronological History of New-England . . . from the Creation* (1736):

> The united Continents of Asia, Africa, and Europe, have been the only Stage of History, from the CREATION to the Y C [year of Christ] 1492. We are now to turn our Eyes to the West, and see a NEW WORLD appearing in the Atlantick Ocean to the great surprize and entertainment of the other. CHRISTOPHER COLUMBUS or Colonus, a Genoese is the 1st Discoverer. Being a Skilful Geographer and Navigator, and of a very curious Mind, He becomes possess'd, with a strong Perswasion, that in order to Ballance the Terraqueous Globe & Proportion the Seas and Lands to each other, there must needs be form'd a mighty Continent on the other Side, which Boldness, Art and Resolution would soon discover.[15]

Whether it was simplified for schoolroom texts or adapted for poetic tribute, such a conception proved an effective way to shape the story of Columbus' initial voyage. In Charles A. Goodrich's *Child's History of the United States* (1827), for example, chapters become "Lessons" designed for "a First Book of History for Schools." Precisely because it is elementary, unambiguous, and intended to instruct children about the "Discovery of America by Columbus," the initial lesson in this little volume assumes importance as a culturally approved *exemplum*. After a brief recital of dates and events, Goodrich comes to the first voyage of Columbus. Prior to 1492, he writes, people did not know there was "any such land as America." How, then, did Columbus know? "He did *not* know. But he thought there must be, to balance the land in the Eastern continent." Although learned men ignored him, Columbus finally sailed westward, returned to Spain with his crew, and "told of the *new world* which they had discovered."[16]

American sketches of Columbus thus use the European idea of "counterpoise" to minimize (and finally ignore) the intent of the original voyage, despite the array of evidence from such sources as Ferdinand Columbus and the influential Scottish historian William Robertson that the Admiral had no conception of a continental land mass between Spain and the Orient. Subordinating the idea of reaching the Indies, Belknap postulates a strain of individualism that makes Columbus an American by temperament. Goodrich (synoptically) and Freneau (in romantic detail) distribute their emphasis differently; their explorer is a man who set out in search of unknown lands he thought were there and found a new world. Finally, from Isaac Taylor in England, comes a children's sketch of a navigator who sailed intentionally for the New World. All doubt of Columbus' goal is removed in *Scenes in America, for the Amusement and Instruction of little Tarry-at-Home Travellers* (published in a popular American edition in 1825), which informs us that "On the morning of October 12 [Columbus] distinctly saw stretched before him, the new world, after which his imagination had so long panted."[17] As Taylor's biographical sketch shows, the impulse to make the Admiral both an intrepid and a romantic hero was not limited to the United States. But a nation that had adapted Columbus to its own purposes welcomed the voyager who had set out to find the New World in which they were going to live.

What was good for Christopher Columbus was bad for Amerigo Vespucci. Those who championed the Admiral had no use for the rival from Florence. Charles A. Goodrich's *Child's History of the United States* is again useful in illustrating the sanctioned view of American history. In Lesson Two, Goodrich takes his didactic narrative to the years after Columbus' famous voyage: "America now being discovered," he writes, "the news soon spread far and wide," and other men sailed in search of additional lands. Among them "was a man by the name of *A-mer-i-cus Ves-pu-cius*." He did not "discover much," Goodrich says bluntly. "But he told so *fine a story,* that America was called after him. It should have been called after Columbus."[18]

With this unwitting tribute to the power of narrative, Goodrich informs his young readers that "America" has been misnamed. His words express a longstanding opinion that Vespucci (or some enterprising Florentine) lied about his voyages. In the *Magnalia Christi Americana* (1702), Cotton Mather observes that "this vast Hemisphere" has been misnamed; in his *History of the United States* (1816), David Ramsey calls Vespucci a "robber" because he had "the country called by his name"; in *English Traits* (1856), Emerson asserts that because Vespucci "baptize[d] half the earth with his own dishonest name . . . broad America must wear the name of a thief"; and in *The European Discovery of America* (1974), Samuel Eliot Morison refers to Vespucci's "colossal" and "well-planned deception."[19] Despite their convictions, however, these writers accepted the name of the hemisphere, the continent, and the nation as a *fait accompli.*

Samuel Whelpley was not so easily reconciled. His *Compend of History, from the Earliest Times* went through twelve editions from 1808 to 1870, carrying with it the most astonishing of all attacks on the name of the continent and of the nation. "The new world has been particularly unfortunate," he asserts, in "the matter of a name." It should "have been called *Columbia*"—a name second "to none in point of dignity, harmony, and convenience." Warming to his subject, Whelpley tells his readers that calling the new continent *America* was "the greatest act of folly, caprice, cruelty, and injustice . . . , that ever mankind were guilty of."[20] Moreover, for obvious purposes of clarity, the nation should have a different name than the continent. But a deeper and more alarming problem is that the nation has no name at all—since the words "United States" designate a collection of states and "of America" means of the continent of America. "Two favorable moments have passed," Whelpley notes, when a name might have been given to the country—the first during the drafting of the Declaration of Independence, the second during the Constitutional Convention. Hopefully, another opportunity will occur soon: for "There are serious and urgent reasons why the United States should have a name."

For all his rhetorical excess, Whelpley raises an issue of considerable importance about naming and identity. He is correct in saying that neither the Declaration of Independence nor the Constitution provides a name for the country. At a later time, Thomas Jefferson proposed to make ten states out of the land between the Ohio River and the Mississippi and to give them such names as Dolypotamia, Metropotamia, and Assenisippia. In the Declaration, however, Jefferson shows no intention of naming the country (perhaps it is just as well). Somewhat forlornly, Whelpley suggests a solution to the problem: "What reasonable objection," he asks, "could there be to calling this country FREDONIA? A name proposed by the greatest scholar in the United States— who *in Europe,* is considered the luminary of this country."

Whelpley's anonymous tribute is to Samuel Latham Mitchill, whose *Pictures of New York* Washington Irving once intended to parody in the Knickerbocker *History of New-York* (1809). Obviously there was more to Mitchill than Irving acknowledged: a distinguished medical scientist who taught at Columbia and later became vice-president of the medical department at Rutgers College, Mitchill served as United States Senator from New York from 1804 to 1809. As a newly elected senator he proposed the name "Fredonia" for the nation, most notably in his Independence Day *Address to the Fredes or People of the United States* (1804). In a note to the printed text of his Address, Mitchill explains that "The modern and appropriate name of the people of the United States is FREDES or FREDONIANS, as the geographical name of their country is FREDON or FREDONIA, and their relations are expressed by the terms FREDONIAN or FREDISH."[21]

Although Mitchill's suggestion did not find general support, twelve states have towns named Fredonia, Richard Emmons' epic poem about the War of

1812 is named "The Fredoniad" (1827), and the Marx brothers' film *Duck Soup* (1933) is set in a beleaguered country named Fredonia. The concern to give the nation an appropriate name, moreover, has had a quixote life of its own. Having decided that "America was discovered by Christovallo Colon," Washington Irving's meticulous Diedrich Knickerbocker announces that the "country should have been called Colonia." Intent on compromise, a member of the New York Historical Society proposed in the 1840s that the nation be called "America" and the continent "Columbia." And in 1846 Edgar Allan Poe asserted that "There should be no hesitation about" calling the country "Appalachia," an indigenous name that would point to a "magnificent and distinctive" section of the land and "do honor to the Aborigines, whom, hitherto, we have at all points unmercifully despoiled, assassinated and dishonored." "At present," Poe contends, "we have, clearly," no name—since "America" signifies not only the entire continent of North America but that of South America, as well. As late as 1958 George R. Stewart echoed the judgment of these writers and suggested that an "evolution of speech" might yield some version of the term "Yank" for the country.[22]

All things, of course, are possible. But some seem unlikely. One may as well appreciate the wit of Garrison Keillor as tilt at the name of the nation. As the citizens of Lake Woebegone realize sadly, Columbus simply "stumbled onto the land of heroic Vikings and proceeded to get the credit for it." Compounding the error, the place was named after another Italian, one "who never saw the New World. . . . By rights, it should be called Erica, after Eric the Red. . . . The United States of Erica. Erica the Beautiful."[23] Although no one has sung "Erica the Beautiful," patriotic hymns can have a powerful effect in establishing the identity of a country. If the matter of a national name was not concluded by default in the final decades of the eighteenth century (and the logical alternative not effectively ruled out when—in South America—New Granada became Grand Colombia in 1819), it was surely ratified by patriotic ritual when Samuel Francis Smith's "America" was sung at a Fourth of July celebration in Boston in 1831. On the birthday of the nation, Americans extolled the "sweet land of liberty" in which they lived. Fittingly, the words of the song did not mention its name.

Vespucci emerges from this brouhaha as a confidence man who invented a voyage to establish priority of discovery and then, confusingly, gave the same name to a hemisphere, a continent, and a country. In whatever form, such charges stem from his letters, extremely popular in Europe, that brought the cartographer Martin Waldseemüller to put the name "America" on the southern portion of his map of the New World in 1507. Along with the poet Martin Ringmann, Waldseemüller had been preparing a new edition of Ptolemy's *Cosmographiae Introductio* when he read Vespucci's accounts of four voyages to the New World (which he appended to his edition). After conventional descriptions of Europe, Africa, and Asia in Chapter Nine, Waldseemüller (or Ringmann, who had written a poem in honor of Vespucci's discoveries) added the famous words:

a fourth part has been discovered by Amerigo Vespucci. . . . Inasmuch as both Europe and Asia received their names from women, I see no reason why any one should justly object to calling this part Amerige, i.e., the land of Amerigo, or America, after Amerigo, its discoverer, a man of great ability.[24]

Waldseemüller may have become aware that Vespucci's claims were not credited by experts: he omitted the name America from a second global map he issued in 1516. But the name stuck, and when Mercator added it to the northern portion of his double cordiform map in 1535, he both validated and extended the province of a name that had received general acceptance in Europe since it was given.

3. PERCEPTIONS OF COLUMBUS

As dedicated to the subject as he was, Joel Barlow was not alone in writing an epic about Columbus' journey to the New World. His *Columbiad* (1807), first published as *The Vision of Columbus* in 1787, was preceded by two other Columbiads, one French and one English, the first by Marie-Anne DuBoccage in 1756, the second by James L. Moore in 1798. Each of these poems becomes a national self-portrait wrought by the voyages of Columbus; each shapes Columbus to its own purposes; each presents a vision of the future—bright with Renaissance glory for France, comfortably prosperous for England, stubbornly millennial for the new United States of America.

La Colombiade, ou, la Foi Portée au Nouveau Monde picks up the adventures of Columbus as he meets the leader of an Indian nation who asks who he is and why he is there. These are, obviously, good questions. Columbus replies in astonishing detail, telling his auditor of "the three continents which form the universe," of the Supreme Being, of European manners and inventions, of his project, of Queen Isabella, of scurvy, of strange "phenomena" of the sea, and of unrest among the sailors. "Merveilleux Etranger," exclaims the chief, no doubt overwhelmed by the barrage of heroic couplets.[25] After many adventures a prayerful Columbus is visited by a tutelary angel who reveals the vast consequences of his enterprise. This prophetic "Vision de Colomb" pays scant attention to the New World; the emphasis is on a renaissance of arts, letters, and science in Europe, particularly in France. To give specificity to her vision, DuBoccage goes on a naming binge similar to that of Barlow when Hesper hails notable Americans: she mentions, among others, Magellan, Francis I, Galileo, Luther—and of course Shakespeare (qui est "regardé," says DuBoccage in a note, "comme le Corneille des Anglois"). In addition to the "immortal genius" Voltaire, the French, Columbus learns, will boast a new Sophocles (Corneille), an Aristophanes (Molière), several Euclids, and sundry other geniuses.[26] What we have in this *Colombiade* is an emphasis on the national and European consequences of New World discovery, with a tribute to the Renaissance as the greatest consequence of all.

James A. Moore's *Columbiad* incorporates three visions, each brought to

Columbus in the western hemisphere, two by archangelic messengers, one by the guardian spirit of the Orinoco River. Behind the authority of the angels is the universal wisdom of the Almighty, who instructs Raphael to assure Columbus that he will soon find a continent and that "Yon northern clime" will yield another to "supremely bles'd" explorers from England who will "spread the commerce of their native land."[27] In this epic, God clearly favors the English. The poem looks past the carefully depicted anguish of the War of Independence to a time of amity between England and a very Anglicized and prosperous United States. In Book 7, Moore assails the evils of slavery during Columbus' brief stay in Jamaica. But in Book 9 he looks forward without a tremor to the elimination of "swarthy" Indian tribes who ravage "infant towns" and spoil "verdant meads":

> Thy veteran armies shall th' invading flood
> Repel, and stain the plain with Indian blood.
> Whene'er they shall thy colonies assail,
> Their numerous sons thy vengeance shall bewail,
> Till, less'ning by degrees, the native race
> Shall lose through all the clime its name and trace. . . .[28]

The cost of settling the continent has seldom been stated more unblinkingly — with a calm more chilling.

Joel Barlow's *Columbiad* offers a third kind of vision, protean and all-encompassing, emanating not from a Caribbean island with Columbus in mid-career but from the mount of vision in Spain with the Admiral's voyaging treacherously concluded. With Queen Isabella dead and "cold hearted Ferdinand" offering stern injustice, Columbus looks back on "a world explored in vain" until the vision brings him to look forward.[29] As one who has already performed his deeds, Columbus stands in the role of observer, more qualified to be a reader of the American epic (as Roy Harvey Pearce acutely suggests) than an actor in it.[30] But Barlow's Columbus is a decidedly active observer, curious, anxious to know more; to some extent Hesper's vision takes its baggy shape because of his questions. The figure of Columbus is *composed* by American history in this poem; the navigator's interest in process as well as progress generates an emphasis on the republican institutions Barlow sees as the product of political evolution.

As might be expected in a poem comprised of visions, Barlow's geographical panoramas are grander in scope than those of DuBoccage and Moore. Moreover, they carry with them rhetorical habits characteristic of a nation that celebrated emptiness as part of its identity. For one thing — naming: whereas DuBoccage and Moore write out of, and about, a world already named, Barlow's "guardian Genius of the western continent" tells Columbus at the outset that this "happier hemisphere" was "Hesperia called, from my anterior claim; / But now Columbia, from thy patriarch name."[31] Hesper does use a number of North American place names. But the deep wonder of the continent lies "in streams without a name" and in primal scenes that can be envisioned only by means of language that negates historical and mythical associations. To the eyes of an appreciative Columbus, Hesper evokes a vision in which

> ". . . hills by hundreds rise without a name;
> Hills yet unsung, their mystic powers untold;
> Celestials there no sacred senates hold;
> No chain'd Prometheus feasts the vulture there,
> No cyclop forges thro their summits glare,
> To Phrygian Jove no victim smoke is curl'd,
> No ark high landing quits a deluged world."[32]

Emory Elliott argues that *The Columbiad,* produced after a seventeen-year absence from an evolving United States, became a "work frozen in time." Less confident in *The Columbiad* than he had been in *The Vision of Columbus,* caught between changing religious assumptions and Enlightenment attitudes, Barlow seems determined to assert "a collective national identity."[33] And that he does, producing out of his determination a poem designed as a national monument. For if *The Vision of Columbus* and *The Columbiad* are two versions of the same poem, the way in which each addresses its culture indicates obvious and instructive differences: the first version, for example, was dedicated to Louis XVI, the second to Robert Fulton; the first was undertaken as a long philosophical poem, the second as a resolute epic; and the first was published inauspiciously by subscription, the second in sumptuous format, leather-bound with gold stamping, and a price (in 1807) of twenty dollars. Cecilia Tichi's description of *The Columbiad* as Barlow's "great act of literary engineering," can be applied to the book as well as to the poem.[34]

But the book and the poem make each other possible: for this "worried-over" epic (as Tichi terms it after examining the text which Barlow used to transform *The Vision of Columbus* into *The Columbiad*) does seem designed in the face of contradictions and anomalies to salute the value of republican institutions in history.[35] At the end of the poem we do not see Columbus; rather, we hear Hesper telling him to complain no more "Of dangers braved and griefs endured in vain," but to "compose" his thoughts in the knowledge that he will be fulfilled by history. With this command Columbus is subsumed by his vision, transformed into the aspirations of the world he discovered.

4. PROLIFERATION

Commemorating an event in which Columbus played the principal role, Barlow's *Columbiad* nonetheless focuses on consequences that exclude the protagonist from direct participation. The burden of the poem is to link event to consequences, to bring the protagonist to appreciate the distinctive merit of American institutions and thereby become a kind of absentee hero because he made it all possible. The measure of Columbus' importance lies in the merit of the consequences.

Washington Irving's *History of the Life and Voyages of Christopher Columbus* (1828) comes at its subject from a different perspective. Under some reproach for his lengthy absence from the United States at a time when American literature was struggling to find a voice of its own, Irving hoped that his expansive biography of Columbus would silence his critics. After almost two years of intense work (with access to the manuscripts of the Spanish scholar Navarette) he completed a study that, according to Jeffrey Rubin-Dorsky, added nothing significant to the accounts already in print.[36]

But if Irving came up with little new information, he did validate the dual image of the Admiral that had been defined in the late years of the eighteenth century and add disquieting meditations on the consequences of Europeans arriving in another hemisphere. Repeatedly during his first voyage Irving's Columbus calms the superstitious fears of his mariners and assures them of the success of the voyage. He is a rational leader, courageous and noble; he is also a "visionary," someone both "practical and poetical," concerned with knowledge rather than exploitation.[37] Yet Columbus is implicated in a larger and darker drama of history, as John D. Hazlett demonstrates: anomalously and romantically (so deep was the habit), Irving uses the term "New World" to refer to the innocence and simplicity of native Americans prior to the coming of Europeans.[38] From the perspective of the nineteenth century he then looks back at what happened once "the white man had penetrated into the land; avarice, and pride, and ambition, and pining care, and sordid labor, and withering poverty, were soon to follow, and the indolent paradise of the Indian was about to disappear forever."[39]

Irving's study of Columbus and his voyages thus posits a new fall from Eden in the New World, with European avarice and ambition embodying the evil. As the representative of Europe and its civilization, Columbus shares responsibility for defiling innocence. As the hero of a biography written to demonstrate Irving's commitment to an American literary agenda, however, Columbus is repeatedly characterized as magnanimous, solitary in his dreams, misjudged in his aspirations, a leader Americans would be happy to follow. What Hazlett calls Irving's ambivalence is genuine and complex. It provides a way of adding one romantic view to another, of extolling Columbus' famous voyage, then seeing it as the beginning of an exploitation of paradise. Recognizably, Irving's misgivings signal an early step toward late twentieth-century attitudes that would cast the Admiral in less heroic postures.

By 1830, the figure of Columbus had been praised, split into male and female components (Columbus and Columbia), and given romantic dimensions that served a variety of expressive purposes. Irving's misgivings, one should note, did not express the popular view. With hyperbole typical of the time, James Kirke Paulding wrote to President James K. Polk in 1845 that "the moment at which Columbus first glimpsed this Continent" yielded consequences "greater and more lasting, than ever emanated from any human being since the fall of Adam. It was the discovery of the lost child of the world."[40] Consequences, we see, even those evoked by this curious analogy, were crucial to self-approbation. The more highly Americans thought of themselves, the more they praised the discoverer of their world.

Few eighteenth- or nineteenth-century novels were devoted to Columbus. Typically, they were flimsy attempts at narrative, unsure of their historical ground. Susanna Rowson's *Reuben and Rachel; or, Tales of Old Times* (1798) and James Fenimore Cooper's *Mercedes of Castile* (1840), for example, are labored efforts that subordinate the Admiral to standard formulas of plot. But markedly different poets found Columbus and the idea of discovery useful to their purposes — among them James Russell Lowell, a Boston Brahmin; Sidney Lanier, a Confederate soldier and accomplished musician; Emma Lazarus, a spokeswoman for Jewish causes whose sonnet "The New Colossus" (1883) is carved on the Statue of Liberty; Paul Laurence Dunbar, a midwestern African American trained as a lawyer; Joaquin Miller, a self-promoting far-Western adventurer from Liberty, Indiana; Ernest Francisco Fenollosa, whose study of Oriental literature and art became a legacy for Ezra Pound (Fenollosa's literary executor); and of course Walt Whitman, self-designed articulator of democracy, who, as Pound once said, "goes bail for the nation."

As one might expect, what these poets wrote was frequently uneven in quality. Lowell's dramatic monologue "Columbus" (1844) portrays the explorer on his first voyage, solitary in his dreams, convinced that "the old world" no longer nourishes the human spirit, inspired by poets who "Speak to the age out of eternity." Replete with romantic intensity, it is in most parts a strong and overlooked poem, arguably Lowell's finest poetic achievement. Lanier's "Centennial Meditation of Columbia: A Cantata" (1876), a musical performance occasioned by the nation's centennial anniversary, ranges over American history in grandiose and wearisome fashion from the point of view of the continent itself. Lazarus' "1492" (1883) describes a year saddened by the persecution of Jews in Spain but joyful at the unveiling of a world that welcomes "all who weary"; interestingly, the poem portrays the "virgin world" of 1492 as a land of compassion in the manner of the lines from "The New Colossus," "Give me your tired, your poor, / Your huddled masses yearning to breathe free." More typically, Dunbar's "Columbian Ode" (written in 1893, the year of the Columbian Exposition) contrasts Old World scholars blinded by superstition and Columbus whose vision fathoms the unknown, while the galloping meters of Miller's "Columbus" (1896) reduce the drama of the Admiral's initial voyage to the ringing imperative, "Sail on!" Crude in its baroque excess yet ambitious in scope and vision is Fenollosa's "The Discovery of America: A Symphonic Poem," an exhausting exercise of some fourteen hundred lines that marks the culmination of a book-length series of meditations on the fated meeting of East and West.

As different as they are in manner and style, these poems tend to treat Columbus as someone who opened up opportunity in the New World because of his alienation from the Old. Poems written for public occasions, such as Lanier's "Centennial Meditation" and Dunbar's "Columbian Ode," function as testimonials and invoke Columbus as a familiar figure identified with an American sense of progress. Lowell's more personal statement portrays a private Columbus ready to become one with a New World because he no longer believes in the Old. Fenollosa's effort, on the other hand, is an excursion into the philosophy of history, replete with ornate apostrophes and internal rhymes that sound like Poe on a bad day ("O list to the treacherous tune of the sirens that swim to the mystical whim of the moon!"), yet poignant in its cameo portrait of a regal Columbus enclosed by the narrator's vision of history:

> He stands
> One instant, like a king that grasps all space—
> Then walks in silence down the savage shore.
> And time flows on as placid as before.
> Ah, hero! has thou felt
> A shadow of the darkness like a belt
> Folding thee close? And wilt thou press it down
> Upon thy forehead, like a thorny crown?[41]

More sustained and resonant in achievement than these poems about Columbus are Walt Whitman's "Passage to India" (1871) and "Prayer of Columbus" (1874), the first of which takes the voyages of the Admiral as emblematic of the quest for "primal thought," the second (a dramatic monologue) which dramatizes Whitman's identification of himself with the discouraged dreamer Columbus became. Along with the more conventional work of other writers, Whitman's well-known poems bring us to see not only the pervasive and sometimes eloquent romanticism that surrounded the figure of Columbus in the nineteenth century but the ways in which it could generate an idiom fresh, personal, and profoundly human.

Short, vibrant allusions show Columbus functioning in a different way—as part of an American metaphorical repertory. "Be a Columbus to whole new continents and worlds within you," enjoins Thoreau, the apostle of self-exploration, in the concluding chapter of *Walden* (1853); "explore the private sea, the Atlantic and Pacific" of your own being. "Do you reckon Tom Sawyer" would pass up a chance to rummage around on a wrecked riverboat, Huckleberry Finn asks Jim in *Adventures of Huckleberry Finn* (1884): "Not for pie, he wouldn't." Tom would land on the wreck with such style that "you'd think it was Christopher C'lumbus discovering Kingdom Come."[42] When such allusions are encoded in the names of fictional characters, they carry deconstructed traces of the Admiral's name into fresh narrative constructs. Wealthy and ingenuous, Christopher Newman in Henry James's *The American* (1877) discovers in Europe a baffling set of Old World conventions and mysteries; innocent and eager for life, Christie Devon in Louisa May Alcott's novel *Work* (1873) is, in the words of Cynthia Jordan, "a sort of female Christopher Columbus, about to leave home and explore the world for the first time."[43] Throughout the nineteenth century, by means of names, allusions, biographical sketches, and poems of tribute and dramatic identification, the figure of Columbus was shaped into images of ourselves. In *The Conquest of Paradise* (1990), Kirkpatrick Sale remarks that by the time of the Columbian Exposition in 1893 the

Admiral was no longer simply a patriotic symbol but a representation of "the official national deity, Progress."[44] During the first century of independence, that is to say, Columbus had become what the United States wanted to be.

Twentieth-century writers such as William Carlos Williams and Hart Crane have reflected on the Admiral's voyages in strikingly different ways. The idea that the American image of Columbus reflects the American view of America is borne out again in Williams' *In the American Grain* (1925), a series of impressionist meditations on the explorers who came early to the North American continent—Columbus, Cortez, and De Soto, among them. Williams portrays Columbus as someone who found a New World of purity and left a legacy of poison that claimed him as well as others. But Williams does not cast specific blame for what became a lethal encounter; rather, his explorers are helpless in their destructiveness, beset with an instinctive evil that haunts both conquerors and victims. Likewise an ensemble piece, though far more mystical in its vision, Crane's *The Bridge* (1930) renders a symbolic portrait of Columbus returning from his initial voyage with the supposed gift of Cathay, the first of the unifiers or "bridgers" who set the conditions for integrating past and present. Whereas Williams plunges Columbus into the plot of a fallen world, Crane presents his mistaken navigator as a prophet lifted above the mundane, ennobled by his consciousness.

The invocation of the New World at the end of F. Scott Fitzgerald's *The Great Gatsby* (1925), the reference to Columbus standing an egg on end in the swirling conversations of William Faulkner's *Go Down, Moses* (1942), the caustic mention of native Americans being taken to Spain in Alice Walker's *The Color Purple* (1982)—such allusions testify to a continued awareness of Columbus on the part of American writers. And with Michael Dorris and Louise Erdrich's *The Crown of Columbus* (1991), the encounter of Europe and America personified in the complex figure of the Admiral once again comes center stage in a way that sifts through the old (and the ancient) and transforms it to the new. In this narrative a protean Columbus is "the accumulation of his causes and . . . of his effects through time," a navigator, a mystic, a slave trader, an official who "acknowledged in his own handwriting" the right of native peoples to govern their territory, a man who brought to the Americas the greatest treasure of Europe: a crown of thorns.[45] Although this is not necessarily *the* crown of thorns, it is an eloquent symbol of Christ brought by Christoforo, the Christ-bearer. And it bristles with implication: Columbus brings to the New World a crown of thorns—a legacy of suffering, a legacy of European pride, glory, and woe. The treasured *object* in this novel lies at the center of a series of circles and enclosures and is found only after one undergoes primal, elemental experience that heightens the wonder of an original world. But the ultimate *treasure* in the novel is a discovery of self stripped of ego, self bonded to others, self whole and bright with promise. After the wind lifts the Crown, then sets it down again, "its circle didn't separate. Only the thorns fell off, every one."[46] What remains is a thornless emblem of unity, refashioned in and by the present.

As *The Crown of Columbus* leads us to see, our perception of the consequences of Columbus' voyages continues to change. As one way of establishing the argument of *Woman in the Nineteenth Century* in 1845 (the same year in which James Kirke Paulding wrote his hyperbolic praise of Columbus to President Polk), Margaret Fuller commended Isabella of Castile for furnishing the Admiral with the means of sailing to the "New World." "This land," she continued, "must pay back its debt to Woman, without whose aid it would not have been brought into alliance with the civilized world."[47] The last part of this statement, fraught with the Eurocentric assumptions of Fuller's time and place, now seems insensitive (if not shocking)—myopic racism in the service of a feminist cause. For we have come to assess the cost as well as the benefits of Western civilization, to doubt the unqualified faith in progress embodied by such a spectacle as the Columbian Exposition of 1893. Given all that archaeologists and historians have taught us about the inhabitants of pre-Columbian America, we can no longer believe that European explorers sailed to an empty world; nor should we refer to "American Indians" without being aware that the very term is a product of Columbus' mistake and Vespucci's masquerade.

Yet with the quincentennial of the Admiral's landing upon us, some writers seem to subordinate knowledge of (and thus respect for) the original inhabitants to a fable of innocence by portraying (once again) the continent as paradise and Columbus as the agent of destruction. In late twentieth-century guise, the dream of paradise turns out to be alive and well, as much an unexamined part of our thinking as the progress-as-paradise credo of 1892 or the New World-as-paradise assumptions of 1792—the difference being that we now locate paradise in the past rather than in the present or the future. The very title of Kirkpatrick Sale's *The Conquest of Paradise: Christopher Columbus and the Columbian Legacy* (1990) suggests the argument of a book that (with considerable passion) bids us step outside our history and live like "original Americans" if we are to save "the earth of America."[48] Sale's ecological commitment is obviously commendable; it deserves to be made our own. But to transform such a commitment into a lament for a New World fall from paradise is to seek refuge in formula, to deny the complexity of a past in which we are all implicated, to forfeit the chance to understand a history that has made us, for good and for ill, what we are.

NOTES

1. Edward T. Stone, "Columbus and Genocide," *American Heritage* 26 (October 1975): 78; *Quincentennial of the Discovery of America: Encounter of Two Worlds* (occasional newsletter issued by the General Secretariat of the Organization of American States), No. 27 (June 1991): 1.

2. *Time* (27 May 1991): 74.

3. *Quincentennial*, No. 26 (March 1991): 2.

4. *Quincentennial*, No. 26 (March 1991): 1.

5. Thomas Hutchinson, *The History of the Colony and Province of Massachusetts-Bay*, ed. Lawrence S. Mayo (Cambridge: Harvard UP, 1936), 1:1. John Daly Burk, *The History of Virginia, From Its First Settlement to the Present Day* (Petersburg, VA, 1804), 5, 19.

6. St. John de Crèvecoeur, *Letters from an American Farmer* (London, 1782), 46. Thomas Cooper, *Some Information Respecting America* (London, 1794), 53. For Web-

ster, see Richard M. Rollins, *The Long Journey of Noah Webster* (Philadelphia: U of Pennsylvania P, 1980), 29.

7. Américo Vespucio, *El nuevo mundo: cartas relativas a sus viajes y descubrimientos*, Estudio preliminar de Roberto Levillier (Buenos Aires: Editorial Nova, 1951), 290.

8. Montaigne, "Of Cannibals," *Complete Works: Essays, Travel Journal, Letters*, trans. Donald M. Frame (Stanford: Stanford UP, 1957), 158.

9. Patricia Caldwell, *The Puritan Conversion Narrative: The Beginnings of American Expression* (New York: Cambridge UP, 1983), esp. Chapter 1.

10. Sylvester Judd, *Margaret: A Tale of the Real and the Ideal, Blight, and Bloom* (Upper Saddle River, NJ: Gregg Press, 1968), 230-31.

11. Margaret Fuller, *At Home and Abroad, or Things and Thoughts in America and Europe* (Port Washington, NY: Kennikat Press, 1971), 373.

12. Jeremy Belknap, *A Discourse, Intended to Commemorate the Discovery of America by Christopher Columbus* (Boston, 1792), 5, 25-26.

13. Freneau, *The Poems of Philip Freneau: Poet of the American Revolution*, ed. Fred Lewis Pattee, 3 vols. (Princeton: University Library, 1902), 1:89-90.

14. Jeremy Belknap, *Biographies of the Early Discoverers of America* (Boston, 1798), 19.

15. Thomas Prince, *Chronological History* (Boston, 1736), vol. 2, Part II, Sect. 2, p. 78.

16. Charles A. Goodrich, *Child's History of the United States: Designed as a First Book of History for Schools*, 2nd ed. (Philadelphia, 1844), 9.

17. Isaac Taylor, *Scenes in America, for the Amusement and Instruction of Little Tarry-at-Home Travellers* (Philadelphia, 1825), 10.

18. Goodrich, 12-13.

19. Cotton Mather, *Magnalia Christi Americana* (Books 1 and 2), ed. Kenneth B. Murdock (Cambridge: Belknap Press, 1977), 119. David Ramsey, *History of the United States, from Their First Settlement as English Colonies, in 1607, to the Year 1803*, 3 vols. (Philadelphia, 1818), 1:30. R. W. Emerson, *Essays & Lectures*, ed. Joel Porte (New York: Library of America, 1983), 849. S. E. Morison, *The European Discovery of America: The Southern Voyages, 1492-1616* (New York: Oxford UP, 1974), 292.

20. Whelpley, *A Compend of History, from the Earliest Times; Comprehending a General View of the Present State of the World, with respect to Civilization, Religion, and Government; and a Brief Dissertation on the Importance of Historical Knowledge*, 2 vols. (New York, 1814), 2:142-43.

21. Samuel L. Mitchill, *Address to the Fredes* (New York, 1804), title page.

22. Washington Irving, *Knickerbocker's History of New York* (New York: Collier, 1904), 41. E. A. Poe, untitled article in *Graham's Magazine*, 29 (December 1846): 312. Poe notes the suggestion by "Mr. Field" of the New York Historical Society on the same page. George R. Stewart, *Names on the Land: A Historical Account of Place-Naming in the United States*, 3rd ed. (Boston: Houghton Mifflin, 1958), 173.

23. Garrison Keillor, *Lake Woebegone Days* (New York: Viking, 1985), 94.

24. Martin Waldseemüller, *Cosmographiae Introductio* (Ann Arbor: University Microfilms, 1966), 70.

25. Marie-Anne DuBoccage, *La Colombiade, ou La Foi Portée au Nouveau Monde* (Paris, 1756), "Second Chant" (Canto), 20-28. The lines in this poem are not numbered. DuBoccage explains in an "Introduction" that the cruel warfare of Cortez and Pizarro in Mexico and Peru led her to refrain from casting either as her protagonist in "un Poëme sur la Conquête du Nouveau Monde" (v-vi). Columbus was her choice because of his courage, wisdom, and popularity in fifteenth-century Europe. Aware of the limitations of her poetic gifts, she nonetheless believes that "ce nouvel Ulysse méritoit sans doute un autre Homere" (vii).

26. *La Colombiade*, "Neuvième Chant," 163, 161.

27. James A. Moore, *The Columbiad: An Epic Poem on the Discovery of America and the West Indies by Columbus* (London, 1798), Book VI, lines 180-87. How the Rev.

Moore came to write an epic poem about Columbus (in the year of the *Lyrical Ballads*), I do not know. Master of the Free Grammar School in Hertford, Herts., author of *A Treatise on the Inspiration of the New Testament* and *A View of the Evidence of the Christian Religion,* Moore is a forgotten (if hardly neglected) writer who is not even represented by an entry in the *DNB.*

28. Moore, *Columbiad,* Book IX, lines 922-32.

29. Barlow, *The Columbiad: A Poem* (Philadelphia, 1807), Book I, lines 37 and 97.

30. R. H. Pearce, *The Continuity of American Poetry* (Princeton: Princeton UP, 1961), 59-69.

31. Barlow, *Columbiad,* Book I, lines 229-30.

32. Barlow, *Columbiad,* Book I, lines 297 and 340-46.

33. Emory Elliott, *Revolutionary Writers: Literature and Authority in the New Republic, 1725-1810* (New York: Oxford UP, 1982), 94, 115.

34. Cecilia Tichi, *New World, New Earth: Environmental Reform in American Literature from the Puritans through Whitman* (New Haven: Yale UP, 1979), 128.

35. Tichi, 115.

36. Jeffrey Rubin-Dorsky, *Adrift in the Old World: The Psychological Pilgrimage of Washington Irving* (Chicago: U of Chicago P, 1988), 221-23.

37. Washington Irving, *History of the Life and Voyages of Christopher Columbus,* 2 vols. (New York, 1861), 1:286 and 2:516.

38. John D. Hazlett, "Literary Nationalism and Ambivalence in Washington Irving's 'The Life and Voyages of Christopher Columbus,' " *American Literature* 55 (1983): 560-75.

39. Irving, *History of Columbus,* 1:401.

40. *The Letters of James Kirke Paulding,* ed. Ralph M. Aderman (Madison: U of Wisconsin P, 1962), 414.

41. Ernest Francisco Fenollosa, *East and West: The Discovery of America and Other Poems* (1893; Upper Saddle River, NJ.: Gregg Press, 1970), 143.

42. H. D. Thoreau, *Walden,* ed. J. Lyndon Shanley (Princeton: Princeton UP, 1971), 321. Mark Twain, *Huckleberry Finn,* ed. Henry Nash Smith (Boston: Houghton Mifflin, 1958), 57.

43. Professor Jordan has made this remark in several conversations with me; the latest occasion was August 9, 1992.

44. Kirkpatrick Sale, *The Conquest of Paradise: Christopher Columbus and the Columbian Legacy* (New York: Knopf, 1990), 350. A more searching analysis of the early contacts between Europeans and Native Americans in North and South America can be found in Stephen Greenblatt's *Marvelous Possessions: The Wonder of the New World* (Chicago: U of Chicago P, 1991).

45. Michael Dorris and Louise Erdrich, *The Crown of Columbus* (New York: Harper Collins, 1991), 204, 265.

46. Dorris/Erdrich, 369.

47. "Woman in the Nineteenth Century," *The Writings of Margaret Fuller,* ed. Mason Wade (New York: Viking, 1941), 143.

48. Sale, 369.

Charlotte Temple's Remains

Eva Cherniavsky

The "we" of the declaration [of independence] speaks "in the name of the people."

But this people does not exist. They do *not* exist as an entity, it does *not* exist, *before* this declaration, not as *such*. If it gives birth to itself, as free and independent subject, as possible signer, this can hold only in the act of the signature. The signature invents the signer. This signer can only authorize him or herself to sign once he or she has come to the end [parvenu au vout], if one can say this, of his or her own signature, in a sort of fabulous retroactivity.

—Jacques Derrida,
"Declarations of Independence"

[The] melodramatic weepie is the genre that seems to endlessly repeat our melancholic sense of the loss of origins— impossibly hoping to return to an earlier state which is perhaps most fundamentally represented by the body of the mother.

—Linda Williams, "Film Bodies:
Gender, Genre and Excess"

Some time after the publication of Susanna Rowson's popular novel *Charlotte Temple* (1791), a tombstone inscribed with the title character's name was erected in Trinity churchyard in New York City. If, as Leslie Fiedler suggests, a certain Charlotte Stanley furnished the inspiration for Rowson's sentimental heroine, the grave of Charlotte's embodied original had no attraction for the novel's readers, who flocked instead to Charlotte Temple's tomb, to the extra-textual marker of this textual construct's remains.[1] Indeed, for a more than a century they littered the gravesite with locks of hair, ashes of love letters, and flowers, and in the words of one late nineteenth-century witness to the scene, kept "the turf over Charlotte Temple . . . fresh with falling tears."[2]

But what exactly shall we say has been interred beneath this monument—what kind of body inhabits Charlotte Temple's grave? With this gesture of memorialization, the builders of the grave simultaneously retrieve a body from the text and mark its loss. By encrypting Charlotte, they *produce* her body *as lost*; that is, they render a body in excess of its discursive articulations, but only as the object of the mourners' melancholic identification. This essay will read *Charlotte Temple* from the vantage of the churchyard scene in order to interrogate the novel's production of this pre- or post-textual body, and the non-linear temporality in which its fabrication of an "original" Charlotte transpires.

The epigraphs to this essay should suggest the political and cultural context(s) in which the novel's temporality interests me. On the one hand, I align *Charlotte Temple* with what Linda Williams identifies as the constitutive belatedness of melodrama, and the phantasm of origins it inscribes on the maternal body. In this respect, the temporality of my own analysis is prospective, locating *Charlotte Temple* in relation to a genre that—particularly in its non-dramatic inflection, as the sentimental novel—emerges in the United States only toward the middle of the nineteenth century. On the other hand, I move to juxtapose *Charlotte Temple* and indeed, by implication, the temporality of nineteenth- and twentieth-century melodrama, with what Jacques Derrida has termed the "fabulous retroactivity" of liberal founding, with a logic of social legitimation that makes "the people" at once the justification for and the result of national autonomy, with a practice of textual self-invention that negates the new political order's historical contingency. I want to suggest that melodrama's essentialization of the maternal as origin needs to be read, not only for its contribution to the emergent ideology of the bourgeois nuclear family, but also as the contestation of a specific refusal of history that grounds this liberal order.

Thus I propose that *Charlotte Temple* inscribes on Charlotte's maternal body, (retroactively) conceived as pre-text, as embodied origin(al), the historical contingency that the emergent political order disavows. More specifically, the novel renders visible the dominant class interests which pre-exist and inform the construction of "the people," renders visible, that is, a class of white, property-owning men whose particular interests the founding texts of the United States make over into "the general interest"—renders the dominant class visible *as* a class by wrenching the category of the "general" from its (collective) grasp.[3] Indeed, Derrida's equivocation about the gender of the self-emancipating signer seems unaccountable: to equivocate in this regard is strangely to endorse the possibility of the signer's spontaneous self-generation, to underwrite the erasure of history it entails, a history of pre-existing social relations that determine who accedes to the status of signatory in the first place. In other words, it is these pre-existing relations that determine the possibility of the white man's disembodiment, his self-abstraction as a metonymy of "the people" in whose name he signs; and that, conversely, effect the designation of non-male and non-white bodies as hopelessly particularized, inadequate to the function of signatory, or citizen, because irreducible to the white masculine generic.[4] I will argue that *Charlotte Temple* at once assumes and contests a portion of the history that renders women unrepresentative of "the general interest" by (re)constituting them as a political body—which is to say, by retracing the limits of the representable.

In a different discursive register, the novel reflects on its own transgressive project. Although the subtitle to *Charlotte Temple*—"A Tale of Truth"— functions most obviously to defend against the moralist's conventional accusation—that the novel as a genre glamorized seduction—it serves more subtly to redefine the possibilities of representing women in an order that denies their political representability. Contemporary criticism of the novel hinged on the juxtaposition of its pernicious influence on the female reader to the benign effects of historical reading. As critics such as Benjamin Rush and Timothy Dwight contended, this impressionable reader would be unable to distance herself from the examples of fallen womanhood she encountered in the novel form. "What can the reader expect," laments Dwight, "after having resided so long in novels, but that fortunes, and villas, and Edens, will spring up every where in her progress through life, to promote her enjoyment. She has read herself into a heroine, and is fairly entitled to all the appendages of this character."[5] On the contrary, when examples of immoral conduct appeared in historical narratives, they effectively deterred the reader from emulation. Thus when Mercy Otis Warren, echoing these male authorities on the subject of female education, exhorts women to put aside all "books that have not a tendency to instill lessons of virtue," she goes on in the same breath to enjoin the reading of "authentic history, which is now written in a style equally elegant to the many volumes of romance, which in the present age croud around the public."[6]

While in one sense Rowson's assertion of the novel's historicity concedes to its moral critics "authentic history['s]" superiority, in another sense it contests their conflation of exemplarity with the singularity of the historical figure, of the woman whose very place in the historical record attests to her eccentricity. If a historical model for Charlotte existed, then she was, like Charlotte, marked out precisely by her lack of singularity, by her resemblance to a character in a seduction novel, her status as a generic figure. Leslie Fiedler observes as much about Charlotte's suggested historical model, quipping that the author of *Clarissa* had of course "invented . . . [Charlotte Stanley's] life before she managed to live it."[7] Insofar as the paradigmatic Charlotte has been divested of the historical woman's distinctiveness, Rowson's claim to historical authenticity remains disingenuous: Charlotte's "tale" is "true," but only because "truth" now lies outside Dwight's ideology of history. Rather than claim morality for the novel, Rowson moves to establish a competing pedagogical code.

As in fact the churchyard spectacle suggests, Charlotte compels the very attachment Dwight attributes to the seduction novel's heroine, if not precisely for the reasons he identifes. While Dwight looks to the material pleasures of a kept woman's existence to explain the reader's attraction to a woman such as Charlotte, an attraction, he seems to surmise, that cannot be explained in terms of her vacuous character, I argue to the contrary that Charlotte's flatness, her merely generic femininity, allows her to stand in for the novel's readership, to be (the) representative of a diffuse collection of readers whom she thereby transforms into a constituency. The graveside mourners refuse to sever their affective ties to the fallen Charlotte, as indeed the moralist argues that they must, not because they have invested her with the aura of social privilege, but because she invests them with a collective identity.

Judith Butler's reading of femininity as masquerade offers a particularly compelling model for understanding the mourners' relation to Charlotte. Masquerade functions in her account, not to conceal a primary or essential identity, but to preserve by way of incorporation a connection that must be refused:

> The mask has a double function which is the double function of melancholy. The mask is taken on through the process of incorporation which is a way of inscribing and then wearing a melancholic identification in and on the body; in effect, it is the signification of the body in the mold of the Other who has been refused. Dominated through appropriation, every refusal fails, and the refuser becomes part of the very identity of the refused, indeed, becomes the psychic refuse of the refused. The loss of the object is never absolute because it is redistributed within a psychic/corporeal boundary that expands to incorporate that loss.[8]

As the mark of the loss that it serves to occlude, the mask constitutes the gendered subject in the image of what she must relinquish. In this frame, we might recast the mourners' refusal to repudiate their bond to Charlotte as their "domination through appropriation" of what amounts to the law's refusal of them—as the mourners' "domination through appropriation" of the loss of their own representative body. Through their melancholic incorporation of the lost Charlotte, that is, the mourners wear "in and on" their bodies the representativeness that the political order denies them. Implicit, then, in the mourners' apparently essentializing gesture, in their production of a pre-textual female body—of a maternal origin—is their engagement with history: their melancholic graveside ritual commemorates, accepts, and dominates a loss of political representation that the narratives of national self-making serve to naturalize.

ALL THE APPENDAGES OF CHARACTER?

In the opening portions of the novel, Rowson rehearses the circumstances of Charlotte's mother's marriage to the young Mr. Temple. This narrative of Lucy's passage from her father's to her husband's house elaborates a model of normative femininity against which Charlotte's fall from virtue is to be read. Yet Lucy represents more than the ideal of republican womanhood, of a particularized and disinterested femininity; her narrative suggests further the way in which republican womanhood assumes the burden of everyone's particularity, of feeling, sympathy in general—assumes the burden of interiority itself within the nuclear family and by extension within the culture as a whole.[9] As a pattern of womanhood, then, Lucy serves as the conduit of private affections; her affecting (and affectingly self-effacing) presence generates the network of affiliations that constitute the bourgeois family. Thus Lucy is normative in the very fact of her sentimental excess, of the only apparently extravagant feelings that function in fact to delimit the domestic. Indeed, we first encounter her, having lost her mother and brother in a series of calamitous misfortunes, voicing the desire to expire with her father. "Oh my father," she exclaims when he seeks to discuss her future, "daily are my prayers offered to heaven that our lives may terminate at the same instant, and one grave receive us both; for why should I live when deprived of my only friend?" (CT, 14). If Lucy remains otherwise mute in the novel's early chapters, her pathetic attachment to a shattered domestic scene—her single, hyperbolic assertion that she has no existence outside of the familial sphere—does not go unnoticed: enchanted with this outpouring of feminine sentiment, Temple moves immediately to appropriate it, to incorporate it in a new familial configuration, in a "Temple" to domestic feeling.

Even before the pantomimic exchange of glances that constitutes her courtship, Lucy's concurrence in the union appears inevitable. Inasmuch as Temple, moved to tears by Lucy's plight, rescues her destitute father from the debtor's prison where he has been confined, he effectively purchases his own domestic felicity. While Temple seems hardly guilty of mere self-interest in this affair—in discharging the father's heavy burden of debt, he depletes his fortune and restricts his own social prospects—sentiment plainly flows along the channels of economic dependencies. Thus Temple can anticipate with apparent propriety and self-assurance the "exquisite transport [it will be] to see the expressive eyes of Lucy beaming at once with pleasure for her father's deliverance, and gratitude for her deliverer" (CT, 21). By predicating Lucy's sentiments toward him on their economic affiliation, Temple imposes the logic of coverture, a principle of republican law—imported, via the British legal tradition, from feudal France—that submerges the wife's legal and economic identity in her husband's, a legal principle that doubles as both the (historical) justification for women's political invisibility and its (naturalized) effect. Coverture follows marriage, Temple reasons; hence marriage should follow coverture.

In this gracefully calculating fashion, Temple acquires in his own name Lucy's affecting feminine presence, whose sentimentality now finds its privileged outlet in the domestic production of the virtuous child. It is in the figure of what Linda Kerber has termed "the Republican Mother" that the covered woman emerges as a force for socialization.[10] Refused political participation, denied her title to property or the right to function in any contractual relation independently of her husband, the white, middle-class woman inculcates the morality of an order that effaces her: through her mediation, as the "expressive" body of private sympathies, public morality is particularized, interiorized. Rowson thus figures the daughter's moral failing as a repudiation of maternal love:

> Oh my friends, as you value your eternal happiness, wound not, by thoughtless ingratitude, the peace of the mother who bore you: remember the tenderness, the care, the unremitting anxiety with which she has attended to all your wants and wishes from earliest infancy to the present day; behold the mild ray of affectionate applause that beams from her eye on the performance of your duty; listen to her reproofs with silent attention; they proceed from a heart anxious for your future

felicity: you must love her; nature, all-powerful nature, has planted the seeds of filial affection in your bosoms.

Then once more read over the sorrows of poor Mrs. Temple, and remember, the mother whom you so dearly love and venerate will feel the same, when you, forgetful of the respect due your maker and yourself, forsake the paths of virtue for those of vice and folly. (CT, 54)

This appeal exemplifies the logic of republican motherhood, which articulates the henceforth idealized power of maternal love as a moral force. If within the bourgeois family the infant finds recognition of its emergent being in the loving maternal gaze, liberal republican culture writes this constitutive look of recognition as an injunction to social duty. The mother's eye here beams applause at her child's assimilation of social norms. In this frame, for the daughter to fall from virtue is to alienate herself, not simply from internalized moral norms, but from the constitutive divisions of her selfhood—from her own interiority. The fall from virtue that severs this maternal tie turns Charlotte inside out; more than a fall from good society, from middle-class to lower-class status, it represents her fall into abjection, the dissolution of her identity.

Thus when Charlotte "falls a victim to her too great sensibility," falls victim, that is, to her own femininity, to her unlimited capacity for sentiment, she literally comes undone; in succumbing to Montraville's pleas she resigns even the power to succumb:

"I cannot go," said she: "cease, dear Montraville, to persuade. I must not: religion, duty, forbid."

"Cruel Charlotte," said he, "if you disappoint my ardent hopes, by all that is sacred, this hand shall put a period to my existence. I cannot—will not live without you."

"Alas! my torn heart!" said Charlotte, "how shall I act?"

"Let me direct you," said Montraville, lifting her into the chaise.

"Oh! my dear forsaken parents!" cried Charlotte.

The chaise drove off. She shrieked, and fainted into the arms of her betrayer. (CT, 47-48)

If this depiction of Charlotte's flight as something between an abduction and an elopement recalls the seminal *Clarissa,* unlike Richardson, Rowson brackets the question of Charlotte's agency altogether.[11] Charlotte is carried off neither against, nor in accordance with her will; once she softens to Montraville's pathetic appeal, she has no will to assert, no power to concur or to dissent. Uncovered and seduced from her father's protection into the embrace of a man who has neither the means nor the intention to domesticate her, Charlotte simply disappears, can no longer be spoken of in relation to a rational model of selfhood premised on individual limits and moral agency. What remains on the scene is not so much a character, and even less a caricature, but a figure of pure affect, uncovered, freed, and abject.

As she sobs, faints, and convulses her way through the cruel twists of a wayward daughter's fate, Charlotte exasperates both the literary critic with a taste for subtle characterization and psychological verisimilitude, and, Rowson insinuates, the consumer of sentimental fiction herself: " 'Bless my heart,' cries my young, volatile reader, 'I shall never have patience to get through these volumes, there are so many ahs! and ohs! so much fainting, tears, and distress, I am sick to death of the subject'" (CT, 98). Yet Rowson goes on to solicit her reader's patience under the banner, precisely, of truth in the novel: "my lively, innocent girl, I must request your patience: I am writing a tale of truth: I mean to write it to the heart: but if perchance the heart is rendered impenetrable by unbounded prosperity, or a continuance in vice, I expect not my tale to please, nay I even expect it will be thrown by with disgust" (CT, 99). To the reader who protests the apparent banality of Charlotte's engagement with the world, that makes each scene in which she figures a repetition of the last, Rowson responds that the "truth of the tale" is vested exactly in the interminable series of affective moments of which Charlotte's history is comprised; dislodged from the scene of familial identification where it organizes a particular set of relations, Charlotte's affect now mediates nothing in particular, constitutes (potentially) her mode of relation to the social in general, and so impels Charlotte into the discursive domain of representative femininity. In order to appreciate the tale, Rowson implies, the reader must transcend domestic morality and melt in sympathy for the lost Charlotte. For the limits which moral and vicious reasoning alike impose inure the individual to the spectacle of dissolution. Both the moralist and the harlot (the "sober matron" with whom Rowson engages in her asides to the reader as well as the willfully licentious La Rue who masterminds Charlotte's elopement with Montraville), constituted in and by the divisions of republican social space, find Charlotte's uncovered feminine affect merely repellent.

In this frame, to write a tale "to the heart" is to appeal to that aspect of republican feminine personality that the economic and symbolic action of coverture at once produces and submerges, to appeal to a Lucy Temple's fund of (familial) sympathies. Those readers whom Rowson distinguishes from the censuring matron and the hardened offender as "my dear girls" perceive in the fallen Charlotte, then, their own excess uncovered, released from the domestic sphere. And thus their melting sympathy for Charlotte at once assumes and produces a sense of distance from the cultural placement of the feminine, an internal distance from their relentlessly privatized selves, a sense of representable identity. Moreover, in this context Charlotte's pregnancy, though anything but unexpected, marks a critical turn in the narrative. The affective bond which binds the reader to this (expectant) mother works, precisely, to *attenuate* the reader's connection to moral norms. As Charlotte moves from girlhood into motherhood, that is, she assumes the full disruptive power of the negative exemplum; if maternal affect in the covered woman is the medium of moral instruction, in the outcast it serves to negate the logic of coverture, to strip away, in other words, the moral imperative from the face of maternal sentiment.

Indeed, in the eyes of the stalwart republican, the helpless Charlotte, destitute and nearing her confinement, is a spectacle, as Rowson tells us, to freeze the blood and turn the heart to stone. "Alas poor Charlotte," she comments on her heroine's vain appeal to a crude landlady's sympathy, "how confined was her knowledge of human nature . . . for when once the petrifying aspect of distress and penury appear, whose qualities, like Medusa's head, can change to stone all that look upon it; when once this Gorgon claims acquaintance with us, the phantom of friendship, that before courted our notice, will vanish into unsubstantial air, and the whole world before us appears a barren waste" (CT, 102). In her "distress and penury," as the outcast mother-to-be, the abject Charlotte acquires Medusa'a deadly aspect, assumes the emblematic form of maternal generativity released from all constraints. And if the lower-class land-lady is proof against the spectacle, perceiving in Charlotte only the laughable posturings of a leisured woman, Mademoiselle La Rue, on the other hand, can take no such distance on her former student and finally succumbs to the mor-alist's terror of retribution: "Take her away," she cries, when the homeless Charlotte turns up in search of a place to bear her child, "she will really frighten me into hysterics; take her away I say this instant. . . . Any where, only don't let me ever see her again" (CT, 109).

READING HERSELF INTO A HEROINE

La Rue's double betrayal, her inability to endure the sight of her own creation, seals Charlotte's expulsion from the social order. The flaunter of morals de-fines herself by the same standards as the moralist, Charlotte discovers, and comments, judiciously for once, "this is too much" (CT, 108). Ironically, La Rue initially justifies her dismissal of Charlotte's pathetic request for shelter by invoking the proprieties of wedded life. Legitimately connected now to the gullible Mr. Crayton, who learns too late of his wife's markedly unsentimental bent, La Rue insists that she could neither afford to impugn her own reputation by seeming to condone the dissipated life of a woman such as Charlotte, nor would she risk incurring for her husband the expense of Charlotte's care. This travesty of feminine morals, La Rue's feigned appreciation of the wife's im-puted moral role, is the fitting prelude to Charlotte's confinement, delirium, and death. While republican assumptions about feminine identity come under open censure in this scene, in which the language of domestic sensibility speaks its own condemnation in the mouth of the hypocrite, Charlotte uncovers in the final stages of her dissolution another modality of feminine "sympathy," freed from the set of social relations that conflate maternal feeling with domestic morality, a modality of identification with the affecting republican mother that affirms the possibility of representative feminine identity.

Realizing that she is pregnant and that Montraville's feelings for her have eroded, Charlotte begs her parents to abet her return, and recounts in a letter a recurrent dream, in which her father first, and then her mother, reproach her for her mother's murder:

> At other times I see my father angry and frowning, point to horrid caves, where on the cold damp ground, in the agonies of death, I see my dear mother and my re-vered grand-father. I strive to raise you; you push me from you, and shrieking cry— "Charlotte, thou hast murdered me!" Horror and despair tear every tortured nerve; I start, and leave my restless bed. . . ." (CT, 81)

In the initial realization of her own impending motherhood, then, Charlotte relives her separation from her mother as a murder, as a violent rupture enacted on the primal ground of "horrid caves." Thus she seems at once to invest this separation from her mother with the painful intensity of parturition, which spares the guilty child in this case and kills the mother, and to imagine that in her own maternal body is taking form only the empty horror of a broken connection. The peculiarity of the scene, however, which at once underscores and complicates the transparent symbolism of this encounter, is the presence of the grandfather, sharing her mother's pain rather than her father's ire. And yet this distribution is central, I would suggest, to Charlotte's symbolization of her motherhood as a rift, as the deadly severance of affective ties: the grandfather's presence in the cave serves to locate Charlotte's experience of loss within the terms of coverture, and more particularly within the construction of motherhood as moral instruction that coverture promotes. If the grandfather comes to occupy the same position as his daughter in the dream, the logic of their pairing is economic; when Temple acquires Lucy as a source of familial affect, he acquires her father in the bargain. Unable to protect either his daughter or his own interest, the grandfather, too, assumes the identity of Temple's dependent, and consequently that of a feminized medium of sentiment in Temple's domestic realm. Insofar as sentimental attachment is governed by the logic of economic dependencies, then, Charlotte's alienation from her mother appears to be of the same order as her alienation from this domesticated, powerless old man.

Charlotte's vision of her wounded mother recurs with a difference after the birth of her daughter, whom Charlotte initially refuses to acknowledge as her own:

> "Oh," said she one day, starting up on hearing the infant cry, "why, why will you keep that child here; I am sure you would not if you knew how hard it was for a mother to be parted from her infant: it is like tearing the cords of life asunder. Oh could you see the horrid sight which I now behold—there—there stands my dear mother, her poor bosom bleeding at every vein, her gentle, affectionate heart torn in a thousand pieces, and all for the loss of a ruined, ungrateful child. Save me—save me—from her frown. I dare not—indeed I dare not speak to her." (CT, 111)

The grandfather no longer figures in this version of Charlotte's dream, and the bleeding mother herself appears to have assumed the father's censuring gaze. But the mother no longer voices her reproach; it is Charlotte in her terror who attributes anger to this "gentle, affectionate" figure, a figure which appears to have transcended, through the anguish of its rent and bleeding heart, through its own slow dissolution, the imperative to moral judgment altogether—it is Charlotte, in short, who sees a "Gorgon" where there is none and recoils in panic from its frown. In fact, the mother's appearance here has assumed all the characteristic marks of Charlotte's own, so that in facing this image of abject womanhood Charlotte faces herself, and the terms of her own motherhood as well.

Yet Charlotte's vision anticipates the tender recognition of her child in the scene that follows. By displacing herself in this vision between the infant's position—in her delirium, she sees her crying child as parted from its mother, like herself—and the mother's, Charlotte realizes the continuity between Lucy Temple, her daughter and herself. She *uncovers*, in other words, the sentimental affiliation that obtains despite her social fall, and that finds its inscription in her child's name: little Lucy restores the broken bond between Charlotte and her mother and reveals a maternal succession that operates independently of republican standards of social legitimation. Thus, significantly, the child that bears Lucy's name shows Charlotte's face, when some years after Charlotte's death, the aging La Rue, whom the wages of sin have left destitute, comes for relief to Charlotte's parents' door. "Heaven have mercy!" she cries, looking at little Lucy, "I see her [Charlotte] now" (CT, 119).

In articulating Charlotte's unbroken connection to her mother, a connection that establishes a ground, in turn, for Charlotte's affirmation of her own motherhood, Rowson "authenticates" Charlotte as exemplum for the female reader: that is to say, by uncovering the sentimental bond that binds Lucy to her fallen daughter and the daughter's illegitimate child, Rowson reveals a principle of feminine connection that obtains in excess of moral boundaries. Inasmuch as the female reader, Rowson's "dear young girl," maintains her affective ties to Charlotte, she bears, like little Lucy, the stamp of this affiliation—discloses, to the eyes of the discerning viewer, the trace of Charlotte's features in her own mild face. The identification of Charlotte's readers with her daughter is in fact suggested in the novel: "if my child should be a girl . . . ," Charlotte instructs her parents, "tell her the unhappy fate of her mother" (CT, 81). Lucy herself, then, like the consumer of this fiction, is imagined as the product of her mother's narrative and conversely, the reader, like little Lucy, wears a melancholic identification with Charlotte on her body. Charlotte's daughter anticipates and thematizes the mourners' incorporation of the novel's encrypted heroine.

THE PENSIONER OF FRIENDSHIP

In response to this conception of a readership, of a community of melancholic readers, Hannah Foster attempts in her novel *The Coquette*—which followed the first American edition of *Charlotte Temple* by just three years—to represent such a collective, to define its practice and its parameters in the frame of women's covered lives. Unlike Rowson, whose historical model for Charlotte—if indeed she had one—never engaged the readers' interest, Foster takes as her pattern for Eliza Wharton a socially well placed figure named Elizabeth Whitman, whose death in childbed in a Connecticut tavern, while unattended by family and friends, and apparently unmarried, had been a well-publicized scandal.[12] So Eliza Wharton's tale opens, symbolically at least, on the scene of Elizabeth Whitman's grave—opens, one might say, where *Charlotte Temple* leaves off, on the affecting image of its heroine's tombstone. The readers' perception of Eliza is thus, in one sense, always retrospective—always already a function of her loss.[13] Yet it is precisely the re-presentation of this loss that the narrative seeks to defer, as though to draw on its pre-text, on the sentimental legitimation of the buried Elizabeth/Charlotte, in order to deflect Eliza's textual reenactment of Elizabeth's fate. In this frame, Foster can be seen to operate on the model of Derrida's liberal founders, who disavow the contingency of their textual self-production. Significantly, then, the better portion of *The Coquette* is concerned, not with the narration of Eliza's fall—of her illicit trysts with Sanford, her concealed pregnancy, midnight elopement, and death—but with her determined attempt to maintain her status as *feme sole,* neither married nor under parental protection, among the community of her female friends.

Put another way, throughout most of the novel, Eliza operates in a state of suspension, poised between Elizabeth's realized fate and her own imminent fall, and claiming, in this state, the right to what she calls her "freedom," and her devoted though skeptical friends refer to as "a play about words."[14] Eliza attempts, in short, the radical divorce of sentiment from the constraints of the privatized domestic sphere, envisions her power to feel, not as *a* medium of connection, but as defining *her own* mode of being in the world. Paradoxically, however, in her attempt at independence, Eliza must rely on the hospitality of her married women friends; she must become, as she puts it, "a pensioner of friendship" in their domestic realms (CQ, 36). As such, as an uncovered feminine presence occupying a kind of social non-space—living under the protection, the coverture, as it were, of women who, being themselves covered, have no protection to extend—Eliza constitutes a female collective with neither social nor economic legitimacy, a community that transcends the constitutive divisions of republican communal space.

Yet contingent on the alienation, or at least the partial alienation, of Eliza's "protectors" from the terms of social morality with which coverture serves to identify them, this society proves unequal to the labor of sustaining Eliza. While she lives, and principally while she still asserts her right to unrestricted sentimental communion, Eliza finds her sphere of influence progressively diminished as "the pleasing scenes of domestic life" (CQ, 97), and, in particular, the duties of motherhood, claim the attention of her friends. Foster's attempt to locate Eliza in the temporality of masculine self-invention, in the Declaration's "fabulous retroactivity," yields to the historical contingency of the sentimental novel's discourse, and its commemoration of women's loss; Eliza's power to form a constituency remains contingent on her replication of Elizabeth's fall. In the closing moments of the novel, at the limits of the narrative as it were, Eliza's fall reintegrates her crumbling community of friends as a community of mourners, which forms again around the locus of an absence, (re)assembles around a grave.

Thus *The Coquette,* for all its grounding in "authentic history," its apparent concession to the terms of republican moral instruction, is a tale about the "truth" of the sentimental tale, a novel that explores the terms of a sentimental pedagogy. Foster's attempt to represent a community of women, centered symbolically on this figure of uncovered feminine affect, works to demonstrate its unrepresentability. The sentimental exemplum signifies beyond the confines of the narrative, signifies in and through the (re)constitution of a readership. The amoral moral remains always in excess of the novel's discourse, then, but finds its inscription "in and on" the reader's body; it inhabits history in the form of an incorporated loss, mute yet resonant—like the fictional Charlotte Temple's buried remains.

NOTES

1. Leslie A. Fiedler, *Love and Death in the American Novel* (New York: Stein and Day, 1966), 95.

2. Cited by Cathy N. Davidson in her introduction to *Charlotte Temple* (New York: Oxford UP, 1986), xiv. Hereafter cited as CT.

3. For a helpful unpacking of the ideological "mirror couple" particular/general interest in Rousseau's *Social Contract*, see Louis Althusser, *Montesquieu, Rousseau, Marx* (London: Verso, 1982), 146-54.

4. Most recently, Lauren Berlant has expanded on this familiar feminist critique in terms particularly relevant to my discussion. See "National Brands/National Bodies," *Comparative American Identities: Race, Sex and Nationality in the Modern Text*, ed. Hortense J. Spillers (New York: Routledge, 1991), 112-13.

5. Cited by Cathy N. Davidson, *Revolution and the Word* (New York: Oxford UP, 1986), 51.

6. Cited by Linda K. Kerber, *Women of the Republic* (New York: Norton, 1981), 246.

7. Fiedler, 95.

8. Judith Butler, *Gender Trouble: Feminism and the Subversion of Identity* (New York: Routledge, 1990), 50.

9. Kaja Silverman offers an excellent account of how psychoanalysis and cinema displace the masculine subject's interiority onto the woman/mother, in order to ensure his discursive authority. See *The Acoustic Mirror* (Bloomington: Indiana UP, 1988), chapter 3.

10. See *Women of the Republic*, especially chapter 9. For Kerber, "Republican Motherhood" represents a more enlightened construction of feminine identity than "the Enlightenment" itself produced: in defining the mother as the cultivator of patriotic offspring, she argues, "the ideology of Republican Motherhood seemed to accomplish what the Enlightenment had not by identifying the intersection of the woman's private domain and the polis" (283). Thus "it justified women's absorption and participation in the civic culture" (284), furnished a strategy for politicizing women's role even as republican law barred their participation in the political order. My use of the term diverges from its author's, then: I contend that the ideology of Republican Motherhood reflects rather than compromises or moderates the logic of women's exclusion from the emergent political order.

11. Cathy Davidson has argued that Rowson shifts the burden of moral responsibility from Charlotte to her society: "She is a victim not so much of her wayward desires but of a shoddy education, of evil advisers (including one schoolteacher), of her legal and social inferiority" (*Revolution and the Word*, 137). I suggest, however, that from the moment of her elopement, Charlotte is not just circumstantially, but constitutively unable to defend herself, to act either in accord with or against the social determination of her "duty."

12. See Davidson, *Revolution and the Word*, 140ff.

13. Cathy Davidson shows persuasively that in transforming the sermonizing newspaper accounts of Whitman's death into Eliza Wharton's story, Hannah Foster restores "the complexity of which she [Whitman] had been deprived in the early allegories of her life and death" (*Revolution and the Word*, 143). While Davidson reads Foster as militating against the reduction of Elizabeth Whitman's narrative to Charlotte Temple's, I

want to explore the (complementary) ways in which *Charlotte Temple,* and the grave-yard spectacle which it produces, are the necessary pre-texts to this novel about the possibilities and limitations of women's community.

14. Hannah Foster, *The Coquette,* ed. Cathy N. Davidson (New York: Oxford UP, 1986), 31. Hereafter cited as CQ.

The Underheard Reader in the Writing of the Old Southwest

James H. Justus

What we *hear* when we read humor of the Old Southwest is funny regional dialect. What we *overhear,* especially in the 1990s, is a system of cultural values that finds great comic turns in what we now understand as sexism, racism, age-ism, and xenophobia—a cluster of biases that necessarily intervenes in both the comprehension and enjoyment of the humor. What we should *underhear* when we read humor of the Old Southwest is its literariness, the substantial noise of generic forms and the casual jumble of conventions. These texts, because they are so rarely subtle in their effects, test the boundaries of the liminal for the reader who responds only to what is heard and overheard. What is underheard may not be heard at all, but even if it reaches us only subliminally, it is the last of these hearings that makes an impression.

In reading this humor, when we become aware of repetitive narrative situations and character types, we tend to process them while responding to the dominant sounds of vernacular speech, deviant language that absorbs the niceties of motivation as well as our curiosity about the relational context of characters who use it. The aural reception of this kind of text is dominant because the specialized idiom appropriates those stable constituent elements that we think of as the glory of the novel as a form—plot and character. With the possible exception of George Washington Harris' yarns about Sut Lovingood, the typical humorous sketch in this body of writing shows no interest in the creation of complex characters engaged in complicated experience. This is true partly because the vehicle of this humor is not the novel but the anecdote, the joke, the tall tale, the piece that fits into limited allotments of newspaper space, but also because they more comfortably respond to the expectations of a related body of affiliated forms: the essay, the travel letter, the sporting epistle, even the "character," that seventeenth-century form that was designed to encapsulate idealized representatives of the human species (which in the Mississippi Valley rapidly became favorite high-profile stereotypes: the half-horse half-alligator; the backwoods innocent; the sexually omniscient widow).

Bakhtin told us that to understand Rabelais we should be prepared to renounce all our deeply ingrained expectations of literary taste. That is, we should be alert to the eruptive presence of "inferior" dialects, disruptive argot, the despised demotic of resolutely nonliterary groups in the shaping of texts that are otherwise written in accepted styles. I would suggest that in the writing with which I have been most recently concerned, we see almost the reverse process. To understand the writing of the Southwestern humorists—that, too, of Mark Twain which was its culmination—we should be prepared to *underhear* the eruptive hum of respectable voices even in the flamboyant orality of backwoods roustabouts whose links are not merely with their inarticulate yeoman cousins but with the very custodians of literary taste.

I.

Southwestern humor is a refraction of one region's demographic upheaval in the second and third decades of the nineteenth century. The literary texts beginning a decade later are one version of that social instability, one in which power relations are oddly comported, an effect of rampant chicanery achieved by the simple device of wretched excess, a compositional habit articulated through obsessive recurrence, unnatural selection, and rhetorical overkill. While particular cultural traits and activities (boasting, say, or courtship rituals) are italicized—sometimes literally—others (say ordinary domestic life among all the classes) are subordinated or omitted entirely. The world of the humorists is specialized and stylized; it is also vulnerable because its cohesive familial and communal relationships are so frail. Fraternization, organization, bonding, groupings of all kinds are premised on expedience. The sketch offers us a condensed reenactment of the exercise of power in the actual geography it celebrates. The point of competition is to establish individual priority within and even despite those fragile group arrangements. There are always winners, which means that there are also losers, those who are "tuck in." From the practical joke to the swindling of widows, however, the winner's material take in all these competitions is always modest: psychological satisfaction and a few dollars to splurge on an oyster supper. The game is everything, because it is the model for the exercise of power. So pervasive is this pattern that the play of power itself becomes a convention.

What I would like to focus on here is a refinement of structure in the kind of sketch in which an educated, sophisticated, and cultivated man of the world confronts a backwoodsman who then recounts an episode out of his experience in the woods. If not exactly a gentleman, the narrator is a respectable, tolerant sort of individual willing to be amused—a stand-in for the author and, from the reader's perspective, "one of us." The backwoodsman—a yeoman farmer, a hunter, a boatman, anyone whose chosen sphere is the relative isolation beyond towns and villages—may be ignorant of some of the most basic kinds of information that the narrator takes for granted, yet he is savvy, tenacious, gregarious, and garrulous—and also willing to be amused. What adds interest to this kind of sketch is that its dynamics of winning and losing are somewhat more complex than those sketches with other structural patterns—the epistolary, say, as in Charles Noland's Pete Whetstone letters and William

Tappan Thompson's Major Jones, whose letters to the editor comprise one single unmediated vernacular discourse. What we see in the sketch that features the encounter between narrator and backwoodsman is the textual representation of how the writer, committed to the values of social stability and civic order, participates in the competitive game of his time and place. As the later arrival on the scene, the narrator assumes all the conventional attitudes of the traveler in exotic newfound territory; the native figure he encounters is seen as a cultural primitive. What is prior is Other. Though the encounter may elicit some mutual good natured scorn, it is not hostile; and indeed that narrator goes out of his way to promote this individual of such different values and habits, opening a space in his sketch for the vernacular figure to become his own hero by taking over the narrative through the sheer stylistic energy of an alternative language.

The best-loved sketch in all the writings from the Old Southwest—and the one that lent its name to what was once perceived as the "school" of Southwestern humor—is Thomas Bangs Thorpe's "The Big Bear of Arkansas," the very model of this narrative pattern. The gentlemanly narrator, on his way upriver from New Orleans on a steamboat, finds his reading interrupted by a genial and voluble backwoodsman by the name of Jim Doggett, who entertains the passengers with stories of Arkansas, a state so naturally fecund that he has found it too dangerous to be a farmer: " 'I had a good-sized sow killed. . . . The old thief stole an ear of corn, and took it down to eat where she slept at night. Well, she left a grain or two on the ground, and lay down on them: before morning the corn shot up, and the percussion killed her dead.' " He has accommodated himself accordingly: " 'natur intended Arkansaw for a hunting ground, and I go according to natur.' "[1]

The narrator hears Doggett before he sees him ("we were most unexpectedly startled by a loud Indian whoop" coming from the bar); with a "confused hum" of broken sentences and a "Hurra for the Big Bear of Arkansas," he verbally propels himself into the steamboat cabin and into the company of a larger audience. His one-liners, all windy tributes to "the creation State," are received with appreciative skepticism by the "heterogeneous" passengers who seem to be from everywhere but Arkansas. The narrator approaches the hunter:

> [C]onscious that my own association with so singular a personage would probably end before morning, I asked him if he would not give me a description of some particular bear hunt; adding, that I took great interest in such things, though I was no sportsman. The desire seemed to please him, and he squared himself round towards me, saying, that he could give me an idea of a bear hunt that was never beat in this world, or in any other. His manner was so singular, that half of his story consisted in his excellent way of telling it, the great peculiarity of which was, the happy manner he had of emphasizing the prominent parts of his conversation. As near as I can recollect, I have italicized the words, and given the story in his own way.

What is to be noted is that Doggett's style is readily identified as the shrill bombast of the half-horse half-alligator figure, derived from an earlier phase of

Mississippi River commercial life (that of the flatboats and keelboats), and whose most artful reconstruction is Mark Twain's rejected raftsman chapter in *Adventures of Huckleberry Finn*; but here it is notably domesticated and humanized. The narrative focus is on the remarkable "creation bear" that the hunter declares was "an *unhuntable bear, and died when his time come.*" Although Doggett typically undercuts his own predictable hyperbole—the champion hunter turns out to be a failure in his biggest challenge—that loss is compensated by the air of a mysterious supernature under whose aegis he operates, one which Doggett acknowledges by his "grave silence" when completing the tall tale and one which the narrator in turn also acknowledges by noting how the audience responds to the teller's awe with its own silence. Thorpe's variation on this pattern, reinforced by the tonal complexities arising out of it, makes "The Big Bear of Arkansas" distinctive among the other humorous sketches; but common to this family structure are (a) the accommodating relationship between the restrained, educated narrator and the garrulous backwoodsman, and (b) the ambiguous status of vernacular speech.

Although speech is a privileged mode according to certain theorists, it achieves that status *after* the advent of a text-centered culture. One of the fictions of the Southwestern sketch is the assumption that backwoods vernacular is rendered in a transparent medium meant only to reveal its spokenness. The celebration of oral culture is accomplished of course through writing. Further, it is not only second-hand (like any representation), its second-handedness comes from the same source as the blander rhythms of the narrator. The authority who complacently situates himself within a telling-and-listening context, who leisurely prepares for us a descriptive introduction to the kinetic show that is about to burst so theatrically upon us, is the same authority who stages and directs the show itself. What we are really getting from the narrator, and from the author whose mouthpiece he is, is a showy gesture of skill: *I'm talking like him, now,* which of course celebrates the *I*, not the *him* he mimics. And as "one of us," the narrator prepares for our reception of the Other, but the truth is, it is announced not by a shift in the *sounds* of English, but by a shift in the material look of the text on the page: the kinds of words or pieces of words (italicized), such as *pre-haps* and *notiony*; phrases of arcane import—*ramstugenous, slantindickler*; and clusters of odd syntax that compel attention if not understanding. Thus, the source of authority remains stable, however chaotic the local linguistic effects may appear to be or however disorderly the society depicted by those effects. There is finally no turning over of authority from a genteel narrator to a rawer, more immediately forceful storyteller.

Enfolded into the larger story of failure, Doggett's boasting mode is more perfunctory than functional, an anachronistic discharging of a debt to convention, as if this Arkansawyer must affirm his place in the Crockett/Fink "character," only to reinterpret himself in the westward declensions of another model—perhaps Jefferson's virtuous yeoman farmer, or the chastened James of Crèvecoeur's *Letters from an American Farmer*. To speculate so is not, however, to grant prior agency to the "Doggett" we see and hear but to grant some creative ambitiousness beyond the formal boundaries that contain him: the faint dissatisfaction with convention, the attempt to reformulate and reinscribe character, is Thorpe's own.

What we remember in the humorous sketch is the vernacular constructions of the narrative, not the substance. We know this in part because the authors of some of the mediocre sketches, ineptly believing that the *done* things of backwoods figures are what make them memorable, concentrate on summarized action with the said things unmemorably paraphrased. The best of the authors knew from the beginning that the *said* things—the way the backwoods men and women recounted their often less than spectacular deeds—were the primary interest. One of the great ironies of Southwestern humor is that a body of writing which purports to valorize speech only emphasizes writing itself as the originating mode. What we are expected to regard as an innocent transparency is a calculated, composed, hyper-conscious system that draws attention to itself as a vehicular agent. And the conductor of that vehicle is a writer—amateur or not—who draws upon a vast range of prior writings to render credible the illusion of a spoken English and, incidentally, the illusion of power-sharing.

2.

The suggestion of Lévi-Strauss—that the function of writing is to enslave—is too solemn by half, but there is no denying that in the competition to possess the Old Southwest, both the theoretical and the practical power were in the hands of the literate: those who recorded land grants, those who wrote regulatory laws in the separate legislatures, those who wrote judicial decisions in the courts at every level—and those who wrote comic versions of the confrontations between the privileged and the subordinated. It does not take great imagination to conclude that verbal authority among the Southwestern humorists is not necessarily committed to the aesthetic freedom of unending experimentation; it is a practical authority, one in which the luxury of time and tireless revision count for very little. What we know of the way so-called primitive types spoke depends almost entirely on these writers—amateur ethnologists, amateur folklorists, amateur anthropologists, but not, I think, amateur writers. They were derivative writers who relied on earlier texts to suggest the scribal means for articulating their experience of observation; their talents were synthetic, amalgamating, traditional, and (soon-to-become) conventional.

The writers of the Old Southwest were not merely literate; most of them were well read. If these preachers, doctors, lawyers, editors, actors, and planters could only incidentally parade their learning in the conduct of their primary callings, they were more than eager to exploit it when they took up their pen. Beginning with A. B. Longstreet in 1835, these writers produced a discourse that reflects less the raw, overheard, spoken language in the Old Southwest than an older turn-of-the-century written language, with its full arsenal of linguistic and rhetorical conventions. Many of the pieces retain the marks of utilitarian seriousness, as the narrating voice alerts us to the kind of information we might like to know: a geographical description (with relevant statistics about population, soil types, mineral deposits, flora and fauna); an anthropological account (with heavy emphasis on Native American culture and artifacts); a sporting episode (with personal experience of a recent hunting expedition); a sketch of a specific site (with notes on massacres, aborted settlements, pioneer trading camps, and other lore that in the 1830s pass for historical interest). But the putatively informational, which easily glides into the non-utilitarian, self-indulgent impulse toward the personal, is displaced by the expression of aesthetic needs: the topographical description, say, assumes romantic heightening according to the now-belated norms of the Sublime; the factual presentation of a hunting party is enlivened by emphatic profiles of backwoods guides and idiosyncratic hunters and trappers in the bush, an exercise in the exaggerations and summary quirks of the character out of (eventually) Webster and Overbury and (more directly) Addison and Irving.

By responding to their literary promptings through humor, these writers freed themselves from the great American cultural expectation that literature be socially responsible; yet their texts are dependent upon prior forms of respectability and prestige. Although the nature sketch, the topographical description, the essay, the public letter were all eminently flexible forms that allowed these authors individualized shaping, they also determined the gentlemanly style (allusive, balanced, complex, witty) with which the amiable amateur could maintain his authority without being an author. But the sway of convention governed not merely the "genteel" portions of the humorous sketch—those featuring the narrator as man of the world—but the depiction of the vernacular protagonist, especially the way he dressed and the way he sounded. Moreover, such convention governs the work now assigned the initiating place in this literary tradition, *Georgia Scenes* of 1835. The discoverer of the backwoods individualist is not A. B. Longstreet; the seaboard colonials in both New England and the South acknowledged his existence and described his eccentricities, and some, notably Timothy Dwight, even made an effort to render his odd speech in certain regularized linguistic forms.

Backwoods speech quickly becomes vernacular set-pieces: verbal displays of folk idioms, malapropisms, neologisms, so striking, so rhetorically revved up that they virtually become material objects. And the maker is an aural poacher, fashioning sounds into marvelous patches of wordplay. For all the editorial pieties from William T. Porter and other influential editors about cultural responsibilities to capture the flavor of natives before the natives disappear into a homogenized population, the native speakers themselves have no control over how they sound once their speech has been appropriated by the writer. What we read is a literary construct at least two removes from actual vernacular: Jim Doggett and Pete Whetstone of Arkansas sound like Jim and Chunky of Mississippi, Daddy Biggs of Alabama, and Yellow Blossom of Georgia. A few typographical tricks—the use of italic font, the apostrophe, phonetic spelling—serve equally for any of the fictionalized sites of the Old Southwest.

3.

One of the inescapable conclusions about this process of conventionalization—
which applies (with certain more discriminating provisos) to canonical writers
of the nineteenth century as well—is the considerable extent to which even a
third-rate contributor of funny sketches to his town's editor participates in the
hegemony of social power. In the competitive games of the Old Southwest between the aggressive settlers and the less favored people whom they encountered in the drive to fill up the newly opened lands, the winners were always
confident of their success. The squatters and marginalized settlers, the riverboat hustlers, the hunters poaching in Choctaw and Cherokee lands, even the
reclusive and suspicious loners in the deep bush were, like their socially privileged betters, interested in their own economic survival; but unlike the settlers,
they had no economic stake in seeing either the backwoods or the frontier
space transformed into deep south versions of Virginia or Carolina. What these
prior residents of the region were up against were determined and ambitious
emigrants, the kind noted in travelers' accounts as *go-ahead* types. The term
derives from Davy Crockett, that quintessential misfit whose "philosophy"
was widely circulated: *Be sure you're right—then go ahead*. The final clause
became a universal recipe for action, even as the first clause was a burdensome
condition to be ignored. Visitors to the flush-times cross-roads and villages applied the term to middle-class artisans, displaced professionals, and shrewd, socially gifted entrepreneurs, but especially to the restless, risk-taking planters
trekking in from the old seaboard states, usually with an extended family and
a slave or two. The competitive spirit in the backwoods was more modest—or
at least it was played in a different key. The activities of rural Georgians that
first prompted Longstreet to a writing career were by and large intramural
competitions—eye-gouging, ear-biting fights; horse-swaps; bouts of marks-
manship; practical jokes—a tendency we see in most of the sketches that followed *Georgia Scenes*.

We can speculate, I think, that one of the reasons why Longstreet, Alex-
ander McNutt, John S. Robb, William C. Hall, Thomas Bangs Thorpe, and
many others found these activities so engaging was that they were not only
largely confined to rivals within the same marginalized groups but they offered
no threats to the planter and professional classes: their truculent deeds, their
explosive games, their extravagant displays of independence were in fact
shadow versions of the larger games ongoing among the privileged classes.
There is of course no evidence that these backwoodsmen thought of their activities as a kind of surrogate, second-best version of those of the settlers—
illiterates leave few records—but they were not stupid. They knew as early as
the 1820s that the wielders of power were Indian agents, land commissioners,
legislators, and judges—many of whom were also planters eager to expand
their holdings. In the context of such larger games, mere bearhunts, fights, and
courting rivalries must have been perceived by the participants as local and
harmless and quaint—as they certainly were perceived by the authors. Even the

backwoodsmen's hardy encroachment on and dispossession of the original in-habitants are half-hearted, frail, and desultory compared to the official pro-gram of dispossession undertaken by the shrewd moderns, the efficient and ed-ucated purveyors of governmental civilization.

The authors, who are also purveyors of that civilization, safely celebrate the games of a marginal people who will become even more marginalized in the years just before the Civil War. What these authors celebrate is the voice of the backwoods, but the celebration is on civilization's terms: writing rather than speech. The theater of the oral performance—on the decks of steamboats, in courtrooms, on village streets—has limited occupancy; the theater of the oral performance rendered in writing reaches beyond those shabby local sites into other shabby local sites, into law offices, parlors, smoking rooms, in every re-gion of the country, into the offices of the New York *Spirit of the Times,* even into the salons of connoisseurs in England. The authority lies not with those primitives who speak with vernacular bite but with the moderns who mimic those idioms in writing.

In that writing the Southwestern author has the satisfaction of control over all the disparate elements of his world, if only in a symbolic way. He unobtru-sively mimics the gentleman, even if he is only a hard-scrabbling newspaper-man or an actor or a middling lawyer in a crowded field, just as he mimics all those vernacular heroes who are not as socially aspiring as he and whom he chooses to see as agents of disorder. Seeing himself in one light and the back-woods figure in another, he uses his power of literacy to assert the priority of order, measure, reason, the virtues of a civilized community, even when the text he produces is laced with irony, self-mockery, and the frequent temptation to succumb to the anarchic freedom he imagines the backwoods to be.

One of the strengths of his time and place is its *in-betweenness.* With the ejection of the native tribes by Jacksonian fiat, the Old Southwest is no longer one thing; and with the process of filling up still continuing, it is not yet what it is destined to be. In the meantime is his time, a transitional era of remaking, reformulating, repossessing; and his place, a transitional space of mobile boundaries and shifting landmarks in which making, formulating, and possess-ing are still provisional attempts. The Southwestern writer—himself an exile, an emigrant, committed to the party of civilization and tempted continually by the party of individualism—is defined by what historians once called the "frontier paradigm," with its "options and tensions between freedom and ne-cessity, safety and danger, liberty and restraint, order and disorder."[2] But these choices are never permanently made in the writing of these humorists. The *in-betweenness* is a psychic space as well as a geographical one, and within the flexible boundaries of that kind of frontier he plays out the game of his own moral amphibiousness.

The sketches from the Old Southwest are interesting to me not for their portrayal of familiar types along the swiftly changing southern frontier but for the revelation of character among the ambitious settlers, among whom the au-thors counted themselves. In the pieces that dramatize competition as the very linchpin of a society, the respectable authors and their narrators identify with aspiring *go-aheaders*. In passages of dialogue and in monologues that internalize and impersonate vernacular culture, the author-narrator is merely a mimic, but in the laws of rhetoric the mimic always remains superior to the speech imitated because he is both originating voice and mimicked voice. Even sympathetically generated dialect in the sketch is edged by parody, the inevitable mark of condescension, because any attempt to record a speech pattern different from one's own can never be a neutral enterprise.

But if in that process the writer most often betrays his self-consciousness, his awareness that in class and political persuasion he is superior to his marginalized hero, he also occasionally shows an often surprising capacity for unfeigned sympathy for him, a momentary suspension of judgment (ethical and political) that allows himself a kind of licensed entry into what he normally regards as the unrestraints of the Other. There is some evidence that this momentary elision of difference in the narrator functions similarly to daydream and fantasy in which transgression can be enjoyed without retribution. The very act of verbal subordination—in which the man of standard received English seemingly turns over control of his medium to one who wields a wild and deviant idiom—denotes attraction: immersing oneself in the pleasures of linguistic deviance is to enjoy the impulse of social transgression. But there is another sense in which the stylistic opposition between narrator and vernacular hero is not as radical or cleanly defined as we often suppose. If we accept the Barthian notion that it is language that speaks, not the author, then the text that constitutes the humorous sketch is a multi-dimensional field in which many "writings" meet and compete with each other. The author behind the narrator, who is also the author behind the backwoods voice, draws upon a vast pool of writings, none of which is original, all of which preexist as convention; and his role—his "only power," in Barthes' words—is to mix those writings, countering one with another "in such a way as never to rest in any one of them."[3]

It is often assumed that the narrator presents himself in a standard English that even in nineteenth-century usage comes across as pretentious, too stiffly formal, and fussily accurate—the better to throw into relief the deviant idiom of his subject. It is a reasonable assumption, but one unsupported by the texts. Here, from Thorpe again, is what a narrator's introduction sounds like:

> Here may be seen, jostling together, the wealthy Southern planter and the peddler of tin-ware from New England—the Northern merchant and the Southern jockey—a venerable bishop, and a desperate gambler—the land speculator, and the honest farmer—professional men of all creeds and characters—Wolvereens, Suckers, Hoosiers, Buckeyes, and Corncrackers, beside a "plentiful sprinkling" of the half-horse and half-alligator species of men, who are peculiar to "old Mississippi," and who appear to gain a livelihood by simply going up and down the river. In the pursuit of pleasure or business, I have frequently found myself in such a crowd.

While there is a pleasing rhythm in this highly controlled and balanced prose, it is more colloquial than formal; and its self-conscious emphasis on parallel substantives contributes to its pictorial density. Here is another example, from Solomon Smith's "The Consolate Widow":

> Between Caleba Swamp and Lime Creek, in the "Nation," we saw considerable of a crowd gathered near a drinkinghouse, most of them seated and smoking. We stopped to see what was the matter. It was Sunday, and there had been a quarter race for a gallon of whisky.

This is an even more serviceable prose. The texture of such "gentlemanly" discourse is not significantly formal; it is not pretentious; indeed, it is a remarkably supple style.

I would suggest that the controlling authorial style, in its very engagement with the vernacular, loses some of the stark correctness that many mainstream writers of the time felt obliged to follow. In the juxtaposition of levels, the vernacular "degrades" the superior style. Orthographically, we do not even need the quotation marks around "plentiful sprinkling" in the first example to know that this process is underway; and in the second example, "considerable of a crowd" has neither quotation marks nor italics to proclaim its vernacular origins—it has already been effortlessly absorbed into Smith's own standard level. The reasons for this stylistic accommodation, I think, are both social and psychological. It is as if the author, while wanting to make clear the differences between his narrator and the backwoods character (a fact that is pretty obvious anyway), wants at the same time to bridge that social and cultural gap. When the narrator's style is ponderously emphatic, it functions as a blatant rhetoric of difference, satirically deflating the narrator himself. And if the purpose of a modulated standard English is to negotiate with the vernacular, to suggest a difference without grotesquerie, that function would actually reflect the situation in the communal life of the Old Southwest. The social milieu was one in which the mingling of classes and ranks was more the rule than the exception. It could hardly be otherwise in a time and place marked chiefly by demographic instability. We may imagine the young lawyer-narrator of Joseph Baldwin's *Flush Times* exclaiming to himself *what a spectacle! what odd types are these in Alabama!* But the words are usually unwritten, and the interacting levels of style are considerably less exclamatory; and what we find are the signs of mutual influence and pervasive accommodation in the heterogeneous mix of the region. In attributing motive to this stylistic accommodation, it does no harm to speculate that what the respectable man of the town wants from the unrespectable man of the margins is the sense of individual integrity and vitality behind the quaint artifice posing as self-confidence.

4.

Despite many of the book titles (*The Flush Times of Alabama and Mississippi; Georgia Scenes; Fisher's River Scenes and Characters*), the humorous sketches only indifferently depict specific cultural customs or the topographical peculiarities of specific locales (a notable exception is Henry Clay Lewis' *Stray Leaves from a Louisiana Swamp Doctor*). Longstreet's Georgia is intended to represent the sparsely settled, raw, and morally unenlightened counties west of Augusta and Savannah; Baldwin's Alabama and Mississippi are geographically interchangeable; Cobb's Mississippi could be any of those states below the Ohio and north of Louisiana. Almost from the first the not-so-reluctant authors wrote and sent in their dispatches datelined Tuscaloosa; Greeneville, East Tennessee; Baton Rouge; Hawkins County, Kentucky; Little Rock, as if the geography mattered; but like many of the backwoods figures that the sketches celebrated, the woods and villages in which their verbal and physical exploits are set all look the same.

For the humorists, landscape is human geography, and the space meriting their attention has in defiance of actuality already filled up: there are too many people, especially lawyers and their clients, and raw nature seems uncomfortably circumscribed. Natural features such as trails, rivers, and canebrakes are as domesticated as cabins, stables, and churches. Landscape, both natural and man-made, is crowded with frolics, courtings, quiltings, faro games, oyster suppers, camp meetings. One curious effect of this symbolic density is not that the backwoods have suddenly taken on liveliness and diversity, those advantages that towns can boast, but that the mythic backwoods have been stripped of their natural definition and function and replaced by glut and disorder, the price that boomtimes exact for more sequenced development.

The world the humorists made is neither urban nor rural; and it is neither civilized nor primitive. It is an artful construct in which everything is foregrounded, people and objects simultaneously clamoring for attention. It is a world in constant motion: greasy playing cards, hunting dogs, steamboats stopping to wood and roaring to race, mourners' benches, trading scams, disappearing fritters, disappearing oysters, disappearing turkeys, bustled girls falling in hot mush, Sut Lovingood's legs. George Washington Harris' backwoods baroque is the culmination of a composed geography that had long ignored its minimal mimetic boundaries. The worlds of the humorists may occasionally differ, but they are all stylized. Baldwin's Alabama and Mississippi seem to be populated by nothing except judges, jurors, lawyers, and clients. Longstreet's Georgia, delineated when the state had already passed its frontier stage, is neatly divided between the social competitiveness of pretentious village matrons and the physical testing of males unmediated by charming creatures or any other carriers of culture. Johnson Jones Hooper's Alabama is a moving frontier where everyone except the Indians deserves victimization at the hands of a shifty rogue. Henry Clay Lewis' Louisiana is one extended swamp of albino blacks, dwarfs, panthers, corpses, and curious landladies.

In short, the world of Southwestern humor is crowded, busy, rowdy, noisy, and filled to overflowing with specialized humanity. Figures move with dispatch over a landscape crowded with other figures. It is, in the words of Melville's Redburn, "a moving world," and it moves in a stylized way. There is no boredom, as there often is in contemporary private documents, because there is no unused time. There are no dispirited stretches of loneliness, or to put it another way, there is no privacy because people are never alone. What we see are groups: two men come together, if only to swap items of trivial value, and they are immediately joined by an audience—to observe, commit, take sides, bet. Even in the hunting stories, the hunter stalks or is stalked by bears, panthers, wildcats in a nature that is as circumscribed and domesticated as Natty Bumppo's wilderness. Houses may be to live in, but they serve mostly as magnets drawing diverse people to their premises, where getting undressed and going to bed is as public an act as fighting or storytelling. Space and time are filled up, a metaphorical congestion that therefore requires self-sufficiency and a vigilant eye trained to detect the soft spots in others. Baldwin's lawyerly sensibility sees chicanery as the spirit of the times, which he deplores even as he profits from it, and chicanery requires the successful practitioner to develop a disposition ever at the ready with a strong nose, a keen eye, and, in Baldwin's phrase, "no organs of reverence." That disposition applies not only to the litigation artists in the Flush Times but also to small-bore swappers and traders, fight contestants, hunters, preachers, quilters, and yarn-spinners.

5.

To what extent is Southwestern humor an accurate reflection of the actual world of the Old Southwest in the three decades before the Civil War? If it is social history we want, the patterns of migration, the quality of social organization, the influence of institutions, the growth of cultural life, and much more can be understood by reading contemporaneous accounts that need no spurious justification: records of travelers both foreign and domestic, those compendia of practical advice known as emigrants' guides, and the odd amalgams of autobiography and topography that we get in such striking volumes as Timothy Flint's *Condensed Geography* and *Recollections of the Last Ten Years in the Valley of the Mississippi* and J. J. Audubon's *Delineations of American Scenery and Character*. Even with firm authorial biases, these works depict a society of real dimensions whose exuberance and energy emerge from its variety, not from the intensification of the same phenomena. These accounts acknowledge the rawness of the new states, but they also record a potpourri of social graces and manners with their own integrity, a wide spectrum of talents both ornamental and useful, and an urgency for establishing a society just like that which had been left behind in the Atlantic South.

This image—or, better, these images—of a more normative society are also confirmed by the writing from the Old Southwest in modes never intended to be made public: commercial daybooks, family correspondence, business journals, and private diaries. If these private documents of the antebellum Mississippi Valley seem inert and placid compared to the public writing by the humorists (or even the published memoirs and travelers' records), it is because they exude an aura relentlessly domestic and utilitarian. The writers of letters and diaries never tire of recording fevers and menus, visits and ceremonials, texts for sermons and responses to them, weather reports and the yield of corn and cotton, the cost of muslin and lace, and laments about sickness, death, and financial failure of cousins and neighbors. But, interestingly enough, this literature of everydayness, however private its origin, also composes itself as written texts, which means that the same conventions learned from prior texts shape its articulation in much the same way as public writing.

One of the more remarkable private texts is a series of diaries by Caleb Goldsmith Forshey (1813-1881), engineer, surveyor, and amateur scientist whose time and place coincided with that of the humorists. Educated at both Kenyon and West Point (though graduating from neither), Forshey pursued his career with all the energy, ambition, and impatience of other go-aheaders who emigrated to the new lands looking for the main chance. At one time or another, he was a promoter of various railroads, a builder of a levee system for the lower Mississippi, a founder of a military institute, a designer of military defenses of the Texas coast during the Civil War, and an ardent advocate of scientific land reclamation in the Gulf South. He was both literate and literary, and he took himself seriously; and while he never relaxed long enough to write humorous sketches for the public's entertainment, he did contribute to respectable journals many technical essays for its edification. Beginning in 1845, he wrote pieces on Humboldt's Cosmos, climatology, the physics of the Mississippi River, the Indian mounds of Louisiana, the meteor showers of 1848-49, and what he calls genetic "depravity" in the children of polygamous Mormons. For obvious reasons, Forshey's extensive diaries are more interesting than his public writing: they reveal an intelligent mind that is assiduous without being innovative—just as the essays do—but they also betray a temperament that ranges with fascinating rapidity from, say, a mournful address to his dead wife to an impromptu voyeuristic letching for a sixteen-year-old backwoods girl.

In the 1840s Forshey settles just across the river from Natchez, in Vidalia, where Thomas Bangs Thorpe is postmaster and editor of *The Concordia Intelligencer*. As an official surveyor of public lands, Forshey lives more in the bush than the Big Bear man ever dreamed of, even when the humorist was assembling his sketches for his first book, *Mysteries of the Backwoods*. Each horseback expedition takes Forshey from ten days to two weeks; a hired guide serves as both companion and provider for campsite food, though Forshey always spends nights when possible with the semi-permanent residents in the remote areas on his route—backwoodsmen whose family, opinions, and eccentric habits provide materials for his daily entries. In towns, Forshey visits acquaintances whose collections of fossils and shells he is always eager to inspect; he sets great store by social affairs, for it is in these years that he is actively seeking another wife. The diaries offer Forshey the means for recording, for comparative purposes, the attributes of each available prospect, accompanied with meditations on each one, internalized debates about their merits and defects, and fantasized projections of what the future with each one might hold.

But Forshey's diaries are all-purpose documents. They are as necessary as his surveying tools for recording land measurements; they function as commonplace books into which he copies bad poems from the newspapers; they are a repository of his scientific observations: descriptions of geological strata, of water temperatures in wells, of wind damage at sites struck by tornadoes, of direction and frequency of meteor showers. He uses diary pages to draft official letters and to index names and dates of his correspondents. And for all personal matters, the diaries function as surrogate companion for absorbing his confidences. Their multipurpose importance is suggested by the title pages that Forshey devises for each:

Diary & Notes
of
Business, Science,
Caprice and Miscellany

Diary and Notes
of Business, fancy
Science &
Miscellany

Journal & Diary
of things & thoughts
by the way

Diary and Notes of
various kinds
Professional, scientific
and
Promiscuous

Diary and Notes
of Business,
of Fancies, & Thoughts
of Science
and Miscellany

Diary & Notes
Scientific & Promiscuous[4]

It is probably needless to add at this point that Caleb Forshey in his private writing shares important traits with his contemporaries among the very public humorists. His racism and sexism are not virulent or especially disfiguring over the course of several years of sustained confessions, but they tend to manifest themselves directly rather than through dramatized anecdote. He shows a Whiggish distrust of poverty and the lack of enterprise he sees as its source; but he is a spirited democrat in his distaste for foreign dandies, snobbish ladies, arrogant gentlemen, and self-serving sycophants in offices of elected officials. And while there is a rhetorical directness missing in the humorists' sketches, he has read them as well as the prior texts they all share as formative models for literary expression: Scott, Addison, Irving, Cooper, Burns, and the ever-popular Romantic poets. The pull of nostalgia and the virtues of sentiment can be triggered easily and often, in "Sweet tears of remembrance [that come] gushing." Forshey pauses often, for two years after the death of his wife, to shed regulated tears, scaled as *sobs, sighs, anguish,* and *melancholy,* in a prose carefully structured to reflect those discriminations. Even though they are thoroughly private entries, his sentences show changes in diction, with appropriate cancellations. Sentiment can overpower him in nondomestic situations, as well. His patriotic sense tells him to weep when, upon visiting Mount Vernon, he finds the grounds neglected and overgrown with noxious weeds; and when passing the tomb of William Henry Harrison on an Ohio River steamboat, he records his response: "an involuntary tear [*gushed* canceled; *dropped from my eyes* canceled] trickled my cheek, as I thought of the virtues reposing there." And he resorts to his chilliest formal prose in reprimanding "a surly & selfish John Bull" who wonders aloud what Forshey could see in William Henry Harrison.

He carries his diary wherever he goes and in whatever degree of society he finds himself, self-consciously noting that *saucy, flirty, black-eyed Sal* is watching him write and speculating about what she must be thinking as he watches her watching "the stranger" write. Forshey also carries in his head a variety of styles of appropriate range to record his diverse entries. It is a solid, reportorial prose when he fills the pages devoted to "professional" or "scientific" matters; but for those pages where he can relax in "Promiscuous" or "Random observations," he draws upon his substantial knowledge of literature, history, classical mythology, and common lore. He shows no hesitancy in thinking of himself as a writer. Literary style for him is the respectable style of an earlier generation. In a word picture of his own sylvan grounds, he notes "the shark of fresh waters . . . devouring their neighbors of the finny tribe." On a journey into Missouri he falls impeccably into the literary mood: "Dawn upon the Prairies, away to the horizon[']s verge the meadows sleep in their pearly covering, & await only the cheering smile of the glorious sun to shake off the dew drops, and wave to the morning wind a fresh salutation—onward steals the morning Light." He sings *matins* and *lays* as his *steed* bears him through the *almost pathless woods*. He is prone to draw lessons from all kinds of spectacles he comes upon—lessons of value in the vein of Longfellow and Whittier—even when the incidents themselves are reported in straightforward fashion.

Caleb Forshey is probably no more representative of the conservative Whig of the Old Southwest than any other single individual in the planter and professional ranks. That his writing shows idiosyncratic traits as richly as it does generic ones makes his case a useful one for questioning the appropriateness of "gifted amateur," the term we continue to apply to the Southwestern humorists. We should not take at face value the humorists' own protestations that their writing was a youthful indiscretion or a hobby to pass idle hours. There were simply too many in this diverse group who persisted in their trifling avocation over a number of years for us to take such claims seriously. The skilled and the clumsy, the well-known and the obscure, the ambitious who published collections of their newspaper writing and the anonymous whose sketches lie forgotten in the files of the *Spirit of the Times*: they were writers, just as Caleb Forshey was a writer. And both the published and unpublished writings are the material residue of a culture of which they were a part just as fully as was the writing of self-confessed professionals like Edgar Poe and William Gilmore Simms. Which is another way of stating that the general climate of antebellum cultural aspiration, with its alternating urgencies of restraint and transgression, touched every person who set pen to paper.

What is to be remarked about the texts from the Old Southwest is not their obvious derivation from the oral folk tradition—the strenuous attempts from Longstreet to Harris to reproduce sounds of yeomen, not sounds of gentlemen, attest to that—but their promiscuous melange of literary influence. It is my thesis that this writing is not so much an exploitation of raw, overheard spoken language as it is the residual flowering of verbal transformations of an old-fashioned written language, some of which derives from canonical writers, some from their popular imitators, and some from those quasi-professional sporting authors of both England and America who carried graceful, indolent, and witty self-consciousness to the racetrack and stables in the towns and to fishing and hunting sites in the wild.

Because it projects a specialized and dense world, stylized and conventionalized, Southwestern humor is a fiercely *made* writing, self-conscious in both its enlargements and its elisions. Though I think the reading of private forms of discourse—letters, journals, diaries, daybooks—of the same time and place helps very little to corroborate the social reality depicted in the humorous sketches, they do provide clues to the dynamics of class relations on the southern frontier and especially to the sense of verbal propriety observed by literate and literary men and women. The writers of personal forms—creatures of piety and propriety whose *writing* presumably departs only minimally from *doing*—inscribe themselves through convention even as they live by convention.

In the hands of the humorists, piety and propriety are filtered, diluted, spiked, and queered by their opposites so intensely, so repetitiously, that impiety and impropriety become the indispensable ingredients in the recipe. Having no organs of reverence is itself a convention. But the sketches are not unbuttoned writing: what holds up even the "inexpressibles" are simply different buttons. Unlike other influential editors in antebellum America, William T. Porter decreed that politics and religion were not appropriate subjects in his paper. Most of the humorists found it easy enough to abide by Porter's prohibition. While some of them did find capital fun in Methodists, in their sketches for the *Spirit of the Times* they generally refrain from specifying party affiliation of the quaintly ridiculous subjects: preachers are just *generically* hypocritical and lecherous and corrupt; local sheriffs and judges and politicians are just *generally* hypocritical and lecherous and corrupt.

But Porter's taboo subjects are only a minor indication of conventional restraints. What importantly shaped the humorous sketch was literary convention itself; though the writers may have satirized the pompousness of the sublime used so relentlessly to describe nature, very few of them in their straightforward moments are entirely weaned from that handy nourishment—not even Mark Twain, who made the most sport of it. Though the humorists knew how to use the approved standard literary style—allusive, balanced, complex, witty—for broadly deflating certain subjects, this was their "normal" style. And in depicting the backwoods protagonist, especially the way he sounded and the way he dressed, not much was added or changed after 1835, when *Georgia Scenes* began the fashion.

All this is not to diminish the achievement of the Southwestern humorists, who until recently have been diminished quite a lot already. It is to acknowledge their achievement as complexly conceived and effectively rendered pieces of writing—not spilled folklore.

NOTES

1. Thomas Bangs Thorpe, "The Big Bear of Arkansas," *Humor of the Old Southwest,* ed. Hennig Cohen and William B. Dillingham (Athens: U of Georgia P, 1975), 273. All other primary quotations from the humorists are drawn from the texts in the Cohen-Dillingham anthology and Joseph G. Baldwin, *The Flush Times of Alabama and Mississippi,* ed. James H. Justus (Baton Rouge: Louisiana State UP, 1978).

2. Berndt Ostendorf, "Anthropology, Modernism, and Jazz," *Ralph Ellison: Modern Critical Views,* ed. Harold Bloom (New York: Chelsea House, 1986), 149. Ostendorf's immediate reference is to the Oklahoma of the turn of the century.

3. Roland Barthes, "The Death of the Author," *Image—Music—Text,* ed. Stephen Heath (New York: Hill and Wang, 1977), 146.

4. Passages from the unpublished diaries of Caleb Forshey are reproduced by permission of the owners, the Mississippi Valley Collections of the Memphis State University Library.

Poe, Plagiarism, and the
Prescriptive Right of the Mob

Jonathan Elmer

I. EPIGRAPH

I begin with an unavoidable and entirely uncontroversial thesis: "William Wilson" (1839) is a psychological drama about the harassments of conscience. The thesis is uncontroversial because it seems to be the accepted interpretation of the tale; for this reason alone, one could argue, it must inevitably be taken into account.[1] But it is unavoidable for a more immediate reason as well, namely, that we cannot enter the tale without first encountering the epigraph Poe places at its threshold, and which imprints with typographical insistence the word "CONSCIENCE" on our reading memory: "What say of it? what say of CONSCIENCE grim, / That spectre in my path?"[2] Although the word "conscience" does not reappear in the rest of the tale, it will henceforth be almost impossible to understand the narrator's double as anything other than his conscience: the double does, in fact, turn out to be rather humorless and "grim," and his meddlesome behavior certainly justifies his designation as "That spectre in [the narrator's] path." Before detailing all the thematic elements which support such an understanding, however, we should note that our interpretation of "William Wilson" as a story about conscience has in an important way been determined in advance. In thus affecting our access to the tale, the epigraph has, as it were, intervened from without; and in this sense the epigraph itself is a "spectre in [our] path," one which will be as hard to evade as Wilson's double.

Poe was fond of epigraphs, and used them in almost all of his tales to delay the introduction of the main narrative and to indicate the key terms in which the story is to be understood. Poe's critical stance with regard to epigraphs, however, was more ambivalent than his ready use of them might seem to indicate. In one of his lengthy reviews of Longfellow's poems, Poe takes up the issue of "prose remarks prefacing the narrative," and concludes that the "practice of prefixing explanatory passages is utterly at variance with . . . unity [of effect]."[3] In a typically acute analysis of the reading experience, Poe explains why this is so:

> By the prefix, we are either put in possession of the subject of the poem; or some hint, historic fact, or suggestion, is thereby afforded, not included in the body of the piece, which, without the hint, is incomprehensible. In the latter case, while

perusing the poem, the reader must revert, in mind at least, to the prefix, for the necessary explanation. In the former, the poem being a mere paraphrase of the prefix, the interest is divided between the prefix and the paraphrase. In either instance the totality of effect is destroyed. (*Essays*, 691)

Poe is talking about poems here, but his conception of the prose tale demanded the same attention to "unity" of effect. In "William Wilson," the epigraph's applicability to the tale certainly seems to give it, retrospectively, the kind of "explanatory" power to which Poe alludes above, even if that power is limited to naming the subject of the narrative—"conscience"—which is not named elsewhere: in this sense the epigraph does put us "in possession of the subject." According to Poe, the precedence of the prefix—a precedence both temporal and spatial since, as Poe emphasizes, the prefix is exterior, "not included in the body of the piece"—does not simply divide our attention (or double it, we might say, given that we are considering "William Wilson"); it also threatens to reverse the normal relation between text and gloss, with the ostensibly "explanatory" prefix becoming the "subject" of which the text itself comes to seem merely the "paraphrase." The preemptive power of the epigraph or prefix, at least in this account, tends inevitably to disturb the reading experience, volatilizing the relation between text and interpretation, doubling and dividing our reading, destroying *from the beginning* the unity of effect.

The effect of the epigraph on our reading of "William Wilson" hardly seems so dramatic; indeed, rather than disturbing our understanding of the tale, the presence of the word "conscience" would seem to confer on it a kind of integrity and coherence. But then we must admit that the effect of the epigraph is to give us the closure before we have the text, the answer before we have the question, the "subject" of the tale before we have the "body" of the text. I am putting pressure on Poe's epigraph because it seems to contain, incognito, an ambiguous dynamic of textual identity that the tale itself elaborates at greater length. For what, after all, does it mean to be "put in possession of the subject" of a tale like "William Wilson," which insistently calls into question the very notions of both "subject" and "possession"? Is it not at least somewhat suspicious that the epigraph grants us so painlessly, so guilelessly, the principle of unity and identity of a text that describes in unusual detail the dissolution of individual identity, the collapse of subjective unity? The critical "subject" *of* the tale—the topic of conscience—is made to seem singular, while the "subject" *in* the tale—William Wilson—is precisely split apart by the advent of the double who apparently embodies that other "critical subject" that is one's conscience. What is division at the level of the *récit,* the narrated content, is unity at the level of the *discours,* or interpretive frame. To be put in possession of the subject of "William Wilson," then, entails a certain confusion between interpretive and moral judgments, between critical evaluations and evaluations of conscience, a confusion that is one important source of the frictional energy of this uncanny tale.

We can already find in the epigraph, then, the interpenetration of questions of subjective identity, property, and textuality which becomes the figural current running through the entirety of "William Wilson." One further oddity of the epigraph points us toward a fuller understanding of what might be at stake for Poe in this interpenetration. The citation from Chamberlayne is incorrectly attributed to his *Pharonnida*: Mabbott surmises that Poe's epigraph is actually a "confused echo" of the following lines from another play by Chamberlayne, *Love's Victory:* "Conscience waits on me like the frighting shades / Of ghosts when gastly [*sic*] messengers of death . . ." (448). Given the importance of naming in the tale, this incorrect attribution should give us pause. Presumably Poe has misremembered the lines from *Love's Victory,* and thus simply attributed his epigraph to the wrong source. But it is also possible that he has fabricated his epigraph quite consciously, dressing it up to look enough like the lines from *Love's Victory* to pass as merely a "confused echo" of them. In either case, we are confronted by a bizarre circumstance. For if Poe *thinks* he didn't write the lines of the epigraph, and Chamberlayne *did not* write them, who did? To whom do these lines belong? And if Poe knowingly wrote the lines of the epigraph and attributed them to Chamberlayne, why should he want to do such a thing? Rather than passing off someone else's work as his own, Poe would thus be passing off his own work as somebody else's. A strange motivation, but not unimaginable: the desire not for appropriation and self-possession, but for the disappropriation and dispossession of the self's textual identity. The lines said to be from Chamberlayne's *Pharonnida,* floating before the entrance to Wilson's narrative, lines which put us in possession of the subject of the tale, are themselves seemingly dispossessed words, not quite the result of Poe's reading nor quite the result of Chamberlayne's writing.

The doubtful status of the epigraph—is it internal or external to the tale "proper"? is its function unifying or divisive? to whom do its words belong?— thus brings into focus the possibility that this tale about doubled identity, dissipation and crime, naming and attribution, property and dispossession, is from the beginning also about reading and its anxieties. And this is to say, as I will argue, that "William Wilson" is about plagiarism, or rather that the problem of plagiarism functions as the horizon for the critical and social anxieties at work in the tale. Only a fuller interpretation both of Poe's stance toward plagiarism and of the tale itself can make this claim convincing, but another curious fact about "William Wilson" is worth considering in this respect. In one of his many charges of plagiarism, Poe accused Hawthorne in May 1842 of including a scene in "Howe's Masquerade" which "resembles a plagiarism" (*Essays,* 575) of the final encounter with the double in "William Wilson."[4] This charge is, from one perspective, patently absurd, since Hawthorne's tale was published a year before Poe's. But it is striking, I think, that the threat of plagiarism would surge forth in Poe's imagination in proximity to his own climactic scene of duelling doubles, in which what had remained until then merely an insidious and doubtful *resemblance* between the characters verges toward a violent unity, or moment of identity. Of course, the temporal absurdity of Poe's accusation—that an earlier text plagiarized a later one—is hard to ignore. On the other hand, once one notices how Poe submits the notion of textual identity in "William Wilson" to a species of retrograde motion and temporal reversal, his accusation conforms to a kind of phantasmatic logic

even in this particular. For in the slippage between interpretive and moral judgments, Poe implies in "William Wilson," one *can't help* putting the cart before
the horse; and indeed, when we turn to a consideration of Poe's anxiety over
plagiarism, we find out that it is often very difficult even to distinguish the cart
from the horse.

2. PLAGIARISM

In an article of several years ago, Neil Hertz offered some explanations for the
"tight-lipped institutional fussiness" with which the academy surveys the
threat of student plagiarism. He described a pamphlet on "A Writer's Responsibilities" that used to be handed out to freshmen at Cornell, in which the author indulged in a minatory fantasy about the plagiarist who "gets away with
it" but who nevertheless "must inevitably" bear somewhere "an ineradicable
mark" of guilt and shame.[5] By means of this fantasized "ineradicable mark,"
the figure who testified to, and exploited, the disconcerting separability of "the
self and its signs"[6] is now imagined as embodying the very opposite: "the 'author' of this mark," writes Hertz in the voice of fantasy, "will be inseparable
from it; here, for once—so the wish would have it—mark, paper and author
will be fused."[7] There is doubtless a kind of satisfaction in the censure of a
discovered plagiarist, in the putting-to-right of the links between selves and
signs. But such a pleasure cannot match the covert love for the one who got
away, since it is only the latter who allows both for this compensatory fantasy
of the integration of self and sign, *and,* as Hertz elaborates, a residual, contradictory but equally wishful *illegibility* of the self:

> [T]he aim of such fantasies of moral legibility, whether they are elaborated by sin-
> ners or judges, is precisely that exciting confusion of ethical and hermeneutical mo-
> tifs; for fantasies are compromise-formations, they seek to have things both ways.
> Our paragraph about plagiarism offers just such a compromise: the ineradicable
> mark is there to satisfy the interpreter's wish to read stable and undeceptive signs,
> while the unknowable suffering is there to satisfy the teacher's wish to be some-
> thing other than a reader—it serves as an acknowledgement of an interiority
> opaque enough to baffle his hermeneutical skills, a residual *je-ne-sais-quoi* that is
> there to remind him of (and, specularly, to confirm him in) his own private human-
> ity.[8]

The teacher's relation to the plagiarist who gets away with it is, as Hertz says,
specular: in investing this figure with both the attributes of pure legibility and
the opacity of a "private humanity," the teacher projects a figure *combining*
the wishful notions of selfhood which are otherwise in contradiction. This is
what provides the "excitement" of the "confusion of ethical and hermeneutical
motifs." And it is this same confusion that lies at the heart of who or what
constitutes the ethical or hermeneutic "subject" of "William Wilson." But this
excitement is the product of an *ambivalence* toward the specular figure of the
plagiarist who gets away with it, for specular doubles—as for instance in Lacan's account of the mirror stage—tend to serve as the focus both of the self's
jubilation before a confirming and "ideal unity," and of the aggression which

arises from the realization that this ideal unity, insofar as it is beyond the self, exteriorized, is also the self's "alienating destination."[9]

To claim that the plagiarist is an instance of the Lacanian specular ego may seem to highlight the figure's containment by a trans-historical or trans-cultural logic. There may be such a logic, but it is not what interests me here. For even if there are specular doubles in all times and places, they do not always have the same features. Hertz's analysis of the institutional "threat" of plagiarism, for example, presupposes certain structures and concepts, such as: an educational apparatus in which culture is "inscribed" on the minds of the more or less anonymous "young"; the acceptance of a split between public and private selves; particular notions of property and intellectual property; and, perhaps most importantly, an imagined relation to a socioeconomic realm of *circulation,* in which texts and ideas and even people can successfully circulate, pretending to be things they are not and *get away with it.* Such structures and concepts determine historically the form in which the seemingly universal figure of the double makes its appearance.

I have laid out in some detail the contradictions and ambivalences arising from one familiar posture toward plagiarism, so that in turning now to Poe he won't look like such a nut. For if there is a quick way to describe Poe's relation to the problem of plagiarism, it would be as outrageous and deliberately provocative. In the series of papers dubbed "The Little Longfellow War," Poe flings about bizarre accusations, tendentious analyses of plagiarism, and generally indulges in an irritating species of innuendo. But Poe's very critical and theoretical incoherence in this episode conforms, I would argue, to the logic of ambivalence identified by Hertz. For as the tediousness of his contributions to the Longfellow War suggests, Poe is less interested in resolving specific conflicts over plagiarism than in having the debate continue: his apparent ambivalence arises, as it does for Hertz's emblematic teacher, from the fact that his interest in exposing specific instances of plagiarism is exceeded by his investment in the problem as such. We might say this investment has to do with Poe's recognition that the debate intrigued the magazine readers, that, publicity-conscious as he always was, he simply knew good copy when he saw it. On one level this is surely correct: Poe was probably more widely known as a contentious critical personality than as anything else (save as author of "The Raven"), and he quite self-consciously exploited this role. But to write off Poe's odd passion for debates over plagiarism as simply a play for what today would be called a larger "market share" is to ignore the way publicity and critical personae were for Poe *theoretical* issues concerning the nature of identity; how plagiarism itself, as a theoretical issue, brought into focus the anxieties surrounding the possibility of a critical identity in what we might call the mass-textual world of publication.

That Poe saw his engagement with the topic of plagiarism as a confrontation between the critic and the world of publicity is fairly clear in his sparring with the anonymous defender of Longfellow, who signed his pieces "Outis" (Greek for Nobody). Outis' recourse to pseudonymy amounts, in Poe's view, to a retreat behind anonymity, a practice common in the magazine criticism of the day, but one which Poe himself spurned:[10] "One of the most amazing things I have yet seen, is the complacency with which Outis throws to the right and left his anonymous assertions, taking it for granted because he (Nobody) asserts them, I must believe them as a matter of course" (*Essays,* 724). Such anonymity asserts its claim to belief, or so Poe fears, through a kind of identification of itself with the voice of the public; because Outis is Nobody in himself, he can, like General John A. B. C. Smith in Poe's "The Man That Was Used Up," figure Everybody. From out the vastnesses of publicity, then, Outis' voice comes forward to challenge not only Poe's specific accusations of plagiarism against Longfellow and Aldrich, but the very grounds of plagiarism itself: "What is plagiarism? And what constitutes a good ground for the charge? Did no two men ever think alike without stealing one from the other?" (*Essays,* 709). After adducing some examples, Outis claims that there can be what Poe had called "identities" of thought and phrasing, without there being anything like plagiarism: "What is more natural? Images are not created, but suggested" (*Essays,* 710). His conclusion: "[N]o circumstantial evidence could be sufficient to secure a verdict of *theft* in such a case" (*Essays,* 711). Outis' argument against plagiarism ends by evacuating the notion of originality entirely, invoking instead an idea of linguistic suggestibility in which language operates men, rather than the other way around: common language (images) arising to separate individuals in common circumstances.

Poe's response to this argument bears some examination. Certainly as sensitive as Outis to the ways in which men are determined by language—inhabit it, so to speak—Poe was nevertheless anxious about this idea. Outis, by contrast, seems quite unruffled by the apparent import of his argument against defining plagiarism; he seems, in fact, indifferent, and it is this "complacency" which most irks Poe. Coupled with Outis' apparent readiness to void his distinctive identity in an identification with a general sameness (Nobody and Everybody are equally indistinct), this indifference and this complacency trigger in Poe an anxious response: "The attempt to prove, however, by reasoning *a priori,* that plagiarism cannot exist, is too good an idea on the part of Outis not to be a plagiarism in itself" (*Essays,* 717). Poe's charge does not demarcate critically the grounds for possible plagiarism; rather it extends those bounds by including as potential plagiarisms the critical voice itself issuing its *a priori* reasonings. Indeed, Poe's central strategy in his effort to provide a "definition of the grounds on which a charge of plagiarism may be based" (*Essays,* 758) consists in rendering such definition a hopelessly difficult task. Poe insists that the *principle* of plagiarism must be maintained and asserted at all costs, even if that means that actual judgments of plagiarism, the final tracing of text to identity, will forever be deferred. Like Hertz's ambivalent teacher, Poe seeks to have things both ways: by troubling the definitional boundaries of plagiarism— notably, so that it includes critical statements about the nature of plagiarism— Poe can assert that the boundaries are always in need of re-articulation. That is, Poe's very insistence that there is no text that is *a priori* free of the suspicion of plagiarism is paradoxically dedicated to the possibility of a non-plagiaristic realm. His duplicitous strategy in the debates about originality and plagiarism is finally motivated by a desire to keep something for criticism itself; it is, in its odd way, a proprietary motivation. Indeed, we might say that, for Poe, an anxiety about plagiarism is the one thing criticism can properly claim as its own. And Outis' greatest outrage in Poe's eyes is not so much his unconcern about property rights, but his unconcern itself; his phlegmatic *lack of anxiety* marks him, in Poe's view, as both duped and duplicated because not critically vigilant.

But criticism, in this account, is opposed not to writing, but to *reading*, for it turns out that reading is for Poe a state of absorption threatening precisely to the self-detachment that seems to be secured by criticism. In Poe's final words on the plagiarism controversy, he describes the nature of this absorption:

> It appears to me that what seems to be the gross *inconsistency* of plagiarism as perpetrated by a poet, is thus very easily resolved:—the poetic sentiment (even without reference to the poetic power) implies a peculiarly, perhaps an abnormally keen appreciation of the beautiful, with a longing for its assimilation, or absorption, into the poetic identity. What the poet intensely admires, becomes thus, in very fact, although only partially, a portion of his own intellect. It has a secondary origination within his own soul—an origination altogether apart, although springing, from its primary origination without. The poet is thus possessed by another's thought, and cannot be said to take of it, possession. But, in either view, he thoroughly feels it as *his own*—and this feeling is counteracted only by the sensible presence of its true, palpable origin in the volume from which he has derived it—an origin which, in the long lapse of years it is almost impossible *not* to forget—for in the meantime the thought itself is forgotten. But the frailest association will regenerate it—it springs up with all the vigor of a new birth—its absolute originality is not even a matter of suspicion—and when the poet has written it and printed it, and on its account is charged with plagiarism, there will be no one in the world more entirely astounded than himself. Now from what I have said it will be evident that the liability to accidents of this character is in the direct ratio of the poetic sentiment—of the susceptibility to the poetic impression; and in fact all literary history demonstrates that, for the most frequent and palpable plagiarism, we must search the works of the most eminent poets. (*Essays,* 759)

Plagiarism has become a problem of reading: the "poetic sentiment" is a heightened receptivity, a susceptibility to beauty and language which is to be separated from the productive aspect of the "poetic power." Poe describes this receptivity as a kind of active "assimilation, or absorption" of "the beautiful" into the "poetic identity," where it becomes "a portion of [the poet's] intellect." The "primary origination from without" then undergoes a kind of repression—"in the long lapse of years it is almost impossible *not* to forget"— and in this way the plagiarizing poet puts forth the assimilated beauty as if it were his own, "with all the vigor of a new birth." But the active aspect of this process may be rather wishful, for as Poe himself points out, the fact that the "poet feels it as *his own*" is an illusory inversion of the actual temporality of ownership: "The poet is thus possessed by another's thought, and cannot be said to take of it, possession." The proprietary language here implies that the "absorption" works the other way, that the poet's abnormal receptivity marks the moment of his own absorption or assimilation into an entirely other realm of property.[11] Such an absorption always implies for Poe a kind of immersion in the realm of circulation, the fusion of identities and the collapse of distinctiveness. What is more, this moment of absorption is also that of the individual's *inscription*: thus Poe writes of the "susceptibility to the poetic impression," which would mark the individual as a stamp marks the receptive wax. According both to an ancient figural logic,[12] and, as we shall see, to the psychoanalytic account of the genesis of conscience, such a stamping constitutes the advent of "character." When Poe speaks of "accidents of this character," then, he draws attention—unwittingly, perhaps, but significantly—to what for him is the intolerable way in which "character" *overtakes* one, catches one unawares—at the moment of susceptibility, the moment of reading.

Small wonder, then, that when the poet puts forth the plagiarism as his own, and is shown that it is not his own, "there will be no one in the world more entirely astounded than himself." He will, perhaps, feel the shivering recognition that is the sign of the uncanny. For his attempt to "regenerate" himself in his own production will have been brought back to him as the evidence of his own generation in a long-forgotten absorption. The "vigor of a new birth" will appear to him as the revenance of his own birth. The fundamental fear attached to plagiarism is not that we will be plagiarized, but that we *are plagiarisms;* and the proprietary anxiety is not that our possessions will be taken from us, but that we are ourselves possessed: we "belong properly to books" as Poe writes in his review of Hawthorne (*Essays,* 583). Small wonder, too, that the literary commodity provokes what Samuel Weber (drawing out Marx's own hints) has called the "crisis of perception and representation active in the uncanny,"[13] for that commodity is precisely riven by a doubleness threatening to the self: the ever-present possibility of plagiarism entails the recognition of the Me in the Not-Me, or rather the recognition that the Self is the effect, or the determination, of the (social) Other, that the original is effected or determined by what we might call the aboriginal. What provokes the concern about plagiarism, in other words, is a social anxiety, the unhappy realization that since, as Hannah Arendt has written, "the essence of who somebody is cannot be reified by himself," we are committed to circulation and publicity; that we are, in fact, determined not so much by the Other as by Others, we are the textual precipitate of the social world.[14] Fantasies of originality and self-generation thus always imply an *agon* with the social, and the drama of self-writing (whether the self is "Poe," "America," or "William Wilson") always contains a covert drama of reading, a reading which returns in uncanny fashion to remind us of our "primary origination from without," in others, by others. "William Wilson" presents this agonized drama of self-writing in the face of the aboriginal.

3. THE ANXIOUS BODY OF THE TEXT

If the epigraph has made anything clear, it is that the beginning of Poe's text is not self-evident. Accordingly, I will postpone the analysis of the opening pages of "William Wilson" and jump right into the fray. More specifically, I will turn first to the gambling encounter with Glendinning, which will allow us to situate the essential features of Wilson's character while also giving us an insight into the mechanism or technique of doubling.

Wilson succeeds in his gambling career by putting into circulation an identity other than his own: to his friends at Oxford, even the "most abandoned associates," he is "the gay, the frank, the generous William Wilson," whose vices are nothing more serious than "unbridled fancy," "inimitable whim" and a certain "careless and dashing extravagance" (440). The image put into circulation is of a character who cannot stop circulating, who like an unbridled horse dashes about in an excessive wandering: the moral stigma attached to Wilson's extravagance, clearly articulated by Wilson himself in the beginning of the tale, is at bottom the recognition of this suspicious propensity to overstep one's bounds, to move beyond one's proper sphere. As the encounter with Glendinning makes clear, the "proper sphere" is first of all defined as one's social sphere. Wilson's class status is rather unclear: as "the noblest and most liberal commoner at Oxford," in possession of an "enormous income" (440), he seems to occupy a position between commoner and noble. Glendinning is a similarly hybridized specimen, a "young *parvenu* nobleman" (440), one who has arrived at nobility by virtue of his money alone. Wilson and Glendinning are thus perfect players in what René Girard would call mimetic rivalry, since each wants what the other wants, namely riches and the social status they seem to guarantee. Wilson decidedly has the upper hand in this contest, however, since he knows that you have to spend money to make money: "I frequently engaged him in play, and contrived, with the gambler's usual art, to let him win considerable sums, the more effectually to entangle him in my snares" (441).

The image of Wilson as "careless," as in some fundamental sense not entirely in possession of himself, is contradicted by his self-characterization as the methodical and systematic "gambler by profession." Wilson informs us that he is acquainted with "the vilest arts of the gambler by profession," and has become an "adept in his despicable science" (440). The combination of art and science required by this "profession" recalls Poe's notion that such a combination and proportion of faculties is displayed by every genius (including of course himself). Dupin, for instance, is both poet and mathematician, and is imaginative precisely in proportion to his analytic capacity.[15] The comparison to Dupin also reminds us that Wilson's success in swindling Glendinning depends upon a kind of doubling of, or identification with, his antagonist, just as Dupin in "The Purloined Letter" is required to identify his reasoning with that of Minister D— —. That is, Wilson must manipulate his opponent into expressing Wilson's own desire to keep the game going and to double the stakes:

> In a very short period he had become my debtor to a large amount, when, having taken a long draught of port, he did precisely what I had been coolly anticipating—he proposed to double our already extravagant stakes. . . . in less than an hour he had quadrupled his debt. (441-42)

The stakes are "already extravagant" even before they are doubled and redoubled at Glendinning's suggestion, and this is because the entire card game and Glendinning's role in it are already the effects of an initial doubling performed by Wilson: "To give to this a better coloring, I had contrived to have assembled a party of some eight or ten, and was solicitously careful that the introduction of cards should appear accidental, and originate in the proposal of my contemplated dupe himself" (441). Wilson's ability to have his own desire "originate" with Glendinning, who as "dupe" is both the victim of the con and Wilson's *dup*licate, is the initial extravagance, the first wandering of his self in the place of another. His mastery of Glendinning and control of the technique of doubling is thus due to his ability to circulate not only a reputation, but his very desires, and to have them come back to him in the form of another's desires. In other words, Wilson's appropriation of Glendinning's fortune depends initially on his capacity to *dis*appropriate himself into the place of the other. Spending money to make money is only the superficial version of this technique of disappropriation: Wilson knows that he must also put into circulation both a certain character and his very desires in order to get what he wants.

The importance of this initial disappropriation can be seen in the disastrous dénouement of this scene. Wilson's double bursts into the gambling den and exposes Wilson's ruses to the others: it is as though the extravagant doubling and redoubling of the stakes have caught Wilson up in the wild exchange, as though he has lost control of the doubling process, which now comes back to haunt him. The scene ends, significantly, with the return of property: " 'Mr. Wilson,' said our host, stooping to remove from beneath his feet an exceedingly luxurious cloak of rare furs, 'Mr. Wilson, this is your property' " (444). For both Wilson and the reader, the uncanny moment resides just here, because the return of property, the setting to right of the extravagant circulation, is not the end of doubling, but rather the restitution of the double to its proper place: that is, the "extravagantly costly" cloak handed to Wilson is not his own, which is "already hanging on [his] arm" (444), but the double's perfect facsimile. The uncanny quality of this moment of exposure resides not in the prospect of Wilson losing his property, but in the return of a doubled property, and its assignment as his own. Wilson's "extravagance," his ability to put himself in the place of the other, returns to him as his own property: he is foiled because he is unable to alienate his own alienability, because his own capacity for disappropriating himself turns out to be what is most proper to him, and cannot itself be disappropriated.

But if the cloak figures Wilson's immoral "extravagance," we must also admit that, by its very doubling, the figure becomes riven by a certain ambiguity. For the return of the double's cloak as Wilson's own property reminds us that elsewhere it is Wilson's "virtue" that is figured by a cloaking "mantle." In the second paragraph of the tale, Wilson writes: "Men usually grow base by degrees. From me, in an instant, all virtue dropped bodily as a mantle. From comparatively trivial wickedness I passed, with the stride of a giant, into more than the enormities of an Elah-Gabalus" (426-27). And in the final scene, we are given the "instant" of this transformation: "It was my antagonist—it was Wilson, who then stood before me in the agonies of his dissolution. His mask and cloak lay, where he had thrown them, upon the floor" (448). When the mortally wounded double falls, his cloak is discarded: the two moments are simultaneously recalled in Wilson's confession that "all virtue dropped bodily as a mantle."

The fact that the cloak figures both a morally suspicious "extravagance" and the "mantle of virtue" volatilizes the nature of the moral confrontation which serves as the thematic frame of the tale. When the exposure of wickedness, in the scene with Glendinning, becomes no longer a kind of laying bare, but rather the forced assumption of a double covering, it is the moral relation itself which seems to be registered as uncanny. Freud, of course, has described the genesis of one form of the uncanny double in terms of the psychic split between ego and superego (or conscience):

> The idea of the "double" does not necessarily disappear with the passing of the primary narcissism, for it can receive fresh meaning from the later stages of development of the ego. A special faculty is slowly formed there, able to oppose the rest of the ego, with the function of observing and criticizing the self and exercising a censorship within the mind, and this we become aware of as our "conscience." . . . The fact that a faculty of this kind exists, which is able to treat the rest of the ego like an object . . . renders it possible to invest the old idea of a "double" with a new meaning and to ascribe many things to it, above all, those things which seem to the new faculty of self-criticism to belong to the old surmounted narcissism of the earliest period of all.[16]

There is a curious about-face in these lines, for at the beginning of the passage we are prepared to view the "new faculty" of conscience as itself the double: "we become aware" of this conscience as something opposed, its appearance "renders it possible to invest the old idea of a 'double' with a new meaning." It turns out, however, that this new faculty looks upon the *original* ego as the threatening double, that the doubling of the self enacted in the advent of conscience entails a temporal reversal, whereby the "narcissism of the earliest period of all" becomes marked as temporally secondary or derived—the "double." Formally, this temporal reversal resembles that which the poet unconsciously performs when he takes as "his own" a phrase by which he had earlier been "possessed"; or it is like Poe's insinuation that Hawthorne had plagiarized his later tale; or it is like the ostensibly secondary epigraph taking over a kind of precedence, and making the body of the text seem *its* gloss. In our most immediate context, what Freud's odd passage suggests is that the "double" who hounds William Wilson may be the *victim* of this reversed ascription, that it may be *he* who is primary. We must entertain the notion that the split between Wilson and his double is not an entirely clean one between conscience and "the narcissism of the earliest period of all": and indeed, even if Wilson is the victim of conscience, he nevertheless *himself* exhibits features of the tyrannical superego, while the "double," for his part, displays in a similarly confused way the intrusiveness of conscience *and* a kind of archaic and impregnable narcissism.[17]

We can maintain, in other words, that the double is still the figure of a kind of conscience, of the narrator's superego, as long as we recognize that certain features of this superego retain what I have called an aboriginal status, that the "advent" of the superego which takes place in this moment of psychic doubling is also simultaneously a kind of archaic return.[18] Such brushes with an archaic or aboriginal source are registered as uncanny, since they are experiences divided between a feeling whose source is strictly unconscious, and the conscious registration of that feeling. Philippe Lacoue-Labarthe and Jean-Luc Nancy have suggested that affect *per se* is essentially divided and divisive, or as they say, ambivalent: it is this argument they make when they write gnomically that "the affect is the unconscious *as* consciousness."[19] In other words, affect as such is uncanny inasmuch as it registers an encounter with an intrapsychic origin which becomes recognizable only in its simultaneous disappearance: it "invokes what one would have to call a 'restraint' or a 'withdrawal' [*retrait*] whose origin is more archaic than that of any repression."[20]

This double movement of the uncanny affect, a movement in which one is touched or marked with an origin even as that origin recedes, suggests that the uncanniness of the relation between Wilson and his double is the sign of our proximity to what I have called an aboriginal sociality. For to say that the moment of the recognition of conscience is marked simultaneously by affect and consciousness is to focus the entire question of the uncanny and conscience on the notion of identification, which Freud characterized as "a very important form of attachment to someone else, probably the very first, and not the same thing as the choice of an object."[21] As "probably the very first" relation to an other, identification stands at the beginning of sociality in general, as Freud makes clear in *Group Psychology and the Analysis of the Ego;* in its role in the construction of the individual psyche, moreover, it performs the crucially socializing function of the installation of the superego. Freud remarks that, through the identification with the parental figure which marks the successful negotiation and outcome of the Oedipal crisis, the child not only assimilates the characteristics of his parents, but also becomes susceptible to all "the influences of those who have stepped in place of parents—educators, teachers, people chosen as ideal models."[22] And indeed, direct parental influence over the contents of the superego seems severely limited by the fact that, as Freud points out, the parents are in turn acting out their own relation to their parental superego: thus, "the child's super-ego is in fact constructed on the model not of its parents but of its parents' super-ego; the contents which fill it are the same and it becomes the vehicle of tradition and all the time-resisting judgments of value which have propagated themselves in this manner from generation to generation."[23] The superego, the conscience, thus becomes less the image of parental restriction than the embodiment of an entire social and cultural system of moral values.

In this regard, it is striking what short shrift is given to Wilson's parents:

> Weak-minded, and beset with constitutional infirmities akin to my own, my parents could do but little to check the evil propensities which distinguished me. Some feeble and ill-directed efforts resulted in complete failure on their part, and, of course, in total triumph on mine. Thenceforward my voice was a household law; and at an age when few children have abandoned their leading-strings, I was left to the guidance of my own will, and became, in all but name, the master of my own actions. (427)

The "complete failure" of Wilson's parents to socialize their child does not result in Wilson's liberation from the social constraints embodied in the super-ego; on the contrary, through the effective erasure of parental influence, Wilson is placed in an unmediated relation to the social origin of conscience, and the conflict thenceforth takes place as a properly social conflict and no longer simply a familial one. In many of Poe's tales, the narrator performs this elision of the familial through recourse to a notion of "heredity" which, passed down through the generations like the contents of the social superego, enlarges family to the point of its submergence in a "race": "I am the descendant of a race whose imaginative and easily excitable temperament has at all times rendered them remarkable" (427).[24] This "imaginative" and "excitable" temperament — so characteristic of Poe's aesthetico-philosophic maniacs — is also quite close to the kind of affective susceptibility, the "abnormally keen appreciation of the beautiful," that Poe associated, in his arguments over plagiarism, with the "poetic sentiment." And indeed, we can see here again the thematics of the inscription of "character" on such a temperament in Wilson's designation of his hereditary trait as that which renders him "remarkable."

The conflict with Wilson's double, the conflict with conscience, accordingly takes place not in the family home, but in the more socially heterogeneous milieu of the school. Wilson's "remarkable" strength of character at first assures his "ascendancy" there: "In truth, the ardor, the enthusiasm, and the imperiousness of my disposition, soon rendered me a marked character among my schoolmates, and by slow, but natural gradations, gave me an ascendancy over all not greatly older than myself; — over all with a single exception" (431). To be a "marked character" is the sign of power, a distinction which, in the relatively equalized social milieu of the school, amounts to a superiority. But to be a marked character also implies one's susceptibility to be re-marked, implies the submission of one's distinction to a law of repetition, a law which is experienced by Wilson as an intolerable opposition, the opposition of equality: "I secretly felt that I feared him, and could not help thinking the equality which he maintained so easily with myself, a proof of his true superiority; since not to be overcome cost me a perpetual struggle" (432). In contrast to Wilson's energy, energy both offensive and defensive, a kind of inertia characterizes the double, a complete lack of positive exertion: "He appeared to be destitute alike of the ambition which urged, and of the passionate energy of mind which enabled me to excel. In his rivalry he might have been supposed actuated solely by a whimsical desire to thwart, astonish, or mortify myself" (432). The double's phlegmatic nature is reminiscent of the complacency of Outis; and, as with Outis, we can suspect that the inertia and indifference characteristic of the double are associated with the social mass of publicity. Thus, it is no surprise that the double's equanimity seems to render him impervious to revenge in the form of social mockery: "my namesake had much about him, in character, of that unassuming and quiet austerity which, while enjoying the poignancy of its own jokes, has no heel of Achilles in itself, and absolutely refuses to be laughed at" (433). This equanimity of the double, his serene assumption of an equality, is experienced by Wilson as the sign of a superiority which he must struggle against. It is the sign of the double's *indifference,* in both senses of the word, and this indifference constitutes the double (and thus the social world of conscience) as a figure of the democratic social ideal, an oppressive and inert abstraction which, in Wilson's words, seems motivated solely by a desire to "thwart, astonish and mortify" the individual's will to differentiate and excel.

Such an analysis explains why Wilson's attitude toward his double is marked by a kind of nervous class antagonism: "I had always felt aversion to my uncourtly patronymic, and its very common, if not plebeian praenomen," writes Wilson, with a fussiness of vocabulary that indicates his desire to distance himself from the "very common" textual identity that is his name, and which his double so intolerably shares with him. As in the scene with Glendinning, there is in Wilson's attitude toward his name a kind of class confusion that he finds appalling, but nevertheless tends to promote: "notwithstanding a noble descent, mine was one of those everyday appellations which seem, by prescriptive right, to have been, time out of mind, the common property of the mob" (431). If Wilson is of "noble descent" here, his nobility is simply unidentifiable, since his name, which as patronymic should signal nobility unambiguously, is itself the "common property of the mob." (The same confusion is at work in Wilson's reference to himself as "the noblest and most liberal commoner" at Oxford). In short, Wilson's distinction of "descent" is indistinguishable, lost in the indifference of the "common property of the mob"; his name, the figure and guarantor of individual and class identity, is not his own, he does not possess it, but is possessed by it. Such are the proprietary and legal connotations of the phrase, "by prescriptive right": the *OED* cites Blackstone in reference to "Lords of manors . . . who have to this day a prescriptive right to grant administration to their intestate tenants and suitors"; that is, the right to certain actions and control based on uninterrupted possession. The *OED* also cites Burke, who draws out this sense of archaic possession "time out of mind": "Our constitution is a prescriptive constitution; it is a constitution whose sole authority is, that it has existed time out of mind."

Burke's usage turns us toward a more etymological understanding of the phrase, as that which is "written before," *prae-scribere.* The British constitution has always been *before;* it is, in fact, as much "before writing" as "written before." Michael Warner, in his provocative analysis of the role of publication in the construction of an America *res publica* of letters, has shown how for the Revolutionary generation the British Constitution served as the scandalous model of a transcendent authority, one standing outside of the system it authorizes. The American Constitution, Warner has argued, strives precisely to undo such authority (understood as "tyranny" by the colonists), or rather it aims to relocate it as immanent *to writing.* Moreover, he shows (and here he follows Derrida) that the indeterminacy which allows for such a relocation of authority is precisely the uncertainty as to whether "the people" existed before the writing of independence, or have come into existence with that writing.[25] To say, on the other hand, that "the mob" retains a "prescriptive right" is to close off this indeterminacy, and to posit the mob as always already before any writing. That the mob has a "prescriptive" right to Wilson's name thus appears as an intolerable obstacle to an effective self-origination, inasmuch as it limits the possibility of self-making through self-designation, or through the signature. "Prescriptive right" is that which always precedes and finally escapes any attempted self-writing. Wilson's attempted erasure of his parents retains the trace of this prescriptive precedence: "I was left to the guidance of my own will, and became, *in all but name,* the master of my own actions" (427, my emphasis). Wilson's independence, his originality, will always be limited by the preemptive naming to which he has been subject, which has prescribed him.

This is why it is not enough for Wilson simply to affirm the "complete failure" of his parents, and remove them from his narration; he must go further and literally name himself: "Let me call myself, for the present, William Wilson. The fair page now lying before me need not be sullied with my real appellation." The essential conflict of the tale is contained in this opening line. For the recourse to pseudonymy attests to the desire to write the self, to retain self-possession precisely through an act of disappropriation: one affirms absolute originality through the act of alienating one's own textual identity—one's given name—like any other piece of property. The gesture is, however, entirely futile, since *whatever* name Wilson gives himself *must be shared by the double* if he is to tell his story; in order to write himself, in other words, Wilson must necessarily succumb to the prescription of the name. Self-writing, as the desire for the disappropriation of the self's textual identity, entails the return to the self of that very capacity for disappropriation, that alienability of identity, as precisely what is proper to the self. Self-writing is unalterably and properly double, it is the *writing of the double,* a phrase in which we can read the undecidable oscillation of identity in the undecidability of the genitive: the writing *by* the double, or the writing *about* the double. If declarations of independence, as Derrida claims, necessarily waver between constative and performative modes, we can in fact see Wilson's pseudonym as the enacted allegory of that undecidability: "William Wilson," as signature, is simultaneously performative—Will-I-am: I proclaim myself Will, faculty of effectiveness and performativity, "master of my own actions"—and descriptive—Will's Son: I am the product of another who has preceded, I am created and not self-creating.

Thus, the power of the double over Wilson is finally simply his power to iterate Wilson's name, or better, to bring home to him its iterability: "The words"—of his name: again, to describe one's name as "words" is a gesture of defamiliarization answering the desire for disappropriation of the self's textual identity—"the words were venom in my ears; and when, upon the day of my arrival, a second William Wilson came also to the academy, I felt angry with him for bearing the name, and doubly disgusted with the name because a stranger bore it, who would be the cause of its twofold repetition . . ." (434). The double's tyranny over Wilson resides in this ability to remind the latter of the iterability of his name, while as the activity of conscience, it is in still another sense the power of prescription. It is striking that, while we are told that the double's "interference often took the ungracious character of advice; advice not openly given, but hinted or insinuated" (435), we are not given enough evidence of such advice to make a judgment about its content. Only twice do we witness such "interference," and in neither case do the double's words look anything like advice. The first case is the exposure of Wilson's cheating in the encounter with Glendinning, which is meddling enough, but cannot properly be called advice. The second though earlier instance is when Wilson is interrupted in his all-night revels at Eton:

> As I put my foot over the threshold, I became aware of the figure of a youth about my own height, and habited in a white kerseymere morning frock, cut in the novel fashion of the one I myself wore at the moment. This the faint light enabled me to perceive; but the features of his face I could not distinguish. Upon my entering, he strode hurriedly up to me, and, seizing me by the arm with a gesture of petulant impatience, whispered the words "William Wilson!" in my ear. I grew perfectly sober in an instant. (439)

Like the return of the doubled cloak in the episode with Glendinning, the double's intervention here consists solely of an uncanny re-minder, the return to Wilson of his own doubleness. If this is "advice," it is of a peculiar sort, not so much a prescriptive order as the simple calling-to-mind of the fact of prescription per se. It is like the "petulant impatience" of a parent who asserts a proprietary power over his or her child by the full articulation of the name he or she has bestowed upon the child: "Edgar Allan Poe, come here this instant!" Such an intervention amounts to the *enforcement of the name,* the appellation which exists only to be sounded and called. The prescriptive power of ideology—"all the time-resisting judgements of value" Freud finds stored up in the superego—may reside less in the content of its prescriptions than in its readiness to remind its subjects that they have been prescribed, already written, always ready to be read.[26]

The "prescriptive right of the mob," then, in all its resonances—proprietary, writerly, ideological—derives from a kind of archaic sociality which, because it both underlies and undoes individual originality, I have called aboriginal. Wilson's erasure of his parents turned us toward this aboriginal sociality, but it is the double who confronts us with its faceless figure. At one point, Wilson senses the double's aboriginality:

> I discovered, or fancied I discovered, in his accent, his air, and general appearance, a something which startled, and then deeply interested me, by bringing to mind dim visions of my earliest infancy—wild, confused and thronging memories of a time when memory herself was yet unborn. I cannot better describe the sensation which oppressed me, than by saying that I could with difficulty shake off the belief of my having been acquainted with the being who stood before me, at some epoch very long ago—some point of the past even infinitely remote. (436)

"The being" whose presence Wilson senses is, in fact, not out of his "earliest infancy" but prior to that, from a time when "memory herself was yet unborn." The point in time prior to memory will always in effect be the "point of the past infinitely remote"; it is the time of aboriginality which lies outside of anything like cognition, "more archaic," as Lacoue-Labarthe and Nancy write, "than any repression." "The delusion, however, faded rapidly as it came," continues Wilson; he means, perhaps, that "the delusion faded *as* rapidly as it came," but his elision of "as" allows us to take the phrase as designating the recognition Wilson here experiences as a moment of pure vanishing, inaccessible to any wakeful consciousness, present only as affect or, as he writes, "sensation." The "sensation" evoked in this moment of pure vanishing is the sign that Wilson finds himself in contact with the aboriginal, the fluid medium of the dissolution of identities which precedes all identity. This aboriginal medium is terrifying because it is objectless, prior to individuation. Thus Wilson's description of his silent encounter with the sleeping figure of his double must not be dismissed as simply overexerted Gothicism: "I looked;—and a numbness, an iciness of feeling pervaded my frame. My breast heaved, my knees tottered, my whole spirit became possessed with an objectless yet intolerable horror" (437). The horror is "objectless" because the double is not an object; what Wilson's "spirit" becomes "possessed" by is the unfigurable matrix of individuality which is not, in itself, individual, but is rather the dissolution, division, and doubling which precedes individuality. This is why the double's "countenance" is described as shrouded in obscurity at his moments of intervention: the face, symbol of the inalienable uniqueness of the personality, does not finally belong to the double; as simultaneous guarantor and disrupter of all the face stands for, the double remains faceless, unfigurable.

But if the double is unfigured, it does not follow that he does not figure. His prescriptive power resides precisely in his power to inscribe. Wilson's sense that the double hearkens back to a time "when memory herself was yet unborn" is terrifying for him because, in keeping with his desire to write himself, he would like to claim a uniquely complete memory:

> Yet I must believe that my first mental development had in it much of the uncommon—even much of the *outré*. Upon mankind at large the events of very early existence rarely leave in mature age any definite impression. All is gray shadow—a weak and irregular remembrance—an indistinct regathering of feeble pleasures and phantasmagoric pains. With me this is not so. In childhood I must have felt with the energy of a man what I now find stamped upon memory in lines as vivid, as deep, and as durable as the *exergues* of the Carthaginian medals. (430)

Wilson's desire to write himself, to affirm his complete originality, is in plain view here: he is "uncommon," an exception from "mankind at large" precisely to the extent that he has not lost himself in the "gray shadow" of "irregular remembrance"; indeed, he implies that he sprang into the world fully matured, feeling everything "with the energy of a man." But the anxiety attending such affirmations is equally legible in this passage, for after all, what Wilson describes as the reason for his total recall is, from another perspective, the testimony of his formation from without, his passive reception of a series of affects which stamp him in a process which is here literally the *inscription of character*.[27]

It is this insistent, though sometimes occluded, troubling of the idea of a time "when memory herself was yet unborn," which leads to Wilson's repeated need to start anew. Any reader of "William Wilson" will have been struck by the apparently excessive length of the introductory pages in which Wilson lingers over the details of his school in all their architectural exactitude (or incomprehensibility). I would suggest that these descriptions indicate that we are to take Wilson's entire narration as in some sense prefatory, and that the attention to architectural details throughout the story provides a half-hidden thematics of what we might call the *preliminary,* in the sense of that which stands before the threshold. Wilson is, at one point, explicit about the preliminary nature of his narrative: "I would not, if I could, here or to-day, embody a record of my later years of unspeakable misery, and unpardonable crime. This epoch—these later years—took unto themselves a sudden elevation in turpitude, whose origin alone it is my present purpose to assign" (426). Wilson's tale is the effort to "assign" the "origin" of his own life, to bracket the series of encounters with his double as the prelude or preface to a life which he will not tell; his recourse to a pseudonym is the performance of this "assignment"; but this self-writing is only possible because Wilson has, in the final encounter with the double, already murdered himself. Wilson can assign his origin only because he has signed his own death-warrant: "*henceforward art thou also dead—dead to the World, to Heaven and to Hope!*" (448); one can describe one's birth only from beyond the grave. In this way, "William Wilson" is like many of Poe's tales which position their writing as simultaneously the record and the result of a passage through death. While the "instant" of transformation at the end of the tale is a pure fusion of identities, what Wilson calls the "most absolute identity" (448), it is also simultaneously a moment of pure dissolution, death, and division. Thus, the confusion of voices Wilson experiences—"I could have fancied that I myself was speaking"—is no mere figure of speech, for if at the end the double proclaims Wilson's death "to Heaven and to Hope," Wilson will repeat that pronouncement at the beginning of the tale: "Oh, outcast of all outcasts most abandoned—to the earth art thou not forever dead? . . . and a cloud, dense dismal, and limitless, does it not hang eternally between thy hopes and heaven?" (426). Both thematically and formally, Wilson's murder of the double is the "origin" of the self-writing he performs in the tale as a whole, and the pseudonymous signature which stands at the beginning of the tale is thus simultaneously an act of self-generation and the pre-emptive repetition of the suicide at the tale's close.

But the circularity of the tale, the way in which the initial signature repeats the final act of self-murder, is perceptible only retroactively: the tale's peculiar temporality is one in which the origin is shown to be a repetition of the end, but always only *after the fact.* In this way, the tale forces the reader to misrecognize its own preliminary nature, forces him to read as the tale itself what is in fact only its preface; the tale forces the reader into putting the cart before the horse. This repetition of the preliminary is thematized in the encounters with the double, which characteristically take place in a closed and confining space of some kind of introductory passage: a "small ante-chamber" (in the final scene), "the vestibule of the building" (in the scene at Eton). "As I put my foot over the threshold, I became aware of the figure of a youth" (439): the recognition of the double is coincident with a kind of transgression, a stepping over the threshold. This architectural thematics is developed in the lengthy description of the various vestibules and subdivisions of the schoolhouse, as well as the careful enumeration of the "periodical egressions and ingressions" (429) from the school grounds. Just as he does in "The Fall of the House of Usher," Poe here develops an identity between his text and the architecture which serves as that text's setting.[28] This identity is most legible in Wilson's first description of the schoolhouse: "But the house!—how quaint an old building was this!—to me how veritably a palace of enchantment! There was really no end to its windings—to its incomprehensible subdivisions. It was difficult, at any given time, to say with certainty upon which of its two stories one happened to be" (429). It is impossible to move around in this house without crossing thresholds; in its "incomprehensible subdivisions," the house demands, as it were, constant transgression. The fact that these partitions are "incomprehensible," moreover, guarantees that such transgression will always be performed unwittingly; one will always unknowingly have stepped over some threshold already. And the situation is finally the same for the reader of this house-text, for we too can never "say with certainty upon which of its two stories" we find ourselves. These "two stories" are not only those of Wilson and his double; they are also the two stories that arise from the reader's recognition at the end of the tale that what he took to be the moment of beginning was in fact the repetition of the tale's end. The "two stories" are those of a doubled origin: the story which tells the origin, and that which, after the fact, tells the story of the origin's repetition of an always already misrecognized, and hence effaced, aboriginality.

The recognition that in reading the tale we have been moving through a series of introductory passages—in both the literary and architectural senses of the phrase—returns us to the problem of the epigraph, which now comes to seem the first prescription, the first threshold passed over unwittingly by the reader. If this epigraph puts us "in possession of the subject" of the tale, that subject must now necessarily seem double. As the subject of the tale, "conscience" has been shown to be merely the power of the double; to be put in possession of such a subject is thus not any escape from doubleness, but rather it is the return of the subject's doubleness—its prior dispossession or essential alienability—as what is proper to it.

But the question now arises: why would Poe be interested in producing such an effect? What does he have at stake in making the reader realize that his or her critical seizure of the tale, as a tale about conscience, is itself the first instance of this misrecognition of the preliminary? It would seem that Poe has a contradictory agenda in the tale. On the one hand, he wishes to *recreate* the temporal confusion he had described, in his articles about plagiarism, as arising from a structure of reading, the confusion whereby we take "as our own" a thought, or idea, or critical prescription that we are in fact possessed by. On the other hand, he wishes to display this confusion, perhaps even to deconstruct it—in any case, to have us *realize* that we have been confused. The uncanniness of Poe's tale, the vague sense of unease, even mild irritation, would seem to be the product of this induced confusion about confusion. As so often with Poe, the reader does not know exactly where to stand. I would even go so far as to say that "William Wilson" aims to produce in the reader a kind of anxiety. And indeed, anxiety itself, as both a theoretical problem and as a passion of the psyche, is finally the undefinable locale of the contradictions Poe's tale enacts. Writing about Freud's difficult negotiations with the problem of anxiety, Samuel Weber has pointed out its inherently paradoxical nature. On the one hand, anxiety is a signal which serves the ego's desire to master through repetition a trauma it could not foresee or prepare for in its first appearance. On the other hand, anxiety itself is a threat which will need a repetition to be mastered. Thus, anxiety submits the ego to a strangely inverted temporality, namely the attempt to delimit or master by anticipation a trauma that has necessarily *already* taken place; and in doing this it reinforces the necessity of always repeating this anticipatory repetition, since it necessarily submits the ego anew to an unmastered affect (of anxiety). Weber writes:

> For as an affect, anxiety "disturbs" and "interferes" with the theoretical effort to identify it, to explain it in terms of cause and effect. What Freud is therefore constrained to do is to separate anxiety from its affect, which is also its effect. For that effect cannot be limited to or determined exclusively as the ego's response to a danger, since anxiety itself can become the danger to which it reacts. Freud's attempt, in seeking to replace his earlier "economic" theory by a "topical" one, is intended to put anxiety in its proper place. But his own discussion demonstrates that anxiety *has no proper place*: it marks the impossible attempt of the ego to construct and delimit such a place, but this place is inevitably displaced, dislocated, enstellt.[29]

I suggested earlier that for Poe an anxiety about plagiarism was the one thing that criticism could properly claim as its own. We can now see the paradox of such a formulation. For if the problem of critical identity entails a vigilance before the possibility of plagiarism, it is a vigilance of anxiety, an anticipation of something that, in Poe's own analysis, *will have already happened*. Such an anxiety is the anxiety of self-ownership, and it is also the undoing of all possibilities of ownership or possession. Poe writes his tale in order to anticipate, in the mode of anxiety, the prescription of the mob, and to redefine this social origin as secondary, just as Wilson redefines his "double," or as Poe himself redefines Hawthorne's tale. But as we have seen, and as Poe's tale displays, such anticipations are themselves doomed to repetition. Plagiarism is impossible to prove but constantly threatened, ceaselessly anticipated as having possibly already happened. To hold fast to an anxiety about plagiarism as properly one's own is to hold on to one's undoing in the social as the only source of one's individual identity. It is simultaneously to submit to and to claim as one's own the prescriptive right of the mob.

NOTES

1. For a typical reading, see Daniel Hoffman, *Poe Poe Poe Poe Poe Poe Poe* (New York: Vintage Books, 1972), 209-13. Three days after finishing the first draft of this essay, I picked up Evan Carton's excellent work. Forty pages into the book, there is an interpretation of "William Wilson" in which Carton emphasizes a great many of the same aspects of the tale as I do: the emphasis on naming, pseudonymy, retroactive tem-

porality, writing as suicide, etc. "I grew perfectly sober in an instant," as Wilson said, soon recognizing the affect as the uncanniness—more than a *frisson*, I should point out—that accompanies encounters with one's double. Carton's interpretation forced me to give up my originality, in a sense, and to admit my own dependence on a kind of aboriginality; the consolation being, of course, that my essay, in its own aboriginal or preemptive way, had already accounted for the experience I was now having in the wake of its completion. See Evan Carton, *The Rhetoric of American Romance: Dialectic and Identity in Emerson, Dickinson, Poe and Hawthorne* (Baltimore: Johns Hopkins UP, 1985), 36-41.

2. Edgar Allan Poe, *The Collected Works of Edgar Allan Poe*, ed. Thomas Ollive Mabbott (Boston: Belknap Press of Harvard UP, 1968-78), vol. 2, 426. Further references to Poe's fiction are to this edition and are given—by page number only—in the main text.

3. Edgar Allan Poe, *Essays and Reviews*, ed. G. R. Thompson (New York: Library of America, 1984), 691. Further references to Poe's criticism are to this edition and are included in the main text.

4. For a fuller account of this accusation, see Robert Regan, "Hawthorne's 'Plagiary'; Poe's Duplicity," *The Naiad Voice: Essays on Poe's Satiric Hoaxing*, ed. Dennis W. Eddings (Port Washington: Associated Faculty Press, 1983), 73-87.

5. Neil Hertz, "Two Extravagant Teachings," in "The Pedagogical Imperative: Teaching as a Literary Genre," *Yale French Studies* 63 (1982): 60-71.

6. Hertz, 63.

7. Hertz, 61.

8. Hertz, 62.

9. The phrase "ideal unity" comes from "Aggressivity in Psychoanalysis," while "alienating destination" can be found in "The mirror stage as formative of the function of the I as revealed in psychoanalytic experience," both of which are collected in Jacques Lacan, *Écrits: A Selection*, trans. Alan Sheridan (New York: Norton, 1977).

10. See Michael Allen, *Poe and the British Magazine Tradition* (New York: Oxford UP, 1969), 47: "only in three articles did [Poe] take advantage of anonymity as the earlier journalists had done."

11. Poe's account of the "anxiety of influence" sounds at moments like a "strong misreading" of Harold Bloom, a temporal reversal which is the peculiar effect of the revisionary ratio Bloom labels "apophrades": successful practitioners of this "most cunning of revisionary ratios . . . achieve a style that captures and oddly retains priority over their precursors, so that the tyranny of time almost is overturned, and one can believe, for startled moments, that they are being *imitated by their ancestors*." See Harold Bloom, *The Anxiety of Influence: A Theory of Poetry* (London: Oxford UP, 1973), 141. It is amusing to consider Bloom as having managed to make Poe sound like an imitator of his, amusing mostly because such a connection implicitly grants that he is engaged in an agon with Poe, whom Bloom has consistently dismissed as a weak writer. On the other hand, Bloom has also quite powerfully characterized Poe as "inescapable," especially for the American reader. It is tempting to see Poe as one of Bloom's strong precursors, in a repressed (because antithetical) composite with Emerson, Bloom's avowed Father-figure. When Emerson writes that "In every work of genius we recognize our own rejected thoughts; they come back to us with a certain alienated majesty," the experience of one's dispossession by books is converted into personal power, as Bloom recognizes approvingly; Poe's own account of the readerly agon, which I have cited above, tends to telescope and conflate the characteristic Bloomian (and Emersonian) moments, so that the poet's strong misreading becomes in fact the first moment of an irrevocable dispossession and loss. On Poe's "inescapability," see Harold Bloom, "Inescapable Poe," *The New York Review of Books*, 11 October 1984: 23-37.

12. For a detailed and provocative account of this logic, see "Typography" in Philippe Lacoue-Labarthe, *Typography: Mimesis, Philosophy, Politics*, ed. Christopher Fynsk (Cambridge: Harvard UP, 1989), 43-138. In the original Greek meaning, "char-

acter" is "a mark engraved or impressed, the impress on coins and seals," from which is derived the metaphoric sense of the "mark impressed (as it were) on a person or thing, a distinctive mark, characteristic." See Liddell and Scott, *An Intermediate Greek Lexikon* (Oxford: Oxford UP, 1983), 882.

13. Samuel Weber, "The Sideshow, Or: Remarks on a Canny Moment," *Modern Language Notes* 88 (1973), 1133.

14. Hannah Arendt, *The Human Condition* (Chicago: U of Chicago P, 1958), 210-11.

15. See "The Murders in the Rue Morgue": "Between ingenuity and the analytic ability there exists a difference far greater, indeed, than that between the fancy and the imagination, but of a character very strictly analogous. It will be found, in fact, that the ingenious are always fanciful, and the *truly* imaginative never otherwise than analytic" (531).

16. Sigmund Freud, "The Uncanny," *On Creativity and the Unconscious* (New York: Harper, 1958), 141-42.

17. For an interpretation of the tale which argues that it is the *narrator* who embodies the conscience or superego rather than the "double," see Ruth Sullivan, "William Wilson's Double," *Studies in Romanticism* 15 (1976): 253-63.

18. Such a notion of the superego's archaic sources is, moreover, in line with Freud's account of the superego in his "second topography": "Thus in the id, which is capable of being inherited, are harboured residues of the existences of countless egos; and, when the ego forms its super-ego out of the id, it may perhaps only be reviving shapes of former egos and be bringing them to resurrection." Sigmund Freud, *The Ego and the Id* (New York: Norton, 1960), 28.

19. Philippe Lacoue-Labarthe and Jean-Luc Nancy, "The Jewish People do not Dream," *Stanford Literary Review* 6 (1989), 198.

20. Lacoue-Labarthe and Nancy, 63.

21. Sigmund Freud, "Dissection of the Personality," *New Introductory Lectures in Psychoanalysis* (New York: Norton, 1965), 56. For the inscription of an originary sociality in Freud's concept of identification, see Lacoue-Labarthe and Nancy, "The Jewish People Do not Dream," and their earlier treatment of the issue in "La Panique Politique," *Confrontations* 2 (1979): 33-57. See also Mikkel Borch-Jacobsen's book-length consideration of the problem, *The Freudian Subject,* trans. Catherine Porter (Palo Alto: Stanford UP, 1988).

22. Freud, "Dissection of the Personality," 57.

23. Freud, "Dissection of the Personality," 60.

24. Thus the narrator of "The Fall of the House of Usher" speaks of the "Usher race" and the congruence, even identity, between the family's estate and the "accredited character of the people" (399). So too Egaeus, in "Berenice," simultaneously erases his immediate family and affirms a greater "racial" inheritance: "My baptismal name is Egaeus; that of my family name I will not mention. Yet there are no towers in the land more time-honored than my gloomy, gray, hereditary halls. Our line has been called a race of visionaries . . ." (209). As early as "MS. Found in a Bottle," Poe makes use of this double maneuver: "Of my country and of my family I have little to say. . . . Hereditary wealth afforded me an education of no common order, and a contemplative turn of mind . . ." (135). Whatever Poe's biographical motivation for this characteristic anti-familial gesture, I would simply underscore that the gesture is not one of repudiation of the social, the sign of Poe's hermeticism, but is rather a technique for bypassing familial mediation in an effort to get more directly at an expanded notion of the social influences on the individual with a "contemplative turn of mind." It is in "William Wilson" that the lineaments of this social world appear most legibly.

25. Michael Warner, *The Letters of the Republic: Publication and the Public Sphere in Eighteenth-Century America* (Cambridge: Harvard UP, 1990). Warner is following through on some reflections of Derrida's on the role of signature and self-writing in

political declarations. See Jacques Derrida, "Declarations of Independence," trans. Tom Keenan and Tom Pepper, *New Political Science* 15 (1986): 7-15.

26. Thematically, this account of the prescriptive power of ideology evidently recalls Althusser's memorable notion of ideological hailing. See Louis Althusser, "Ideology and Ideological State Apparatuses," *Lenin and Philosophy*, trans. Ben Brewster (New York: New Left Books, 1971), 127-86.

27. Mabbott notes that Poe derived his interest in exergues from Bielfeld's *L'Erudition Universelle*, which defines the exergue as "the portion of the design [on a coin] found beneath the ground on which are placed the figures portrayed" (449). According to the *OED*, the exergue has an affinity with the signature, since it is the "space . . . for any minor inscription, the date, the engraver's initials, etc." The *OED* further notes that the English word was probably fabricated from Greek roots (*ex-*, [out] plus *ergon* [work]) to approximate the French *hors-d'oeuvre;* in French, exergue retains this sense of material which is prefatory in nature. The exergue thus combines a number of motifs centering on the outside of a work, that which lies "beneath the ground" of the "figures portrayed," which precedes that portrayal as a prefatory inscription. When Poe has Wilson liken his own formation to the inscription of an exergue, he draws attention to the way in which Wilson's origin is itself preceded by, indeed effected by, an aboriginal marking: it is an admission that one's signature, that which grants identity and the possibility of the self's circulation, is written by others in a prefatory prescription. To liken the self to a coin is, of course, also to emphasize the necessity of that self's circulation, its commitment to publicity; and to describe the self as a prefatory inscription is to make that circulation a textual affair.

28. For an account of Poe's architectural thematics, see Joseph Riddel, "The 'Crypt' of Edgar Poe," *Boundary* 2 7 (1979): 117-41.

29. Samuel Weber, *The Legend of Freud* (Minneapolis: U of Minnesota P, 1982), 58.

Hawthorne and the Making
of the Middle Class

Michael T. Gilmore

The currently fashionable triad of American literary studies, race, gender, and
class, a triad born of the egalitarian dethroning of the white, male, largely Anglo-Saxon canon, contains its own tacit hierarchy and rests on its own unenun-
ciated principles of exclusion and privileging. Disagreements abound over
whether race or gender should occupy the top tier in the new cultural ranking,
but about the subordination, even the effacement, of class, there can be no
doubt. Few working-class authors have been recuperated — George Lippard,
author of *The Quaker City* (1845), is a notable exception from the antebellum
period — and no programs in class and its multifarious manifestations have entered college curricula to compete for students with women's studies and African-American studies. Class as a thematic or formal consideration, once the
obligatory nod has been made, usually recedes to the background, if it does not
vanish altogether, while the critic goes about the business of interpreting *Uncle
Tom's Cabin* (1852), *Clotel* (1853), or *Pierre* (1852) in the light of racial and
feminist concerns.

One might speculate about the reasons for this omission. It could be argued
that the assimilation of the children of working-class parents into the white-
collar professoriate has dulled academic sensitivity to the reality of socioeconomic difference. Or it might be claimed that the historic dominance of the
middle class in the United States has produced a relatively homogeneous society in which class conflicts have been muted to the point of unimportance. Or
if one balks at the notion of an ideological monolith, a related hypothesis offers
itself. One might still hold that the United States, in contrast to the stratified
nations of Europe where social and economic alterity erupted into armed com-
bat in 1848, subsumes its class divisions under the sign of gender and/or race.
What we find in nineteenth-century American writing, goes a version of this
argument, is not economic struggle but a clash of gender styles, not a confrontation between social groups but the displacement of a patrician ideal of masculinity by an entrepreneurial or marketplace model.[1]

This paper takes issue with the critical consensus that relegates class to the
margins of antebellum American literature. It does so not by examining the
novels of a certified labor activist like Lippard, but rather by turning to a familiar and much-analyzed classic of the American Renaissance, *The Scarlet*

Letter (1850). Nathaniel Hawthorne, perhaps our most "canonical" nine-teenth-century novelist, the writer, indeed, in whom the canon is given birth, maps the emergence of middle-class identity and simultaneously reveals the self-contradictory and unsettled nature of the new configuration. Behind this claim lies the work of historians and students of gender and the family who have shown, convincingly to my mind, that the period when Hawthorne was writing saw the appearance of the middle class in its recognizably modern form. These scholars dispute the idea of an unbroken ideological or class he-gemony in the United States. They recount the development of a social forma-tion that declared itself, in part, through gender arrangements, the separation of public and private spheres, and the substitution of naturalism for historical contingency. Their work suggests not so much that class was submerged in gen-der, but rather that gender and the family were imbued with the determinants of class.[2]

Yet Hawthorne's text complicates the findings of these scholars. *The Scarlet Letter* points not simply to the development of an American middle class but also to the highly ambiguous character of that construction. It makes clear that the category of class, at least as the category arises in the Age of Jackson, does not march under the banner of essentialism. Hawthorne's masterpiece amounts to a warning that, in rescuing class from erasure, we must dispel any notion of its being a self-consistent entity.

The social indeterminacies of *The Scarlet Letter* problematize the current view of Hawthorne as an important figure in the formulation of a conservative brand of liberal individualism. According to the interpretation put forward most forcefully by Sacvan Bercovitch, Hawthorne contributed to the building of an ideological consensus that complemented the middle class's coalescence.[3] But the class loyalties knitted into *The Scarlet Letter* seem altogether too un-stable to authorize so unambiguous a cultural function for the narrative. And recognizing the textual vacillations fosters a certain skepticism about the crit-ical method of reasoning by analogy or homology. The case for Hawthorne's "liberalism" often seems to rest on structural resemblances between literary and social states of affairs, a mode of demonstration that commonly suppresses evidence of dissimilarity.[4] The resemblances are undeniably there in *The Scarlet Letter,* but the differences are no less real, and Hawthorne's text can be usefully studied to bring out the historical and gender oppositions concealed within lit-erary-social congruity.

It remains true that *The Scarlet Letter* participates in the project of shaping middle-class identity. The novel registers the exfoliation of a socially specific way of life. It encodes the deep structures of the middle class within its discur-sive patternings and to some degree labors to win consent to that class's dom-inance by validating its claims to universal legitimacy. But at the same time *The Scarlet Letter* obscures the boundary lines it seems to posit as impermeable. The book undoes its own synchronizations of gender roles, private and public spaces, and socioeconomic categories. Hawthorne's notion of what constitutes middle-class personhood turns out to be internally beleaguered. Patterns of male and female behavior, as pictured in the novel, slide into inversions of themselves, and the tale's image of the present is disrupted by pressure from the past and foreshadowings of the future. To borrow the terminology of Raymond Williams, we might say that Hawthorne's middle class incorporates both residual and proleptically oppositional elements,[5] but because gender is so integral to middle-class character as it crystallizes in the text, sexual ambiguation necessarily accompanies ideological and vocational exchange. The middle-class mother assumes a relation to the social like that of a free-market individualist, while the middle-class father embraces feminized sentiment. Hawthorne's new class threatens to come apart even as it comes into being.

Doubtless these inconsistencies can be traced in part to Hawthorne's own anomalous class position, a matter to which I will return at the end of the paper. But insofar as Hawthorne can be taken as an influential maker and articulator of nineteenth-century American culture, it is possible to generalize from the inconstant allegiances of his greatest work. The reversals and impasses of *The Scarlet Letter* betoken not merely his own unsettled status as an impoverished patrician trying to earn a livelihood by literature. They attest to the instability, the persistent vulnerability, of the ideological closure of the antebellum middle class.

I.

Like the word adultery, the name of the middle class is never mentioned in *The Scarlet Letter*. The only socioeconomic groupings Hawthorne refers to are the rich and the poor, or, in the antiquated vocabulary the novel sometimes adopts, the high and the low. Hester Prynne is said to receive abuse equally from the poor on whom she bestows her charity and from the "[d]ames of elevated rank" for whom she plies her needle.[6] The mass of Puritans are distinguished from their rulers only by being designated "the people," with little detail provided about their material condition.

Yet like the act of adultery, the middle class occupies a crucial position in Hawthorne's narrative. Following Roland Barthes—who defined the bourgeoisie as the class "*which does not want to be named*"—one might see the avoidance of nomination as the proof of textual centrality.[7] Hawthorne's labeling of those who are presumably neither rich nor poor as "the people" would be in keeping with this universalizing or self-excising impulse. Fortunately, there is more to go on than deletion. Hawthorne writes that the Puritan order supplanted the "system of ancient prejudice" associated with "nobles and kings" (164). He invites us to view the inhabitants of seventeenth-century Boston as the precursors of post-feudal—that is, bourgeois—civilization. But historical commonplace dissolves into anachronism, and anticipation gets conflated with actuality as the Puritan past merges into the American present. For Hawthorne presents colonial Boston as a preindustrial settlement sheltering a contemporaneous middle class, and he inscribes his major characters, above all Hester, with attitudes and modes of behavior that did not become normative until the entrenchment of commercial and industrial capitalism in the nineteenth century.

It might be useful to summarize some of the salient features of that emergent social and economic organization. Perhaps most important for *The Scarlet Letter* is the increasingly rigid segregation of work from the household, a divorce accelerated by the decline of domestic production and by the rise of factories and offices. Along with this change came a revaluation of female personality. Excluded from the public and male preserve of "productive" labor, women began to be identified with, and supposedly to derive their nature from, the private space of the home. They shed their traditional image as lustful and socially disruptive and were now believed to find fulfillment in moral purity, self-sacrifice, and caring for others. This revision, it should be emphasized, centered on middle-class women, who have been pictured—by, among others, Mary Ryan in history, and Nancy Armstrong in literature[8]—as the principal makers of middle-class lifestyle. The dominant values obviously penetrated working-class culture as well, but many laboring people retained residual or eighteenth-century perspectives on work and the family. Working-class women, for instance, were slower to assimilate domestic ideology because they typically sought employment in manufactories or carried paid work into the home.

The Puritan commonwealth depicted in Hawthorne's early chapters, and at various subsequent moments throughout the text, looks decidedly premodern in its emphasis on hierarchy and patriarchy and in its blurring of the boundaries between public and private. It is a community of rulers and ruled, of ministers, magistrates, and soldiers exercising authority over a deferential and largely undifferentiated people. Hawthorne says that seventeenth-century Boston takes its character from "the stern and tempered energies of manhood, and the sombre sagacity of age" (64). He distances its customs from his own time by observing that the Puritan elders regularly intervene in the most intimate details of moral and family existence. This patriarchal world antedates the Victorian model of domesticity and assumes the primacy of fathers in governing the family. Governor Bellingham, the Reverend Mr. Wilson, and other civil authorities contemplate removing Pearl from Hester's care because they assume the public's right to oversee the socialization of children. And just as the public intrudes into what came to be seen as a private and female enclave, so Puritan women in the novel think nothing of "stepping forth into the public ways" and loudly proclaiming their opinions of Hester's misdeed. For these New England matrons, writes Hawthorne, "the man-like Elizabeth"—not, one might add, the modest and sentimental Victoria—"had been the not altogether unsuitable representative of the sex" (50).

Although Hester emerges out of the seventeenth-century past, her Elizabethan qualities belong mainly to the narrative's prehistory. Hester, the sexually sinful female, exemplar of traditional womanhood, seems outdated when the action commences. Her refusal to identify her lover in the marketplace reveals the heroine as someone who is already in transition toward a post-Puritan order which guards the private from public exposure. Dimmesdale is also revealed in this opening scene as a Janus-like figure with one eye on a future respectful of the separate spheres. He tells the Reverend Mr. Wilson, much to the older man's bewilderment, "that it were wronging the very nature of woman to force her to lay open her heart's secret in such broad daylight, and in the presence of so great a multitude" (65).

The later pages on Hester's psychological metamorphosis are read too narrowly if we make out in them only the account of one unhappy woman's accommodation to repression. The celebrated descriptions of Hester's change "from passion and feeling, to thought," of her once sensual but now forbidding aspect "that Passion would never dream of clasping in its embrace" (163-64), condense into the span of a few years and a single chapter the reconstruction of feminine nature that required roughly a century to complete. Hawthorne dissolves the transgressive, appetitive Eve into her sexless opposite, replacing concupiscence with the condition that Nancy Cott has accurately labeled "passionlessness" and that underwrites the age's ascendent ideal of self-negating motherhood.[9] He historicizes, as it were, the dark lady/fair lady split in classic American literature by portraying Hester as a dangerous adulteress recasting herself into a model Victorian saint. In the course of the story, she assumes all those mother-related callings available to nineteenth-century middle-class women, winning the people's reverence for her selflessness as a volunteer nurse and self-ordained "Sister of Mercy." The townspeople forget the "original signification" (161) of Hester's letter because that original meaning—of woman as fallen Eve—has been eclipsed historically by middle-class woman's role as self-sacrificing dispenser of nurturance.

Just as Hester is a woman in transition, so *The Scarlet Letter* itself can be understood as a text mutating from one generic category to a second, historically posterior, literary form. The tale, like the heroine, appears anachronistic at first, an eighteenth-century seduction story that has somehow strayed into the age of *Uncle Tom's Cabin* and *The Wide, Wide World* (1850). But Hawthorne's narrative quickly shows its hybrid character as a contemporaneous sentimental novel superimposed upon that obsolete seduction plot. It is remarkable how much of the book approximates the fiction of the "scribbling women" Hawthorne famously disparaged in his correspondence. The structure of the antebellum middle-class family is replicated, or rather disfigured, in the novel's central human reality, the mother and daughter who spend all their time together while the father absents himself at work. The many scenes involving Hester and Pearl parallel the sometimes affectionate, sometimes troubled, mother-daughter relationships familiar to readers of domestic literature. Hawthorne admits that the wearer of the letter behaves more like a mother from the permissive present than from the rigid Puritan past. Loving her daughter "with the intensity of a sole affection," she lacks the resolve to discipline Pearl severely and expects little return for her tenderness other "than the waywardness of an April breeze" (179). This domestic Hester almost lives up to Hawthorne's description of her as "the image of Divine Maternity" (56).

But Hester, even in her maternal avatar, is not, or not merely, the Victorian angel in the house, the woman Dimmesdale hails as his "better angel" (205). The proto-feminism into which her alienation modulates is, in Hawthorne's treatment, the corollary to her solitary mothering and doing of good. Thrust into a modernized family arrangement by her infraction, Hester experiences as compressed personal history the gradual sundering of realms—public disjoined from private, male separated from female—that by the mid-nineteenth century constituted middle-class existence. One need only contrast the gawking, vociferous matrons who surround the scaffold in the early chapters with the mother and daughter who retire into the background while Dimmesdale delivers his election sermon. The now fully modern heroine, clinging to the margins of the marketplace, feels overwhelmed by a sense of her lover's remoteness "from her own sphere." Despite their private interview in the forest, Dimmesdale seems to have no connection to her; in his public, professional capacity, he is "utterly beyond her reach" (239). Such stark compartmentalizing underlines the rigid genderization against which antebellum feminism rebels but which simultaneously empowers feminist protest by making women cognizant of themselves as a separate human category and interest group. Hester is a female reformer two hundred years before her time because alone among the Puritans she is able to conceptualize "the whole race of womanhood" (165) as a branch of the human race apart from men.[10]

Dimmesdale is Hester's male counterpart as middle-class father and "new man" emancipated from the paradigms of an earlier cultural system. Unlike the Puritan patriarchs, he expresses admiration for Hester's unwillingness to speak in public: what for them is a failure of religious and civil duty is for him the mark of true womanhood. The split between public and private defines masculine identity for Dimmesdale too. He internalizes the fundamental rupture of modern social life as a division between his inner and outer selves. The self he displays in public to his parishioners is sharply differentiated from—it is the contradiction of—the private self that the reader knows to be Pearl's unacknowledged father and Hester's soulmate. The minister is tortured by "the contrast between what I seem and what I am" (191) and struggles to take his place beside his "wife" and child before the public gaze. But every attempt to confess, to overcome the breach between family and workplace, founders on his fear of the consequences of exposure. As we shall see, Dimmesdale does succeed in mediating between the private and the public, but he does so in ways that controvert his characterization as middle-class male.

Dimmesdale is further set apart from Boston's ruling elders by his having risen in the community through ambition and ability. "It was an age," Hawthorne writes, "when what we call talent had far less consideration than now, but the massive materials which produce stability and dignity of character a great deal more" (237). Dimmesdale has acted the part of a Jacksonian man on the make and pushed ahead of his seniors through assiduous cultivation of crowd-pleasing verbal skills. The homology to Hawthorne's own situation as a professional author trying to win fame and affluence through his linguistic gifts is evident enough.

Indeed, Dimmesdale's curious dwelling arrangements both highlight his post-Puritan professionalism and epitomize the text's enforcement of gender sequestration. The minister lives not with his "family" but with Hester's former husband, Roger Chillingworth, a man who, like himself, has a university education and practices an intellectual calling. Their lodgings resemble a workspace or office building more than a home. In one half is Dimmesdale's library, crammed with "parchment-bound folios" and writing materials, in the other the physician has installed his "study and laboratory," and the "two learned persons" daily settle down to their specialized vocations, at the same time "bestowing a mutual and not incurious inspection into one another's business" (126). Hawthorne has written into the narrative a graphic image of male professionals "married" to their work in the era after family production, when mental and manual forms of labor were segregated almost as sharply as men and women. Or better yet, he has given us a picture of the intensifying rivalry between the two great healing professions of the nineteenth century, the clerical attendants of the soul and the medical doctors of the body. Only Hester, in her gendered and unpaid role as charity worker, is entitled to treat spiritual as well as physical ailments.

Hawthorne is able to render the world of middle-class professionalism so vividly because he endeavors to enter it. His ambition to write for a livelihood, to become that invention of modernity, an independent author, gives him sympathetic understanding of his two male characters even as it figuratively places him in competition with them for status and income. As a young man about to matriculate at Bowdoin College, Hawthorne already pictured himself as a professional; in a well-known letter to his mother, he weighed the pros and cons of a career in law, medicine, and the ministry, ending with the question, "What would you think of my becoming an Author, and relying for support upon my pen?" As a writer who specialized in character analysis, Hawthorne did not flinch from rivalry with the other professions but positively cultivated it, as he ventured into territory traditionally reserved for clergymen and doctors. Reviewers, repelled or amazed by his psychological penetration, regularly compared him to a preacher, a Puritan, or an anatomist. "[H]e shows the skillful touches of a physician in probing the depths of human sorrow," exclaimed an admirer of the tales, and a reader of *The Scarlet Letter* was uttering a commonplace when he remarked that "of all laymen he [Hawthorne] will preach to you the closest sermons."[11]

Just as Hawthorne the novelist would lay claim to professional standing, so his novel apes the mores of the white-collar paradigm. *The Scarlet Letter* is formed by the same structural divisions that beset Hawthorne's principal characters. The book reproduces the separation of spheres most palpably in the line isolating "The Custom House—Introductory" from the ensuing narrative. The preface encloses the reader in the public and male domain of the Salem customhouse, "Uncle Sam's brick edifice" (15) symbolizing government and commerce. Here Hawthorne introduces us to his fellow workers, all of them men, describes his duties as Surveyor of the Revenue, and sets forth a kind of professional primer for writers, a detailed account of the genesis and composition of his romance. This sketch abuts but does not encroach upon the family romance of Hester, Pearl, and Arthur. Affective life quarantines itself in the tale of frustrated love, with its copious notation of female domesticity and private suffering. Holding in tension the oppositions endemic to nineteenth-century capitalism, the text as an entirety organizes itself as an instantiation of middle-class experience.

A similar splitting operates on a smaller scale within the romance proper, once the opening scene of Hester's punishment on the scaffold has run its course. Thereafter imperceptible lines of gender division radiate throughout the plot and give the tale its exemplary character as a kind of microcosm of the divergent forms of antebellum American storytelling. Chapters track Hester and/or Pearl on the one side, and Dimmesdale and/or Chillingworth on the other; mother and daughter inhabit one fictional space, the two males work and reside in another. When gender intersections occur, they do so outside society or in highly privatized settings that do not disturb the developing barrier between the familial and the public—places such as a jail cell, the scaffold at midnight, the seashore, or the forest. *The Scarlet Letter's* spatial demarcations point to its double character as feminized domestic tale and canonical "drama of beset manhood."[12] The novel's divisions miniaturize respectable—that is, middle-class—literary culture's bifurcation into the two subgenres of sentimental fiction and the fiction of male bonding and competition.

2.

Thus far we have been concerned with the parallels or homologies between Hawthorne's fictional universe and the historical details of middle-class formation. *The Scarlet Letter,* according to the argument, reinscribes the spatial and gender divisions constitutive of middle-class identity in the era of its rise. A change of focus is now in order, for it will bring to light some of the dark spots that concentration on similarity has ignored. The "dark spots" are complications and contradictions whose effect is to destabilize the particular alignments posited between textual and historical patterns. A first step toward correcting these occlusions would be to note that the gendered locus of class membership wavers in the novel and that Hester and Dimmesdale change places by donning the other sex's social characteristics.

The Scarlet Letter, for example, contains an American Adam figure who bears comparison to other Adamic heroes of nineteenth-century male sagas, heroes like Natty Bumppo, Ishmael, and Henry David Thoreau. This character, writes Hawthorne, "roamed as freely as the wild Indian in the woods" and criticizes the institutions of Puritan Boston "with hardly more reverence than the Indian would feel for the clerical band, the judicial robe, the pillory, the gallows, the fireside, or the church" (199). The character conceptualizes freedom and autonomy as qualities existing apart from the social order. For Hawthorne's Adam figure, the individual is defined not as a member of some larger unit but primarily in opposition to community; he is self-made and owes allegiance only to his own values and interests.

The character, of course, is Hester, but Hawthorne's account of her fierce independence suggests less Victorian womanhood than the Jacksonian individualist. It is appropriate to use the pronoun "he" in describing such a person because to Hawthorne's contemporaries, the solitary subject was necessarily a

man. Ralph Waldo Emerson's representations stand as typical. In that most famous of treatises on the mid-century summons to autonomy, "Self-Reliance"
(1841), the seeker after independence is always gendered as male. The iterated
nouns and pronouns do not mask but instead proclaim the cultural exclusions.
"The nonchalance of boys who are sure of a dinner, and would disdain as
much as a lord to do or say aught to conciliate one, is the healthy attitude of
human nature." Emerson's masculine insistences implicitly invert the clauses in
his declaration, "Whoso would be a man, must be a non-conform-ist."[13]

In actuality, this virile nonconformist conformed to the social practices of
his time. He was more entrepreneur than Transcendentalist or sourceless
Adam. Karl Marx's comments in *Grundrisse* on Robinson Crusoe, a literary
avatar for the Adam myth, are illuminating not just about Hawthorne's tale
but about the disjunction between the individual and civil society generally, a
separation which provides so recurrent a feature of American masculine writing. Marx explains that the presence in eighteenth-and nineteenth-century literature of the isolated, apparently pre-social individual—a figure he himself
likens to Adam or Prometheus—entails a massive forgetting or ignorance. En-
tering the novel "[n]ot as a historic result but as history's point of departure,"
the Robinson Crusoe character reverses the actual circumstances of his appearance. He belongs to, and can only arise in, a "society of free competition"
where "the individual appears detached from the natural bonds etc. which in
earlier historical periods make him the accessory of a definite and limited human conglomerate."[14] Some of the bonds Marx has in mind, like clans or feudal hierarchies, never existed in America, but Hawthorne's rendering of the Puritan commonwealth reminds us that on this continent too the human
community involved a dense network of responsibilities and connections. The
autonomous individual who dominates antebellum narratives of male rivalry
and maturation is a corollary to the acceleration of market capitalism in the
Age of Jackson, not a reflection of humanity unencumbered by history but a
product of the breakdown of republican commitment to the common welfare
and its displacement over the century by laissez-faire ideology. The bearer of
this historical change was Jackson's man-on-the-make, vocal opponent of cus-
tomary restrictions on economic development and building block of the new
middle class. But in *The Scarlet Letter*, paradoxically enough, this quintessential individualist and free-thinking pioneer in regions forbidden to women is
herself a woman and otherwise the antithesis of Jacksonian man.

Hester's dissident side, as noted earlier, associates her with antebellum feminism. Recent critics have construed Hawthorne's strictures on his heroine as a
repudiation of the movement for women's rights that was gathering force while
he composed his romance, less than two years after the Seneca Falls Convention of 1848.[15] While this may be an accurate appraisal of Hawthorne's conscious purpose, it slights the historical volatility of his characterization of
Hester. The heroine's assumption of masculine traits—which Hawthorne obviously intends as a disparagement—encodes a shadowy hint of future developments in female reformism. For a brief moment at the end of the story,

Hester appears to overshoot, as it were, the domestic feminism of Hawthorne's own day and to verge on the androgynous "New Woman" of the post-Civil War period.

As Carol Smith-Rosenberg has pointed out,[16] the feminism of the late nineteenth and early twentieth centuries thrived outside conventional social arrangements. It broke with the ideology of domesticity. The "New Woman" differentiated herself from her mother's generation by rejecting marriage and opting for a career. She braved the charge of "mannishness" by choosing a life not in the traditional family but in female institutions like women's colleges and social settlements, the best-known example of which was Hull House in Chicago, and she strove to cultivate autonomy as in a nondomestic environment.

Hester's denial of her (hetero)sexuality can thus be viewed not simply as a de-eroticizing but as a prefigurement of the Gilded Age woman reformer. Such a reading would be patently anachronistic, but my point is that Hawthorne's portrait of Hester as self-reliant individualist converts her, in the novel's "Conclusion," into a prophecy of supercession. She never remarries after Arthur's death and, upon returning to New England from Europe, assembles around her a community of women who console and advise each other in the face of masculine oppression. In this liminal, nonfamilial setting, Hester creates an alternative institution to patriarchal structures. Her stated message, in which she assures her followers of a "brighter period" when "the whole relation between man and woman" will be established "on a surer ground of mutual happiness" (263), is far less radical and less meaningful than her example. Hester endures as an independent being who separates herself from the prevailing social order—her cottage lies on the distant periphery of the Puritan settlement—and who finds fulfillment in the company of other females. The image of her in the book's final pages seems as much an historical postscript as a textual coda to the action.[17]

Just as Hester undergoes a series of social and sexual mutations, so Dimmesdale, exemplar of mid-century manhood, alchemizes into a communal being who looks remarkably like a sentimental novelist. The minister, according to Hawthorne, could never join Hester—or the Deerslayer, or the hermit of Walden Pond—in "the hardships of a forest life." His "culture, and his entire development" as a man of the cloth forbid it (215). Standing at "the head of the social system," Dimmesdale derives his very identity from its framework; he internalizes the community's "regulations, its principles, and even its prejudices" (200). Whereas Hester discovers her authentic self in isolation from the Puritan colony, Dimmesdale—to revert to Marx's formulation—knows himself to be "the accessory to a definite and limited human conglomerate." He is a residual presence in the commercial and industrial middle class, a product as much of the eighteenth or seventeenth century as of the Age of Jackson and Hawthorne. The minister can be seen as demonstrating the accuracy of Hawthorne's historical imagination—he is supposed to be a Puritan, after all—but more interestingly, his portrayal underscores the persistence in the text of loyalties and assumptions about individuality that clash with the ideology of liberalism. As a man, Dimmesdale is an anachronism from the past, as Hester as a woman is a potential anachronism from the future.

But Dimmesdale is not just a man; he also completes Hawthorne's fictionalization of middle-class womanhood. From the outset, he is delineated in terms that typify nineteenth-century femininity more than conventional maleness. First beheld on the balcony during Hester's punishment, he has "large, brown, melancholy eyes," a "tremulous" mouth, and a "nervous sensibility." His diffidence ill suits public office and causes him to feel most at ease in "shadowy by-paths." Dimmesdale is said to keep himself "simple and childlike" and to retain "a freshness, and fragrance, and dewy purity of thought" that affects many people as the manner of "an angel" (66). It would appear from his description that the angel is domestic, the pure and retiring homemaker of Victorian ideology.

Besides physically resembling a woman—much as Hawthorne does in surviving daguerreotypes—Dimmesdale is identified with the female realm of the emotions. His feminine qualities tally with his (residual) immersion in the social; he and Hester swap positions dramatically in this respect. Hawthorne, speaking in his most naturalizing mode, observes that her years of isolation have stripped Hester of the capacity for affection and passion, the preservation "of which had been essential to keep her a woman" (163). But what Hester has temporarily forsaken, Dimmesdale, nominally a man, has possessed all along. The feeling evident in his voice when he addresses the Puritan populace works so powerfully on the hearts of his auditors, that the minister's words weld them "into one accord of sympathy" (67).

Dimmesdale's skill at deploying and manipulating sentiment enables him, like the popular women novelists of the 1850s, to bridge the gap between private affect and public occupation. The young preacher is conscious of the rift between the two realms, an awareness that certifies his modernity and places him apart from the Puritan patriarchs, who act as though the closet and the marketplace are synonymous. Dimmesdale's attempt to surmount the division rhetorically, through the mediation of language appealing to the emotions, inflects his nineteenth-century contemporaneousness toward the feminine and allies him, as an artist figure, with Stowe or Warner rather than Cooper or Melville. For the minister's sermons, delivered "in a tongue native to the human heart" (243), constitute a sentimental literature; they validate and make public—they publish—the inner feelings that the text denominates as female or domestic. Hawthorne tropes the heart as a chamber or residence, a space that only a woman can humanize and make inhabitable. He has Chillingworth observe to Hester, "My heart was a habitation large enough for many guests, but lonely and chill, and without a household fire" (74). Dimmesdale's "Tongue of Flame" suffuses the public world with affectivity; he feminizes culture by lighting a hearth fire in the popular heart.

Dimmesdale's volte-face, from rising male professional to domestic novelist reaching out from the private sphere to engage "the whole human brotherhood" in the language of sentiment (130), alerts us to the fact that the neat structural divisions of Hawthorne's own novel tend to lose their resolution upon closer scrutiny. Hawthorne himself is a male fiction writer redoing the seduction formula as a domestic love story of mother, daughter, and missing father. Moreover, the partition between public and private, male and female, encapsulated in the break between "The Custom-House" and the romance proper, inverts itself with a slight alteration of perspective. Hawthorne terms the preface an indiscreet surrender to the "autobiographical impulse" (3). Not only does he lay out his theory of romance, he divulges intimate details about his struggles with a writer's block. He gives an account of his personal affairs, including his resentment at being dismissed from office—the kind of washing one's laundry in public that Hawthorne well knew would create a stir. He even conducts the reader into a chamber of his home, with its "little domestic scenery" of doll, child's shoe, and hobbyhorse (35). The tale that follows, on the other hand, is an impersonal commodity contrived for sale on the literary marketplace. Hawthorne, who addressed his readers as "I" in the introduction, now extinguishes the private self and assumes the mask of omniscience as a third-person narrator. The pigeonholing on which the text seemed to rest its articulation of social life under expanding capitalism proves impossible to maintain. *The Scarlet Letter*'s formal separation into preface and narrative operates to exhibit *and* to dissolve the structures of middle-class existence.

These migrations demonstrate the lability of structural parallels between text and history. They testify to the overflow or supplement that class brings to gender. Hester is a female denizen of the private sphere, but she is also an isolated individualist whose stance toward the social mimics laissez-faire doctrine rather than the cult of domesticity. Dimmesdale is an absent father and male co-worker, but he is also a domestic author. Both characters, in both their avatars, inhabit positions in the middle class—positions that did not emerge as ubiquitous until that class jelled in the Jacksonian Era. Yet the two characters hold those places as occupational and ideological transvestites.

Class refuses to be permanently absorbed into gender in Hawthorne's text. For while gender style is always tethered to class, class exceeds the capacity of gender to contain it. The refusal of fixed gender roles returns upon class, as it were, to advertise a problem in Hawthorne's attitude toward middle-class identity. The mid-century middle class proscribed the very gender ambiguity he sponsors in his novel. To be a "masculine" woman was to veer toward the attributes of the working class; to be a feminized male was to ape the manner of the social aristocracy. Hawthorne's sense of occupational and gender mutability connotes a refusal to abide by the dominant class's sexual and spatial requirements. The novel's constant shifting of boundaries betrays authorial doubts about the middle-class ethos. The shifts intimate, not Hawthorne's collusion in the liberal consensus, but rather his indecision about an historical emergence that his art commemorates but simultaneously chafes at as stultifying.

3.

The ending of Hawthorne's novel precipitates a last effort to confront the com-
partmentalizations of market culture. The ending can be read in either of two
ways, as an undoing of middle-class conventions or as their apotheosis. The
final tableau on the scaffold, with Dimmesdale joining Hester and Pearl as he
had failed to do at the beginning, reconstitutes the intimate nuclear family. T.
Walter Herbert, in an influential article on gender in Hawthorne, calls this
scene a recreation of "essential manhood and essential womanhood."[18] And
there's no doubt that the last chapters contain some of the narrative's most
ideologically sanitized pronouncements. A consolidating of gender stereotypes
and cultural boundaries appears to signal Hawthorne's complete capitulation
to middle-class ideals. He projects the fissures of his time into the afterlife. Not
Hester and Dimmesdale, he suggests, but Dimmesdale and his male rival, "the
old physician," will find themselves reunited in the "spiritual world," their
"antipathy transmuted into golden love" (260-61). Pearl's shedding of tears at
her father's dying kiss is construed, in the best sentimental fashion, as "the
pledge" that she will cease to "do battle with the world, but be a woman in it"
(256). The reader learns that Hester's hope of reforming gender relations will
have to wait upon an "angel" of unblemished character, "a woman indeed, but
lofty, pure, and beautiful"; and capable of "showing how sacred love should
make us happy, by the truest test of a life successful to such an end!" (263).
Though Hester delivers this prophecy to a community of women, Hawthorne's
words imply that his heroine's feminist longings are to find fulfillment in the
dream of a perfect marriage.

If at moments the ending strives to naturalize the doctrine of pure womanhood, however, it never does so without equivocation. Pearl's defection to Europe, where she reenters the gentry from which her mother's family descended,
hints at a persistent and unmastered distaste for the confinements of middle-
class life. The same impatience hovers behind Hawthorne's disclosure, in the
tale's final paragraph, that on the tombstone of his ill-starred lovers "there appeared the semblance of an engraved escutcheon" bearing a heraldic device
(264)—feudal and aristocratic residues that affront middle-class closure.
Moreover, Hester's insistence on reassuming the scarlet letter, on advertising
her youthful sinfulness, acts as a reminder of the premodern understanding of
woman's character. The letter reminds us that nineteenth-century female essentialism is a temporally bounded, post-Puritan construct, not an eternally existing ideal. Contemporaneous gender roles can be thought of as universally desirable only by repressing the historical differences that the tale itself has
documented.

To put this more positively, Hawthorne seems as intent on rending the bar-
riers of Jacksonian culture as he is on legitimating its norms. The scaffold
scene, with its reuniting of the middle-class family unit, illustrates the point.
The apparent essentialism of this episode is qualified, not to say undermined,
by the physical setting of its occurrence. Hawthorne brings together the Victo-

rian trinity of mother, father, and child in the very site where domestic ideology proscribes it: before the stares of the multitude in the marketplace or public stage. Understood in this way, the building of the entire narrative toward the climactic reconstruction of the family indicates a wish on Hawthorne's part, not to uphold, but to challenge nineteenth-century binary logic. The scaffold scene marks a trespassing of the industrial order's boundaries, a reversion to older patterns of behavior and an anticipation of future struggles to insert familial or domestic issues into the political sphere.

A glance at Hawthorne's own circumstances, and another look at Hester's standing in the community, may help to elucidate his oscillations. The author of *The Scarlet Letter* occupied a highly irregular class position. As he impresses upon us in "The Custom-House," he was descended from one of New England's most distinguished families. The Hathornes (spelled without the "w") were long-standing members of the Massachusetts elite and perhaps the closest thing the non-slave-holding states boasted to an aristocracy. The novelist's ancestors journeyed to the New World with the first wave of Puritan immigrants. They were prominent jurists and magistrates whose deeds—or rather, misdeeds—were recorded in histories of the country's earliest settlement. But like Poe's mythical Ushers, the line's fortunes have declined precipitously. When the future novelist was a child of three, his own father, a merchant, died at sea, and he was raised on the charity of relatives. As an author, he has not escaped dependency. He has continued to receive handouts to support his family; indeed, as we know from the preface, he has failed so miserably as a writer that he has had to accept employment as a government functionary. Little wonder that he imagines his forefathers dismissing him as a mere "writer of story-books! . . . Why, the degenerate fellow might as well have been a fiddler!" (10).

Like his fictional minister, Hawthorne the dependent patrician seemed to have an equivocal sexual identity that inclined toward the female. Many contemporaries commented on his extraordinary good looks, Elizabeth Peabody (the sister of his wife) pronouncing him "handsomer than Lord Byron"— another aristocratic figure renowned for almost feminine beauty. Reviewers detected "a large proportion of feminine elements" in the work—to quote Henry Wadsworth Longfellow—and heaped up adjectives like quiet, passive, pure, arch, delicate, lovely, and sensitive. They called the novelist "Gentle Hawthorne" in recognition both of his genteel roots and demeanor and of his womanly tenderness. Hawthorne's celebrated reclusiveness reinforced these impressions. The description of Dimmesdale as lingering in "shadowy by-paths" can be applied to the notoriously shy and aloof creator who withdrew into his mother's home for a decade after graduating from college. And of course Hawthorne's lack of financial independence cast him in a feminized position. Like women throughout history, he had to rely on others to provide the money for his family's maintenance.[19]

Compounding the feminizing of aristocracy, Hawthorne's pauperism highlights the mutability of his location in the social order. He represents a notable instance of antebellum declassing: he is an impoverished scion of the American patriciate, an aristocrat driven to subsist on public charity. But he is also, precisely as the author of the text we are reading, on the verge of redefining his social position as a member of the rising professional class. He aspires to, and with this fiction finally attains, the economic independence that comes from appeal to the marketplace and not to a patron. He belongs to the first generation of self-supporting writers in the nation's history, the men and women of the 1850s who proved it possible to live by the pen. Hawthorne is at once a professional male, an erstwhile aristocrat, and a failed laborer at literature reeling from the loss of his government sinecure. Ideological uncertainty and ambivalence toward the new middle class seem hardly surprising in his case. He stands within the emergent social formation, but he stands above it and below it as well.

And Hester shares his categorical instability as *declassé* aristocrat. When first forced to mount the scaffold, she thinks back to her paternal English home, "a poverty-stricken" dwelling over the portal of which hangs "a half-obliterated shield of arms . . . , in token of ancient gentility" (58). Convicted of adultery, required to wear the badge of shame, Hester's regal bearing nevertheless invests her with an aristocratic air. The servant who admits the heroine to Governor Bellingham's mansion is so struck by her manner, and by "the glittering symbol on her bosom," that he imagines she must be "a great lady in the land" (104). But in fact Hester's sexual transgression only completes her family's social collapse, arguably into the laboring class. She ekes out a subsistence for herself and Pearl with her needlework, a Puritan forerunner of the nineteenth century's favorite emblem of downtrodden womanhood, the seamstress.

Seen from a different angle, Hester evokes the middle class in the making, but, like her creator, she stands outside as well as within the nascent configuration. Her ties to the working class are particularly significant in this regard. For the Jacksonian working class was both residual and sexually problematic in its behavior; its female members were mannish and unfeminine, as well as old-fashioned, by bourgeois standards. They departed the family for workshops or toiled in the home for wages at the very moment when the middle-class dwelling was becoming equated with leisure and with exemption from the rapacity of the marketplace. Female laborers approximated women of the past or men of the present more than the wives of antebellum lawyers, retailers, and manufacturers. Hester's erasure of her femininity and adoption of free-market attitudes may thus stem as much from the ambiguities of her class status as from the sliding of her gender position and historical specificity.

But these ambiguities do not negate the evidence linking Hester and Arthur to middle-class formation. As much as the overt allegiances, the instabilities in their respective characterizations announce the entrance into American literature of a new historical phenomenon. For the slippages are not unique but were in actuality common to the antebellum middle class. It is hardly a coincidence that the novel's version of that class materializes as a consequence of sin. To Hawthorne, middle-class emergence is a fraught difficulty, not a matter for congratulation. His two principal actors reflect his own, and presumably many other people's, incomplete incorporation into, and continuing uneasiness with, the social revolution of his time. Hawthorne's lovers proclaim the circumstance that at a time of profound sociological dislocation, Americans who were acquiring middle-class values and lifestyle were by no means unanimous about the process. Some retained older loyalties and patterns of behavior that could generate internal disaffection; others developed commitments that could lead to open resistance. Hester and Arthur's permutations bespeak the still fluid nature of an ideological ascendancy that hardened into dominance only after the Civil War—and did so, moreover, in relation to an increasingly restive and militant working class.

Gender and race have been rightly reinstated at the center of American literary history. We have learned, thanks to the insights of feminists and African Americanists, to revise our thinking about the supposedly essential qualities that determine those two rubrics. It is now accepted that gender and race are social contructions with indeterminate boundaries that fluctuate over time and are shaped by historical circumstances rather than by anything innate. In the case of class, the situation in the United States has traditionally been the reverse. Americans have long taken for granted the proposition that there was no such thing as class in the country's past; unlike gender and race, it simply didn't exist. If this reading of *The Scarlet Letter* accomplishes nothing else, it is meant to suggest that here too change is necessary. Class, no less a social construction than gender and race, has been just as fluid and difficult to ascertain exactly. But its existence has been just as real, and it is time that we admitted its importance in the making of our cultural inheritance.

NOTES

1. I refer here specifically to the formulation of David Leverenz. See his book, *Manhood and the American Renaissance* (Ithaca: Cornell UP, 1989). The elision of class, usually in favor of gender or race, is so pervasive in criticism on antebellum literature that to illustrate the practice, one could simply call the roll of leading Americanists: Jane Tompkins, Philip Fisher, Richard Brodhead, etc. Some "second generation" New Historicists have argued for greater attention to class, although their own writing tends to marginalize it. See, for instance, Gillian Brown, *Domestic Individualism: Imagining Self in Nineteenth-Century America* (Berkeley: U of California P, 1990). A recent article that attempts to recuperate class more centrally in relation to several Hawthorne short stories is Nicholas K. Bromell, " 'The Bloody Hand' of Labor: Work, Class, and Gender in Three Stories by Hawthorne," *American Quarterly* 42 (1990): 542-64.

2. Of the many writers who could be mentioned here, I would single out Stuart Blumin, *The Emergence of the Middle Class: Social Experience in the American City, 1760-1900* (New York: Cambridge UP, 1989); Bruce Laurie, *Artisans into Workers: Labor in Nineteenth-Century America* (New York: Noonday, 1989); Mary P. Ryan, *The Cradle of the Middle Class: The Family in Oneida County, New York, 1790-1865* (New York: Cambridge UP, 1981); and Eli Zaretsky, *Capitalism, The Family, and Personal Life*, rev. ed. (New York: Harper, 1986). On the English side, see Leonore Davidoff and Catherine Hall, *Family Fortunes: Men and Women of the English Middle Class 1750-1850* (Chicago: U of Chicago P, 1987).

3. Bercovitch has developed his position in essays published over a number of years and drawn together in *The Office of "The Scarlet Letter"* (Baltimore: Johns Hopkins UP, 1991). A somewhat similar interpretation of Hawthorne's novel as a document of

ideological compromise has been advanced by Jonathan Arac in "The Politics of *The Scarlet Letter,*" *Ideology and Classic American Literature,* ed. Sacvan Bercovitch and Myra Jehlen (New York: Cambridge UP, 1986), 247-66.

4. This form of argumentation has become identified with the New Historicism and is illustrated, in criticism on Hawthorne, by Walter Benn Michaels' essay, "Romance and Real Estate," reprinted in his *The Gold Standard and the Logic of Naturalism: American Literature at the Turn of the Century* (Berkeley: U of California P, 1987), 85-112. On the totalizing character of Michaels' book, see Brook Thomas, *The New Historicism and Other Old-Fashioned Topics* (Princeton: Princeton UP, 1991), 117-50.

5. See Williams, *Marxism and Literature* (Oxford: Oxford UP, 1977), esp. 108-27.

6. Nathaniel Hawthorne, *The Scarlet Letter* (Columbus: Ohio State UP, 1962), vol. 1 of *The Centenary Edition of the Works of Nathaniel Hawthorne,* 84. Subsequent page numbers given in the text refer to this edition.

7. See Barthes, *Mythologies,* trans. Annette Lavers (New York: Hill and Wang, 1972), 138.

8. I refer to Ryan's *Cradle of the Middle Class* and to Nancy Armstrong, *Desire and Domestic Fiction: A Political History of the Novel* (New York: Oxford UP, 1987).

9. See Cott's essay, "Passionlessness: An Interpretation of Victorian Sexual Ideology, 1790-1850," *A Heritage of Her Own,* ed. Nancy Cott and Elizabeth H. Pleck (New York: Simon, 1979), 162-81.

10. I should perhaps qualify this statement by noting the conspicuous seventeenth-century exception (that proves the nineteenth-century rule?) of Anne Hutchinson. On the continuities between Hutchinson and Hester, see Amy Lang, *Prophetic Woman: Anne Hutchinson and the Problem of Dissent in the Literature of New England* (Berkeley: U of California P, 1987).

11. Letter to Elizabeth C. Hawthorne, 13 March 1821, *Letters, 1813-1843* (Columbus: Ohio State UP, 1984), vol. 15 of *The Centenary Edition,* 139; see the reviews collected in *Hawthorne: The Critical Heritage,* ed. J. Donald Crowley (New York: Barnes, 1970), esp. 78, 193.

12. I am paraphrasing the title of Nina Baym's article, "Melodramas of Beset Manhood: How Theories of American Fiction Exclude Women Authors," *American Quarterly* 33 (1981): 123-39. *The Scarlet Letter* is fairly unusual among the classics of the American Renaissance in encompassing both male and female domains.

13. The quotations are from *Essays: First Series* (Cambridge: Belknap Press of Harvard UP, 1979), vol. 2 of *The Collected Works of Ralph Waldo Emerson,* 29.

14. References are to the selection from *Foundations (Grundrisse) of the Critique of Political Economy, The Marx-Engels Reader,* ed. Robert C. Tucker, 2nd ed. (New York: Norton, 1978), 222.

15. See Bercovitch, *The Office of "The Scarlet Letter,"* 106.

16. See particularly Smith-Rosenberg, "The New Woman as Androgyne: Social Disorder and the Gender Crisis, 1870-1936," *Disorderly Conduct: Visions of Gender in Victorian America* (New York: Oxford UP, 1985), 245-96.

17. This is not to suggest that the argument for a nondomestic feminism wasn't made in Hawthorne's day. Margaret Fuller's *Woman in the Nineteenth Century* (1845) is a case in point. But as a widespread cultural movement, the phenomenon belongs to the latter third of the century.

18. Herbert, "Nathaniel Hawthorne, Una Hawthorne, and *The Scarlet Letter*: Interactive Selfhoods and the Cultural Construction of Gender," *PMLA* 103 (1988): 285-97, esp. 289.

19. Peabody is quoted in James R. Mellow, *Nathaniel Hawthorne in His Times* (Boston: Houghton, 1980), 6; the Longfellow review appears in *Hawthorne: The Critical Heritage,* 80-83, esp. 81. Although I invert his emphases, I wish to acknowledge here the work of David Leverenz on types of antebellum masculinity. See *Manhood and the American Renaissance.*

"Margaret Garner":
A Cincinnati Story

Cynthia Griffin Wolff

All history becomes subjective; in other
words there is properly no History, only
Biography. Every mind must know the
whole ground. What it does not see, what
it does not live, it will not know.

—Emerson, "History"

After *Beloved* was published in 1987, Toni Morrison spoke eloquently about
the nightmare of silence that had been thrust upon slave women. Not merely
the denial of literacy and the refusal to permit a "decent" woman to speak in
public. Not merely a code of chastity that ostracized any slave woman who
gave an honest account of the sexual exploitation and degradation to which
she had been subjected. But the diabolical punishment of the "bit," an ingenious device that yanked back swollen lips, clamped tongue to jaw, and dried
the spittle so thoroughly that even after the "bit" had been removed, speech
remained more a wild memory than a cherished possibility. Morrison also
spoke about her fascination with the Margaret Garner affair, a flight from slavery that attained brief, sensational currency among abolitionists in those years
just before the Civil War.

There are some stories whose intrinsic nature seems bounded by silence—
stories that no one wants to tell and no one wants to hear. Sometimes there is
a fundamental problem with "facts": villains and violators generally keep only
self-serving records of their crimes, and the victims of extreme brutality often
retain sanity only by explicit *failures* of recollection. (Thus women who have
been sexually molested in childhood by their fathers have a lethal propensity
for "forgetfulness": they carry the "memory" of their degradation not as a
narrative to be told, but as a collection of symptoms whose origin remains mysterious.) Sometimes, even if there is a knowing teller for the tale, the forms of
available narrative will allow very little to be told that society is not already
predisposed to hear. And always, when these tales *untell* the myths by which

Reprinted by permission from *The Massachusetts Review* 32 (1991): 417-40; c. 1991 The Massachusetts Review, Inc.

society has justified its power, both victim and teller are reviled. Unwelcome stories demand a reconstruction of "reality" and of the distribution of social power: castigating these victims and tellers is society's way of resisting the change.[1]

One such story is that of the slave mother. Driven to distraction by violations and torture—helpless and of necessity silent—loving children she does not "own" and "protecting" them by the desperate strategy of infanticide. "It was not a story to pass on," Morrison has observed.[2] Nonetheless, it is a vitally important story, for the anguish and near insanity of its lineaments remain as inescapable evidence of the slave system's daemonic destructiveness. Certainly Morrison intends to speak to this moral need, both urging and enacting the process that she has named "rememory"; and her immense aesthetic achievement is a reconstruction of this element of America's history—a retrospective that replaces the slave woman's silence with eloquent language.

Perhaps, then, there are some stories that must be told by "others" and "outsiders" and "inheritors," stories that can never be exact or correct or firsthand; and because these stories must be told (imperfectly) by others, "truth" can come only from telling and retelling. Telling these stories—eventually making such stories *tellable*—is necessarily a communal effort. And perhaps that is why Toni Morrison was not alone in her determination to formulate the morally vexed tale of the slave mother's terrible quandary. Instead, one might say that she has completed an effort that was begun in 1851 by Harriet Beecher Stowe. Not retrospectively, but by some miracle of moral imagination, Stowe was able to comprehend the anguish and impotence and rage that lay coiled at the heart of the slave mother's enforced silence. Like Morrison who would follow her, she was determined to replace that silence with eloquent language.

Above all, the achievements of Stowe and Morrison urge the necessity of community. In this case, it is a union of women—both black and white—who are resolved to liberate the slave woman from the bondage and isolation of her silence. And it begins, as it ends, with "Margaret Garner."

Only one short description of her remains. It was written by Levi Coffin, head of the Underground Railroad in the crucial border city of Cincinnati—a man who is said to have been personally responsible for leading three thousand slaves to freedom. She was

> a mulatto, about five feet high, showing one-fourth or one-third white blood. She had a high forehead, her eyebrows were finely arched and her eyes bright and intelligent. . . . The African appeared in the lower part of her face, in her broad nose and thick lips. On the left side of her forehead was an old scar, and on the cheekbone, on the same side, another one. When asked what caused them, she said, "White man struck me." That was all. . . .
>
> She appeared to be twenty-two or twenty-three years old. . . . She was dressed in dark calico, with a white handkerchief pinned around her neck and a yellow cotton handkerchief, arranged as a turban, around her head. The babe she held in her arms was a little girl, about nine months old, and was much lighter in color than herself, light enough to show a red tinge in its cheeks.[3]

Inevitably, perhaps, the representation conveys the habits of mind in mid-nineteenth century America. This is an African-American madonna: Mother and Child.

Well before the beginning of the Civil War, this country had begun to elaborate a pseudo-religion, "The Cult of True Womanhood," and the focus of "worship" was a stereotype of perfect, loving comfort—the "Angel of the Hearth"—The Mother. It was, in all of its particulars, fraudulent—cruelly hypocritical toward white women and barbarous toward blacks.

Throughout most of the nineteenth century, when a married woman who was white bore children, she had no legal claim to them. The father was their sole and absolute guardian: he had the legal right to make every meaningful decision in their lives; and if his wife dared to leave home (fleeing from drunkenness or abusiveness), the father retained custody. Thus although idealized images of "Mother" and "Motherhood" had been endowed with national reverence, actual mothers had no *real* power to protect the babies that they had borne—little legal claim to them at all. For white women, unlimited moral responsibility had been combined with *de facto* impotence.

For African American slave women, the situation was immeasurably worse. When a married slave woman bore children, the father had no legal claim to them—even if he happened to be a free man and even if he happened to be white. In deference, perhaps, to the necessities of nursing and infant-care, small slave children generally "travelled with the mother," but she had no legal claim to them. A slave woman and her children all "belonged" to her white owner. He was free to use them in any way that suited his desires, however cruel or perverse. He could dispose of them at will, could sell or trade them separately whenever and wherever he wished. The law offered no protection whatsoever. And what of that cherished image—"The Angel of the Hearth," the "Mother"? According to the apologists for slavery (and to all others who were simply indifferent to the moral dilemmas that slavery had produced), these ideals could not be applied to African American women: their nature was more primitive and less refined than that of white women; they were not "civilized"—not really "attached" to their children.

America's crude hypocrisy regarding motherhood served one useful end; it created the possibility for "community" among black and white women. No white woman would know the horror of the slave mother's ordeal; however, every woman whose moral sensibility was tied to her role as a mother could sympathize with their plight, and it is this deep bond among women that lies at the heart of "Margaret Garner's" story.[4]

The first part of it begins before Margaret Garner ever came to Cincinnati—begins, in fact, with the woman who was the period's most eloquent story-teller, Harriet Beecher Stowe. The explicit connection between the two women is tenuous—a local legend that was dutifully recorded in 1941 by Forrest Wilson, Stowe's most thorough biographer. In examining the possible real-life sources for Eliza's flight over the ice in *Uncle Tom's Cabin*, Wilson noted: "In southern Ohio there exist[ed] other versions of the . . . story put forward by reputable and sincere people. One Margaret Garner, an ex-slave woman who lived in Cincinnati after the Civil War, escaped over the frozen

Ohio River and thought she [had] inspired Mrs. Stowe's story." Such a claim, put forth by the woman herself, is both puzzlingly anachronistic and deeply intriguing.[5]

When Harriet Beecher moved from New England to Cincinnati in 1832, very little in her experience had prepared her for life in an exotic, unruly river-town. Her father, Lyman Beecher, had come to preside over the Lane Theological Seminary, and he had optimistically expected the town to be a "London of the West." The sixth largest city in America (in 1850, it would still be the country's fastest-growing), Cincinnati was dirty and violent. Ohio was a free state. Kentucky—just across the river—was a slave state. Laid out along the river that divided the two states, Cincinnati was a city with a considerable number of black residents, some free and some escaped slaves, and their number was rapidly increasing—690 in 1826, and 2,255 by 1840, about 5% of the total population.[6] The businessmen of the area, who had regular and profitable dealings with the slave-holding states, were vehemently opposed to the efforts of Garrison and the abolitionists; and bounty-hunters, who seized putative runaways by force (sometimes fugitive slaves, but sometimes free blacks) and took them to be sold in the deep South, roamed through the city, pursuing their prey virtually without challenge. The pestilential atmosphere of violence and degeneracy erupted frequently in racial incidents (and riots) or in bodily attacks on abolitionists. No one could be immune to the problem, and few could remain neutral.[7]

Living in Walnut Hills, six or seven miles from the noisy city-center, Harriet Beecher Stowe could avoid many of the disagreeable features of this violent river city. However, she could not shirk the moral quandaries that an intimate view of slavery offered. The public issue was not so troublesome to her: slavery was wrong, it ought to be abolished, and the attendant problems were pragmatic, not moral. By contrast, the network of private dilemmas that slavery had created was almost impossible to puzzle out. And the ultimately *unanswerable* question was this: until slavery and every lingering trace of it had been abolished, how might anyone who had been ensnared by its toils lead a "good" life? In the shadow of slavery, in the tight grasp of slavery, what *was* "goodness"? In her day-to-day life, what did a "good" woman do?

Between the time of her marriage in 1836 and the time she began to write *Uncle Tom's Cabin* (in 1850), Harriet Beecher Stowe bore seven children. Her daily world was populated largely by women, and a great many of them were black. She employed them—to help with laundry, cooking, cleaning, and sewing; she taught black children side by side with whites in the "family school" and became acquainted with their mothers; and she visited back and forth with free black families who lived as neighbors in Walnut Hills.[8] This was an extended domestic realm, a little society in which women worked together and gossiped to pass the time; here, the young mother, Harriet Beecher Stowe, learned about the degradation of slave women—tales of cruelty and perversion that had been unimaginable in far-away New England. She learned from Eliza Buck, for example, as they worked in the kitchen together.

. . . In her youth she must have been a very handsome mulatto girl. . . . She was raised in a good family as a nurse and seamstress. When the family became embarrassed, she was suddenly sold on to a plantation in Louisiana. . . . She has told me of scenes on the Louisiana plantation and has often been out at night by stealth ministering to poor slaves who had been mangled and lacerated by the lash. [Later] she was sold into Kentucky, and her last master was the father of all her children. On this point she ever maintained a delicacy and reserve that always appeared to me remarkable. She always called him her husband; and it was not till after she had lived with me some years that I discovered the real nature of the connection. I shall never forget . . . my feelings at her humble apology, "You know, Mrs. Stowe, slave women cannot help themselves."⁹

After a while, Stowe had heard so many tales of despair that she often remarked that comprehending the realities of slavery might drive anyone mad: women advertised as "good breeders" and "mothers, whose children were about to be sold from them [who] have, in their desperation, murdered their own offspring to save them from this worst kind of orphanage." Eventually, she developed a bitter contempt for the so-called "patriarchal stability and security" that was said to protect the welfare of "the slave population."¹⁰ Yet the final step in Stowe's emotional education did not occur until 1849.

Periodically, Cincinnati was swept by seasons of cholera; however, none was more destructive than the cholera epidemic of 1848-49, which held the city in a state of surrealistic captivity for more than six months. No one knew what caused the disease — or what might be done to avoid it — and soft coal fires stoked with sulphur were burned at every corner (even during the hot, humid summer months) because this smoke was thought to neutralize the poisonous miasma in the air. At its height, between May 1 and August 30, the epidemic killed 4,114; when the final tally was taken, there had been one death for every fifteen residents. One of the victims was Charley Stowe, aged eighteen months, Harriet Beecher Stowe's youngest child.

Sometimes the disease was merciful and dealt death almost immediately, but in Charley's case, dying took a long time. He began vomiting on July 12, and they wrapped him in wet sheets to prevent dehydration. Days went by. He would seem to rally, only to sink back into febrile fretfulness. On July 15, Aunt Frankie, who did the family's laundry, took sick while she was washing their clothes; she died the next day, and Harriet sat with her daughters, sewing Aunt Frankie's shroud and caring for Charley. On July 17, even the family dog was seized with spasms and died in an hour. But Charley still clung to life, his disease more painful each day. He did not succumb until July 26, after a sickness of two full weeks. For most of that time his mother had fought to save him. By the end, however — distraught by suffering that she could do nothing to relieve — she had begun to pray for his death. On July 26, she wrote: "At last it is over."

My Charley — my beautiful, loving, gladsome baby . . . now lies shrouded, pale and cold in the room below. . . . Many an anxious night have I held him to my bosom and felt the sorrow and loneliness pass out of me with the touch of his little warm hands. Yet I have just seen him in his death agony, looked on his imploring face when I could not help nor soothe nor do one thing, not one, to mitigate his cruel suffering, do nothing but pray in my anguish that he might die soon."[11]

Years later, Stowe recollected this moment as a turning-point. "I have often felt that much that is in [*Uncle Tom's Cabin*] had its root in the awful scenes and bitter sorrows of that summer." She had discovered how it felt to be utterly helpless to protect a child. "It was at [Charley's] dying bed and at his grave that I learned [a little of] what a poor slave mother may feel when her child is torn away from her. . . . I felt that I could never be consoled . . . unless this crushing of my own heart might enable me to work out some great good to others. . . ."[12]

Harriet Beecher Stowe realized that no one in her position could ever fully appreciate a slave mother's anguish. Indeed, the course of her marriage had been relatively smooth, and she had never even thought to ally herself with the suffragists who wanted to alleviate a woman's lot (usually focusing on white women). Still, she was heartbroken by the loss of this child, devastated by her inability to respond to his pleas or relieve his pain. Afterwards, she had an entirely new vision of the black woman's profundity of suffering. Might this not, then, enable her to be of unique assistance to them?

In his own brilliant autobiography, Frederick Douglass had put the African American male into American history; he had told the slave man's story—told it unforgettably and in written form. And after the publication of that book, the United States could never again discount the black man's suffering or deny his moral autonomy. Now Stowe would make a similar effort in behalf of black *women*; she would write the slave mother's story, claiming the black women's right to moral autonomy. And by inscribing the African American woman into history, she would assure these women a place in the nation's account of itself—never to be erased, never again to be forgotten. Such was the mission of *Uncle Tom's Cabin*.

There are dozens of black mothers and children in the novel, and after the passage of the Fugitive Slave Act in 1850, there was nowhere in America for them to find safety. Surely the best-known "mother and child" are Eliza and her baby, for their melodramatic escape over the ice from Kentucky to Ohio became a sentimental icon in mid-nineteenth-century America almost as soon as the novel was published. Little wonder. The novel deliberately presents Eliza iconographically, as "The Mother," and she is portrayed in ways that make her all but indistinguishable from the sentimental heroines of domestic fiction.

Having a clear-headed notion of her explicitly political mission, Stowe wanted to engage the reader's sympathetic identification with her black characters, and this reaction could never be enticed by an abrupt confrontation with slavery's most extreme forms of oppression and brutality. Thus Eliza's passage toward freedom, which occurs early in the novel, is presented with a tone and a series of details that might have come from the works of Fenimore Cooper or Sir Walter Scott. The slave mother's immediate opponent is not a slave holder, not a human at all, but "Nature" at its most "Sublime": "she vaulted sheer over the turbid current by the shore, on to the raft of ice beyond. . . . The huge green fragment of ice on which she alighted pitched and creaked as her weight came on it. . . . With wild cries and desperate energy she leaped to another and still another . . . leaping, — slipping, — springing upwards again!"[13]

The reader would do well not to be lulled by this moment of Romantic adventure. In the following chapter (only five pages after the heroic crossing), Eliza's pursuer is calculating the amount of money he has lost because of her escape, and he is reminded of a similar financial mishap.

> "Last summer, down on Red River, I got a gal traded off on me, with a likely lookin' child enough, and his eyes looked as bright as yourn; but, come to look, I found him stone blind. . . . Wal, ye see, I thought there warn't no harm in my jest passing him along, and not sayin' nothin'; and I'd got him nicely swapped off for a keg o' whiskey; but come to get him away from the gal, she was jest like a tiger. . . . I tell ye, she made all fly for a minnit, till she saw 't warn't no use; and she jest turns round, and pitches head first, young un and all, into the river, — went down plump, and never ris." (*UTC*, 1:84-85)

Here is something a good deal truer to life, a woman whose "escape" by means of the river has been accomplished not by crossing it, but by plunging into it with her child and drowning. Considerably less memorable than Eliza's escape (the nameless woman's story is told in a single paragraph), this episode is a foretaste of the unromantic tragedy to come: by gentle steps, Stowe's narrative escorts the reader down to hell.

There is Prue who was bought "to breed chil'en for market" (*UTC*, 1:284). There are Susan and Emmeline, "gentlewomen" by any measure, now waiting in a slave warehouse to be auctioned off: "Susan had . . . the same horror of her child's being sold to a life of shame that any other . . . mother might have; but she knows that tomorrow any man, however vile and brutal, however godless and merciless, if he only has money to pay for her, may become the owner of her daughter, body and soul" (*UTC*, 2:98). And there are others, many others — as many accounts of violation as there are females in the slave system.

These many narratives culminate in the second iconographic tale of a slave mother's dilemma: "The Quadroon's Story." If Eliza's heroism had been cleanly Romantic, the heroism of "the quadroon," Cassy, is turgid and violent. Softened by no pieties or platitudes, its moral boundaries transcend those of conventional Christianity. Cassy is familiar with every outrage, every degradation of the slave trade: "In her eye was a deep, settled night of anguish . . . hopeless and unchanging" (*UTC*, 2: 125). Long ago, Cassy had loved a white man. Naive and trusting, she had borne him two children and believed in his promises of fidelity and protection. But when his affections wandered and his funds ran low, " 'he sold us. . . . He sold both those children' " (*UTC*, 2:142, 143, 145). Her son and daughter, then — both lost to the vast anonymity of the slave system.

Passed casually from owner to owner, Cassy eventually had another baby:

> "Oh, that child! — how I loved it! How just like my poor Henry the little thing looked! But I had made up my mind, — yes, I had. I would never again let a child

live to grow up! I took the little fellow in my arms, when he was two weeks old, and kissed him, and cried over him; and then I gave him laudanum, and held him close to my bosom, while he slept to death. How I mourned and cried over it! . . . But it's one of the few things that I'm glad of now. I am not sorry to this day; he, at least, is out of pain." (*UTC*, 2:145)

Murder. A merciful murder, but murder, nonetheless. A terrible, *explicitly perverse* assertion of moral agency. And nothing in the novel suggests censure or recrimination. It is a horrifying truth that Cassy's decision to kill her child was an enactment of the only form of "mother-love" that slavery *reliably* allowed.

In the *Key to "Uncle Tom's Cabin,"* Stowe stipulated her method in hard-headed, unmistakeable terms. The novel had given "a very inadequate representation of slavery; and it is so, necessarily, for this reason,—that slavery, in some of its workings, is too dreadful for the purposes of art." How did she gather material? Stowe begins the answer with an archetypal confrontation that is starkly devoid of the prettifying softness in her fictions.

> Several years ago . . . a colored woman . . . was ushered into the nursery. . . . This woman was thoroughly black, thick-set, firmly built, and with strongly-marked African features. . . . [She was accompanied by her child.]
>
> "Here are some papers," said the woman. . . . [They stated that a] trader in Kentucky . . . had waited about as long as he could for her child. . . .
>
> [The woman] had been set free by the will of her owners; . . . the child was legally entitled to freedom, but had been seized on by the heirs of the estate. She was poor and friendless, without money to maintain a suit . . . .

Both the beginning and the absolute center of moral urgency. Harriet Beecher Stowe with her child and an anonymous black woman with hers—just such a meeting, reenacted many times; the tales of brutality so often told in half sentences and embarrassed whispers—all the mingled concerns, hesitant friendships, and unthinkable dangers that brought white and black mothers together in the border town of Cincinnati. This is the human quandary that provided a beginning for *Uncle Tom's Cabin.*[14]

Little wonder, then, that Margaret Garner had claimed some part in the genesis of that singular work—some part that spoke the essence of her woe. Some part that might affirm, "Yes, this is *my* story. This is the book that put my story into history. And after this book, I can never be erased."

Strict chronology invalidates such a claim: Stowe moved from Cincinnati to Brunswick, Maine, in 1850; *Uncle Tom's Cabin* was published in 1852; and Margaret Garner did not cross the river into Cincinnati until 1856. Yet the nature of "relatedness" cannot be so easily dismissed, for the story of "Margaret Garner" remains—complex, compelling, and mysterious.

On Saturday, January 26, 1856, a blizzard blanketed the city of Cincinnati; there had been snow on the ground for nearly five weeks, and the thermometer during this extraordinary cold spell had hovered between zero and twenty degrees below. The river was frozen solid. Sunday evening, the most recent snowfall had ended, young people took the snow-clogged thoroughfares as an invitation to minor mischief, and the city's police were called to answer numerous complaints about snowball fights that had frightened horses into bolting with the sleighs they pulled.

Across the border in Kentucky, several miles back from the Ohio line, seventeen slaves who had been planning escape for a long time managed to get hold of a sleigh and two strong horses. On Sunday night, after everyone else was asleep, they jumped aboard and took off for the river.

It was no short journey, and they drove like blazes. By the time they reached Covington, just across from Cincinnati, the sun was already coming up, and they were in danger of appearing conspicuous. They parked the sleigh outside the Washington Hotel, crossed the river on foot, and divided into two separate groups as soon as they had reached free soil.

The larger of the two groups was successful: they made their way up town, found safe hiding places, and eventually followed the Underground Railroad up to Canada. The members of the other group were not so fortunate. They had become confused and had to ask directions several times. By mid-morning, they finally found concealment in the house of a free black man named Joe Kite, but they had already called attention to themselves. As soon as he had fed them breakfast, Joe Kite went out to seek Levi Coffin's help, and the two men made arrangements for the slaves to join the "Railroad" going North. However, during the short time Kite was absent, his house had been identified by the pursuers; and Kite had scarcely gotten back inside before the posse began to storm the exhausted fugitives, who had barricaded themselves inside. It was a small group, eight members of a single extended family: a husband and wife in their mid-fifties (Simon and Mary), their son Robert (sometimes called young Simon), his four children, and his wife—Margaret Garner.

The ensuing battle dominated the front page of *The Cincinnati Daily Enquirer* the next day; its headline read, A TALE OF HORROR :

> The city was thrown into much excitement yesterday morning by the information that a party of slaves . . . had made a stampede from Kentucky to this side of the river. Other circumstances . . . have imparted a degree of horrible interest to the affair. . . . Three of the slaves, who bore the relationship of father, mother and son . . . were the property of Mr. James Marshall, of Richwood Station, Boone County . . . and five others, consisting of a woman named Peggy [Margaret Garner] and her four children, the oldest about five years of age, the youngest an infant at the breast, [were the property of] Mr. Archibald K. Gaines, who resided in the immediate vicinity of Mr. Marshall. Peggy was married to young Simon, the slave of Mr. Marshall, and the son of the old couple. . . .
>
> Early yesterday morning, Mr. Gaines, accompanied by a son of Mr. Marshall, arrived in this city in pursuit of the fugitives. . . . [These two men, accompanied by a posse of "officers," followed the family to Joe Kite's house, but when they arrived there], they found the doors and windows fastened. . . . Upon thundering at the door, Kite looked out of a window, and at first agreed to admit them, but afterward refused to do so, and at this juncture, as they were about to force an entrance, Simon fired from the window with a revolver. . . . Upon this the door was burst in, when Simon fired three more shots at the party. . . . Mr. Gaines seized him by the wrist and wrenched the pistol from his hand before he could shoot [again]. But a deed of horror had been consummated, for weltering in its blood, the throat being

cut from ear to ear and the head almost severed from the body, upon the floor lay one of the children of the younger couple, a girl three years old, while in a back room, crouched beneath the bed, two more of the children, boys of two and five years, were moaning, the one having received two gashes in its throat, the other a cut upon the head. As the party entered the room the mother was seen wielding a heavy shovel, and before she could be secured she inflicted a heavy blow with it upon the face of the infant, which was lying upon the floor. . . .

The only information derived from the eldest boy, in reply to who had injured him and the other children, is that the folks in the house did it. . . . The fearful act lies between one of the other of the miserable parents, perhaps both. . . .

. . . The mother of the children is a good-looking, hearty negress, while her husband bears the appearance of having been well cared for. . . .[15]

The wounded children, whom *The Enquirer* referred to as "little sufferers" (without the least hint of irony), were given medical attention; and the entire family was subsequently lodged in the County Jail.

On the following day, after local abolitionists had obtained counsel for the fugitives, a Coroner's hearing took depositions from those who had witnessed the act.

Mary Kite, the wife of the occupant of the house, testified that the people arrested [had come] to the house about eight o'clock in the Morning. . . . [Somewhat later], she heard a shot fired, and going in, found the youngest woman attempting to cut her boy's throat, while the child exclaimed, "Oh mother, do not kill me!" . . .

Elijah Kite . . . corroborated the evidence of his wife. [Both testified] that when they entered the room where the fugitives were, during the time the woman was attempting to cut the boy's throat, the father of the boy was pacing the room wringing his hands and screaming, as if bereft of reason. . . .

Mary Garner, one of the blacks being claimed by Marshall . . . testified [that when a parcel of men began to lay siege to the house, Margaret Garner rushed in and said]: "Mother, before my children shall be taken back to Kentucky I will kill every one of them." She ran to her child, a little girl, three years old, and cut its throat; she said, "Mother, help me to kill them." I said, "I cannot help you to kill them."

The hearing concluded with an indictment: "We find that the said child, Mary Garner, was killed by its mother, Margaret Garner, with a butcher's knife, with which she cut its throat."[16]

The legal situation was not so simple as this statement might suggest. For many years, the Cincinnati courts had consistently ruled that slaves who had been taken by their masters to live in the free state of Ohio were "emancipated" by virtue of their residence under the jurisdiction of that place. Even if they were subsequently returned into a slave state, they remained "liberated," and if they escaped, they could not lawfully be pursued and recaptured as "fugitive slaves." It was Margaret Garner's contention that "when . . . she was a girl, she was brought from Kentucky into the city of Cincinnati . . . to nurse Mary Gaines, daughter of . . . John Gaines."[17] If this assertion could be substantiated, neither she nor her children could be reclaimed into slavery. Yet any victory would be dubious, for she would then have to stand trial for the murder of her daughter. Of the two options, Margaret Garner preferred to remain in Cincinnati so that her children could be free, even if it meant a murder trial. Hence her lawyer pressed the claim of prior residency.

Each of the captured adults made a similar claim, and a series of public hearings ensued to determine the status of the fugitives. For the next two weeks, the newspapers carried day-by-day accounts of the proceedings, almost as if they constituted some sort of serialized novel. Yet the events that inform these journalistic accounts have none of the aesthetic intensity or moral coherence of fiction: instead, they are a concatenation of confusion and despair that do not come together into a "tale."

Margaret Garner's hearing was the last to be held. It began on February 8 and lasted for four days. Her children were with her in the courtroom for the entire period.

Most of the time, she sat despondently, holding her nine-month-old daughter, Silla. The baby

> was continually fondling her face with its little hands, but she rarely noticed it, and her general expression was one of extreme sadness. The little boys, four and six years old . . . were bright-eyed . . . little fellows, with fat dimpled cheeks. During the trial they sat on the floor near their mother, playing together . . . unconscious of the gloom that shrouded their mother, and of the fact that their own future liberty was at stake. The murdered child [had been] almost white, a little girl of rare beauty.[18]

None of the other fugitives had testified in their own defense (under the terms of the Fugitive Slave Law of 1850, they had no right to do so); however, Margaret Garner's attorney discovered an ingenious loophole. Although she could not take the stand to speak in her own defense, she was allowed to speak briefly on behalf of her children.

Her remarks were simple, almost flat. They confirmed that she had already visited Ohio with the approval of her owner; yes, "I came here with John Gaines and his wife"; no, she could "remember nothing very particular that happened when I was brought over." And "these three children . . . are mine; they were born since I was in Ohio with John Gaines."[19] It was as if her anger and hope, even her passion to protect the children—all the comprehensive, vitalizing elements of her character—had been spent in that flight from Kentucky and the slaughter that followed it. This was the last testimony to be heard. Afterwards, the court was adjourned to await summation the following day.

Throughout the two weeks of public hearings, there had been an eager audience: the courtroom had been packed, and crowds outside greeted the prisoners every day as they entered and again as they left. On the day following this testimony, counsels for the owners and for the slaves began their summation. During the remarks of Margaret Garner's lawyer, Lucy Stone [Blackwell] slipped into the courtroom and quietly took a seat.

The most eloquent orator of the female suffrage movement, Lucy Stone was traveling through the city as part of a lecture tour, and she had arranged to stay for several days—in part to visit the members of her husband's family who still lived there (Cincinnati had been the home of the famous Blackwell clan), and in

part to join the abolitionists' efforts to assist these fugitives. A week earlier, she
had written to Henry Blackwell from Indiana, "I suppose you have seen the
notice of that horrible slave capture in Cincinnati where the heroic mother
killed her child.

> No hall could be had for a meeting of sympathy. . . . My brain burned at the
> thought that *anybody* could for one moment weigh the safety of property in the
> scale with that which might have secured LIBERTY to those who have proved so
> well that they deserve it. I received a letter yesterday . . . asking me to accept the
> guardianship . . . of one of the wounded little ones. I wrote him, that I hoped they
> would all get their freedom, in which case, *such* a mother, was all the guardian they
> needed.[20]

Of course, she added, in the sad event that it should prove necessary, she would
be more than happy to become the child's guardian.

Unlike Stowe, Lucy Stone had not yet lost a baby, but she had spent many
years fighting for a mother's right to protect her children. So deep were her
feelings about the matter that her marriage ceremony in 1855 had contained an
extraordinary "formal protest." Among its stipulations were protests against
the laws which gave a husband "1. the custody [and unlimited use] of the
wife's person and 2. The exclusive control and guardianship of their children."
Lucy Stone was more a politician than Stowe, but in this Cincinnati courtroom,
her motivation was personal. As a white woman and a free woman, she had
been accorded a courtesy that had been denied to Margaret Garner, who was
not permitted to speak in her own defense. She could try to tell some part of the
slave mother's story.[21]

At the conclusion of the first day's summation, Stone accompanied the de-
fendant back to jail, and the two women spent several hours together. Stone
attempted to offer consolation: "I told her that a thousand hearts were aching
for her."[22] She offered the more tangible comfort that she would attempt to
negotiate the purchase of the mother and children—with the purpose of setting
them free. Indeed, the colloquy lasted so long that afterwards, wild stories were
circulated claiming that Lucy Stone had smuggled a knife into the prisoner's
cell, urging her to kill herself and her children rather than return to the degra-
dations of slavery. In the end, there was little substantive help to be given, and
Lucy Stone resorted to her most reliable weapon—impassioned public address.
She took the incomprehensible "facts" and gave them story-shape.

Thus it was that when the formal proceedings had been concluded and
Margaret Garner and her children were removed, Lucy Stone was allowed to
address the still crowded courtroom.

> . . . I returned to town only yesterday or I should have been here during every day
> of this trial. When I came here and saw that poor fugitive, took her toil-hardened
> hand, and read in her face deep suffering and ardent longing for freedom, . . . I told
> her that [thousands of friends] were glad that the child of hers was safe with the
> angels. Her only reply was a look of deep despair—of anguish such as no word can
> speak.
>
> I thought then that the spirit she manifested was the same with that of our an-

cestors to whom we had erected the monument at Bunker Hill—the spirit that would rather let us all go back to God than back to slavery.

The faded faces of the negro children tell too plainly to what degradation female slaves submit. Rather than give her little daughter to that life, she killed it. If in her deep maternal love she felt the impulse to send her child back to God to save it from coming woe, who shall say she had no right to do so? That desire had its root in the deepest and holiest feelings of our nature—implanted alike in black and white by our common Father. With my own teeth would I tear open my veins and let the earth drink my blood rather than wear the chains of slavery. How then could I blame her for wishing her child to find freedom with God and the angels, where no chains are?

In order to create an *acceptable* "story" from the anguished chaos of the events, Stone appropriated the structures of that one narrative about which all Americans could be presumed to agree—the account of our own Revolution. Then, having established the moral parameters of the case, she concluded with an epic flourish: "I told [Margaret Garner's owner] that these were heroic times, and that this heroic action of his slave might send his name to posterity as her oppressor—or if he chose—as the generous giver of her freedom."[23]

With this, the episode ended. The magistrate who had been presiding announced that he would render no decision until March. The fugitives were given over to their owners, a small procession followed their progress to the river, and a large delegation of Kentucky friends was there to meet the owners on the other side. The slaves were held in the Covington jail for a few days until the publicity had quieted down, and then their owners spirited them back into the anonymity of the slave system. A requisition was made in Ohio for Margaret Garner, but her master, unwilling to sell her into freedom, declared that she had already been sent down the river. Nothing remained but a local rumor: "It was reported that on her way down the river she sprang from the boat into the water with her babe in her arms; that when she rose she was seized by some of the boat hands and rescued, but that her child was drowned."[24]

Did Margaret Garner disappear into the plumbless depths of Southern slavery after killing her one remaining female child? And if she did, what of that story "put forth by reputable and sincere people" that there was "an ex-slave woman who lived in Cincinnati after the Civil War . . . [who] thought she [had] inspired Mrs. Stowe's story?" The Cincinnati census records from 1870 (when Margaret Garner would have been about fifty) list only one Garner—Mary J. Garner—a white woman with a ten-year-old child: another person altogether. Did Stowe tell "Margaret Garner's" tale? Did Lucy Stone? Did any of the avid reporters and onlookers? Did all—or any—of them tell the story of this woman whose life was so bereft of words and so surfeited with turmoil and swift, decisive reaction?

Readers who know Toni Morrison's novel *Beloved* may feel that they have finally met "Margaret Garner" in that novel; certainly her "tale" is told here as never before. The time has finally come (almost a century and a half after the event) when the mediating pieties of Stowe's contemporary account can be cast aside. Indeed, Toni Morrison's retrospective account can do two things that were not possible in Stowe's era: it can present an entirely unsentimental account of slavery's brutality, and it can deal with the tragic inheritance that slavery has bequeathed to African American women.

This Cincinnati story dissects the *after-birth* of slavery's tragedy in a three-generational tale of mothers and daughters.

The grandmother, Baby Suggs, is dead by 1873 when the novel begins; her son's wife, Sethe, and Sethe's daughter, Denver, still live in her house at 124 Bluestone Rd., Cincinnati. They share it with only one other, a baby ghost ("the soul of her baby girl. Who would have thought that a little old baby could harbor so much rage? . . . fury at having its throat cut.") This baby ghost has invented a kind of palavering haunt—a way of rejoining her mama and brothers and sister, to squall and fret in her own way. (Baby Suggs had been a breeder: " 'Be thankful, why don't you,' " Baby Suggs had used to say to Sethe when she worried about the baby ghost; " 'You lucky. You got three left. Three pulling at your skirts and just one raising hell from the other side. Be thankful, why don't you? I had eight. Every one of them gone away from me' " [*Beloved*, 5]. But by 1873, the two boys, Howard and Buglar, had run off, and Baby Suggs had died, and only Sethe was left to live on Bluestone Road with her two daughters—one alive and the other a baby ghost.

So much in this novel resurrects the "Margaret Garner" who fled across the Ohio River in 1856 that it matters very little how many historical details have been altered. The essential elements remain: a mother and child who are entrapped by an impossible moral maze, and a one-woman massacre when the slave-catchers corner them:

> Inside, two boys bled in the sawdust and dirt at the feet of a nigger woman holding a blood-soaked child to her chest with one hand and an infant by the heels in the other. She did not look at them; she simply swung the baby toward the wall planks, missed and tried to connect a second time. . . . Outside a throng, now, of black faces stopped murmuring. Holding the living child, Sethe walked past them in their silence and hers. (*Beloved*, 149, 151)

One daughter dead, the head almost severed from the body (Sethe's finger held "her face so her head wouldn't fall off"), two boys wounded, and a baby girl still nursing at the breast. The almost anonymous casualties of what Morrison has called the "sixty million and more"—victims and survivors of our American holocaust.

Without the necessary sentimentality of Stowe's great work, this novel captures something of the unpretty confusion that must have been Margaret Garner's reality—something of the form of human degradation that is so unplanned and casual that it eludes even tragedy. And yet the two novels come together in telling the story of that anguished moral urgency that baffles a mother's moral judgment—powerless to protect her babies and yet desperate to do so. Sethe's confused misery more explicitly reiterates Cassy's: " 'It ain't my job to know what's worse. It's my job to know what is and to keep them away from what I know is terrible' " (*Beloved*, 165). What had Sethe's own mother done to keep them away from what was terrible? She threw her babies away—all except Sethe, the only one she kept:[25]

> She told Sethe that her mother and Nan were together from the sea [on the passage over from Africa]. Both were taken up many times by the crew. "She threw them all away but you. The one from the crew she threw away on the island. The others from more whites she also threw away. Without names, she threw them. You she gave the name of the black man. She put her arms around him. The others she did not put her arms around. Never. Never. Telling you. I am telling you, small girl Sethe." (*Beloved*, 62)

And so the baby ghost, Beloved ("she my daughter. She mine. See. She come back to me of her own free will and I don't have to explain a thing"). This baby *was* "beloved"—so dearly beloved that "she had to be safe and I put her where she would be" (*Beloved*, 200).

In Cincinnati, the crucial border city. Harriet Beecher Stowe, Lucy Stone, and Toni Morrison—Eliza, Cassy, Baby Suggs, Sethe, and Beloved. Agents and actors in the complex process by which history and biography merge into unforgettable understanding. All "real" in a community of women, black and white. All united in the compassionate act of conferring "reality," at least, upon "Margaret Garner" (who was never allowed to speak for herself) by *making the "story."*

NOTES

1. For an account of amnesiac symptoms in adult women who were abused as children see Richard P. Kluft, M.D., *Incest Related Syndromes of Adult Psychopathology* (Washington: American Psychiatric Press, 1990), esp. 55-61 and 209-20. The book is helpful throughout by providing an "analogue" model for understanding the ways in which a *slave woman* might have been specifically deprived of the ability to tell her own tale. At the beginning of *Their Eyes Were Watching God*, Zora Neale Hurston writes, as an aftermath of the slave experience, "Women forget all those things they don't want to remember." (And survivors of the Holocaust have similar problems with "remembering.")

The notion of "killing the messenger with unwelcome news" has ancient origins, and the implicit social model that informs it is a simple one. More sophisticated models of society as a complex nexus of powers carry more sophisticated elaborations of the ways in which power protects itself by carefully delimiting the general use of language. Such formulations can be found throughout Michel Foucault's work. His "Discourse on Language," is most useful here.

> . . . We know perfectly well that we are not free to say just anything, that we cannot simply speak of anything, when we like or where we like; not just anyone, finally, may speak of just anything. . . . It is always possible one could speak truth in a void; one would only be in the true, however, if one obeyed the rules of some discursive "policy" which would have to be reactivated every time one spoke. . . .

We tend to see, in an author's fertility, in the multiplicity of commentaries and in the development of a discipline so many infinite resources available for the creation of discourse. Perhaps so, but they are nonetheless [at the same time] principles of constraint, and it is probably impossible to appreciate their positive, multiplicatory role without first taking into consideration their restrictive, constraining role.

See Michel Foucault, "The Discourse on Language," *Critical Theory Since 1965,* ed. Hazard Adams and Leroy Searle (Tallahassee: Florida State UP, 1986), 149, 155.

2. Toni Morrison, *Beloved* (New York: Knopf, 1987), 274.

3. Levi Coffin, *Reminiscences of Levi Coffin* (1898; New York: Arno Press, 1968), 562-63. It is interesting to note the way in which the details of this description reveal Levi Coffin's own self-conscious preoccupations with "racial differences."

4. See Nancy Cott, *The Bonds of Womanhood* (New Haven: Yale UP, 1977), esp. Chap. 2. Fanny Fern's novel, *Ruth Hall* (1854; New Brunswick: Rutgers UP, 1988), gives a vivid account of the educated *white* woman's dilemma. Practitioners of the slave trade routinely dismissed the feelings of *black* mothers, claiming that African Americans were little more than savages—without "human" affections. See, for example, Samuel B. How, *Slaveholding Not Sinful* (1855; Freeport: Books for Libraries, 1971). Jean Fagan Yellin's splendid book, *Women and Sisters* (New Haven: Yale UP, 1989), studies this kinship from a somewhat different vantage. Elizabeth Fox-Genovese makes a convincing argument that *Southern* women often felt more kinship with the male hierarchy than they did with slave women. See *Within the Plantation Household* (Chapel Hill: U of North Carolina P, 1988).

Stowe's own awareness of the hypocrisy of this ethic insofar as *white* women were concerned was undoubtedly limited in 1851. Never so conservative as her sister Catherine (nor so liberal as her sister Isabella), Stowe's attitude toward the possibilities for women—toward the nature of their "appropriate" role—changed a good deal over the years. By 1871 when she published *My Wife and I,* Stowe was able to write a convincingly impassioned plea for a woman's need for a life that contained much more than wifehood and motherhood; however, in 1851, when *Uncle Tom's Cabin* was written, she remained deeply committed to the ethic of "motherhood" (she had, after all, just borne her seventh child). For a discussion of Harriet's discourse with her two sisters on such subjects, see Jeanne Boydston, Mary Kelley, and Anne Margolis, *The Limits of Sisterhood* (Chapel Hill: U of North Carolina P, 1988).

I am deeply sympathetic with some of the contemporary criticism that has been aimed at Stowe. I am thinking, for example, of Richard Yarborough's criticism of Stowe's failure to challenge black stereotypes ("Strategies of Black Characterization in *Uncle Tom's Cabin* and the Early Afro-American Novel")—or of Jean Fagan Yellin's condemnation of Stowe's failure to counsel (perhaps even condone) *feminine* rebellion against the patriarchal hegemony ("Doing It Herself: *Uncle Tom's Cabin* and Woman's Role in the Slavery Crisis"): both essays to be found in *New Essays on "Uncle Tom's Cabin",* ed. Emory Eliot (London: Cambridge UP, 1986). Still, on the whole, I am more sympathetic with Elizabeth Ammons' notions in "Stowe's Dream of the Mother-Savior: *Uncle Tom's Cabin* and American Women Writers Before the 1920's" (to be found in the same collection) or Jane Tompkins' views in *Sensational Designs* (New York: Oxford UP, 1985) or Philip Fisher's notions in "Partings and Ruins: Radical Sentimentality in *Uncle Tom's Cabin,*" *American Studies* 28 (1987): 279-93. That is, I see Stowe as a strategist, using the *tools* of her age to undermine what she perceived as the greatest *evil* of her age—perhaps of any age.

However, my principal point of departure is this. In 1851, the *female* slave had very little cultural "existence": Frederick Douglass scarcely mentions her plight (as Mary Helen Washington has observed); the publications of Theodore Weld, especially *American Slavery as It Is,* first published in 1839, do not dwell upon the particular horrors of the African American *woman.* Perhaps more important, when *she* is rendered, she is rendered as the *object of torture* (only very obliquely as the *"object of lust"*). In short, in 1851, the *voice* of the slave woman had never been written into American culture. Even more crucial: *the shocking, unresolvable dilemma of the slave* MOTHER *had never been dissected.* Those who cared to think about the issues of abolition had heard (perhaps) that mothers were separated from their children. However, the extremities of "moral behavior" as the issue presented itself to slave mothers was not thrust into American consciousness until the publication of *Uncle Tom's Cabin.*

It is unfortunate that Stowe was not prepared to assist Harriet Jacobs in the publication of *Linda Brent*: Jacobs appealed to Stowe at a time when the author was drowning in her own obligations. Still, it is significant that Jacobs *did* appeal to *Stowe*—and that when her own story was published, it was regarded for so many years as a PIECE OF FICTION. The first of these suggests the importance of *Uncle Tom's Cabin* as an initiator of the explicitly female voice of slavery; the second suggests how long it has taken for American culture to credit the "reality" to that experience.

5. Forrest Wilson, *Crusader in Crinoline: The Life of Harriet Beecher Stowe* (Philadelphia: Lippincott, 1941), 146-47.

6. See Wendell P. Dabney, *Cincinnati's Colored Citizens* (Cincinnati: Dabney Publishing Company, 1926), 15.

7. In July of 1838, a pro-slavery mob made a number of assaults upon the building in which James Birney published his abolitionist newspaper, *The Philanthropist.* Finally, on July 30, they demolished it, dumped the presses in the river, and concluded the night by rampaging through the black section of town, terrorizing its residents. Twenty-seven year-old Harriet Beecher Stowe, now married and the mother of eighteen-month-old twin girls, monitored the protracted siege with impotent fury: "I wish [Mr. Birney] would arm [his building] with armed men, and see what can be done," she wrote in early July; "If I were a man I would go, for one, and take good care of at least one window." See *Life and Letters of Harriet Beecher Stowe,* ed. Annie Fields (Boston: Houghton, 1899), 95.

8. *Life and Letters,* 142. "In her own family she had a private school for her children, and as there was no provision for the education of colored children in her vicinity, she allowed them [to attend]."

9. *Life and Letters,* 175-76.

10. Harriet Beecher Stowe, *A Key to "Uncle Tom's Cabin"* (Cleveland: Jewett, Proctor & Worthington [London: Low and Company], 1853), 48, 133.

11. *Life and Letters,* 119.

12. *Life and Letters,* 173.

13. Harriet Beecher Stowe, *Uncle Tom's Cabin Or, Life Among the Lowly,* 2 vols. (Boston: Houghton, 1896), 1:78.

14. Stowe, *A Key to "Uncle Tom's Cabin,"* 5-6. In every culture, the issues of moral authority and autonomy tend to be organized around particular actions or activities. Whatever else is true about the focus upon "Motherhood" in America during the nineteenth century, this preoccupation served to center the culture's notions about women's moral activity—their authority and autonomy—specifically around the rights and duties pertaining to that relationship. It is important for a contemporary critic to recognize this fact. In some significant sense, claiming the right to active moral activity within the boundaries of "motherhood" in 1850, was the necessary prerequisite for claiming authority and autonomy in other areas of life. No one understood these "facts" of culture in mid-nineteenth-century America more thoroughly than such suffragists as Elizabeth Cady Stanton and Lucy Stone.

15. *The Cincinnati Daily Enquirer,* 29 January 1856.

16. *The Cincinnati Daily Enquirer,* 30 January 1856.

17. *The Cincinnati Daily Enquirer,* 31 January 1856. A similar claim was made for all the other adults—Mary, Simon, and Robert Garner.

18. Coffin, 563.

19. *The Cincinnati Daily Enquirer,* 12 February 1856.

20. Leslie Wheeler, *Loving Warriors: Selected Letters of Lucy Stone and Henry B. Blackwell, 1853-1893* (New York: Dial Press, 1981), 155.

21. Wheeler, 136. Lucy Stone bore her only daughter in the fall of 1857—about a year and a half after this trial; she miscarried a baby boy about fifteen months later, and this loss (with the accompanying probability that she would bear no more children) was a blow that affected her in much the same way that Harriet Beecher Stowe had been affected by Charley's death.

22. Coffin, 565.

23. *The Cincinnati Daily Gazette,* 14 February 1856.

24. Coffin, 567.

25. I am indebted to Hortense Spiller's sensitive discussions of Morrison's work for helping me to understand the consequences of the black mother's "heritage" of "heroism."

The abortion of interracial fetuses ("throwing them away") and of infanticide is not a problem that has been limited to black women. In the Harriet Jacobs narrative, she speaks of *white girls* who conceive children by *black male slaves.* "In such cases the infant is smothered, or sent where it is never seen by any who knows its history." See Harriet A. Jacobs, *Incidents in the Life of a Slave Girl,* ed. Jean Fagan Yellin (Cambridge: Harvard UP, 1987), 52.

Antinomies of Liberalism: The Politics of "Belief" and the Project of Americanist Criticism

Cary Wolfe

There's an old joke that has always had, for me at least, an unnervingly familiar feel to it—a sensation generated, as in most jokes, by the countervaling
forces of my self-recognition in the protagonist on the one hand, and the critical distance (the distance that lets me laugh *at* him) that the concept of self-
recognition implies on the other.[1] The short version of the joke goes like this: A
guy walks into his doctor's office one day and makes a startling announce-
ment. "Doc," he tells his physician of many years, "I don't know how to tell
you this, but I think I'm dead." The doctor, understandably taken aback, can
see that in the face of such extraordinary symptoms, an unusual brand of treatment is needed. And so he tells his patient to come back in a week, but in the
meantime to repeat to himself over and over this one phrase: "Dead men don't
bleed, Dead men don't bleed." The patient, skeptical but desperate, agrees to
give it a try.

A week later, the patient returns. Doctor: "Well, did you follow my instruc-
tions?" Patient: "Yes, yes I did." Doctor (barely able to disguise his satisfaction
at the elegance of prescribing *mere words*): "So, how do you feel *now*?" Patient: "Well, to tell you the truth, I feel about the same." At this point the doctor abruptly rises from his Socratic repose and calls the patient over to him,
purposeful but a little secretive, concealing something. "All right, hold out your
hand," he tells the sick man (now impatient as the moment of the Cure approaches). And when the patient obeys, the doctor whips out a needle, pricks
the patient's index finger, and observes triumphantly the small dome of blood
which now holds his patient's riveted attention. "There!" the doctor exclaims,
almost giddy with the moment, "*now* what do you think of your condition?"
And the patient replies—not even blinking as he gazes, astonished, at the burn-
ing evidence at his fingertip: "Well what do you know, Doc—dead men *do*
bleed!"

I like to think of this joke—for reasons that I hope won't seem entirely personal by the end of this essay—as a strong reading of what an older critical
vocabulary would call the deep structure of the Liberal subject and its episte-
mology, or at least of the variety of Liberalism that is reconstructed—even as it

appears to be *de*constructed—in some of the more sophisticated historicist work in recent Americanist criticism. Indeed, the study of American culture—in its founding, its institutionalization, and its usual modes of practice—is so intertwined with the foundational assumptions of Liberalism that you have to wonder at times if it is possible to do Americanist criticism and *really* talk about anything else.[2] The protagonist in our joke, though, gives us good reason to try to do otherwise. Aside from the fact that he thinks he is dead, the distinguishing characteristic of our Liberal hero is not so much his imagined freedom to believe anything that he "personally chooses" (in this case, to believe that he is dead) but rather his ability to immediately transform any evidence to the contrary—any evidence that might unmask the imaginary nature of that freedom—into further evidence of that selfsame freedom.[3]

From this vantage, then, Liberalism must be viewed not as a specific kind of content, but rather as a containing structure or logic which relegates questions about cultural politics and history which it itself cannot answer to the realm of the transcendent, the idealistic, the totalitarian—to a realm, in short, whose distinctive feature will always be its infringement on that freedom to be nothing in particular which is both Liberalism's exhilarating promise and its politically truncated terminus.

Another way of putting it is to say that the problem with Liberalism is not that it cannot think difference—something, in any case, which it does quite expertly, as the Liberal subject's appetite for the new and original items of commodity culture will testify—but rather that the difference it thinks is always reified.[4] For the ideology of Liberal pluralism, the *value* of that difference, in other words, is to be found in the freedom to be and believe whatever you want (including, for the man in our joke, dead), the freedom in which we are all "the same" in spite of (because of?) our differences. But that freedom, of course, is wholly *abstract*, and we are not all the same; the freedom of choice to buy a Maserati instead of a BMW is not the same as the freedom of choice to sleep under an overpass instead of on a sidewalk heating grate. And the only way to think *that* kind of difference, I want to suggest, is to think precisely what the Liberal problematic prevents: a kind of difference which is not expressive of the subject's freedom, but is rather constitutive of it, and which makes it possible to think that social and historical change which is nothing other than *difference across time*.

My characterization of the Liberal problematic ought to make it clear that I cannot in this context begin to address the full range of positions which share the fundamental structure of Liberalism's "negative freedom." So let me, instead, adopt an alternate strategy by focusing upon powerful and provocative critiques of the antinomies of Liberalism in recent American criticism, with special attention to the work of Walter Benn Michaels. Michaels' work is doubly useful for my purposes here, because it constitutes both an implacable critique and a kind of demonized reproduction of the Liberal problematic. Michaels' anti-Liberalism is both polemical and, on the face of it, theoretical, but I want to argue that it is nevertheless framed and contained by the conceptual structures and limits of Liberalism from the outset in much the same way that declarations of the "end of ideology" are ideological through and through.[5] Those sorts of pronouncements have traditionally sought to capture the political and cultural specificity (which is to say *transcendence*) of American-ness itself—and nowhere more powerfully than in the interpretations of the central works of the American Renaissance (Richard Chase's "romance," R. W. B. Lewis' "American Adam") sedimented by the founding generation of American Studies during the Cold War.[6] And Michaels, in a way, situates himself squarely within this critical topography when he notes that "belief"—his proposed alternative to the continental concept of "ideology"—is "One of the few problems in literary theory which Anglo-American critics can with some justice claim as our own."[7]

Whether or not this is good news will be part of what is at issue here, but in any case there are (as my mention of Chase and Lewis already indicates) some immediate institutional and disciplinary stakes in this discussion. These debates throw into relief not only the critical politics of competing modes of contemporary theoretical discourse (in this case, Marxist, Pragmatist, and New Historicist), but also the historiographical possibilities produced or foreclosed by those discourses. In this instance, what is under contention is not only the general intellectual lineage of Americanist criticism, but in particular the meaning, authority—in short, the cultural capital—of one of Liberalism's most attractive and yet troubling figures, William James. And as if the social, biographical, and institutional status of James weren't enough, his major work, *The Principles of Psychology,* rivets our attention on what may be viewed as the primal scene of Liberalism: the conception of autonomous selfhood in accordance with the language and structure of private property. To discuss the genealogy of American critical politics, we must deal, it seems, with James. And to deal with James we must, in other words, confront his Lockean Liberalism. In a sense, then, these discussions turn out to be—this time on the terrain not of Modernism and Marxism but of "Naturalism" and Jamesian "Pragmatism"—the American counterpart of the so-called Brecht/Lukacs debate.[8] And as that comparison suggests, what is finally at stake here is nothing less than the imperative of thinking historical change itself and the American intellectual's responsibility to the shape of that change.

POLITICS OF "BELIEF": THE EXAMPLE OF WALTER BENN MICHAELS

To view Walter Benn Michaels' work as squarely within the Liberal problematic would seem to be, on the face of it, a doomed proposition. After all, what distinguishes the Liberal view, as Fredric Jameson puts it, is "the belief that the 'system' is not really total . . . , that we can ameliorate it, reorganize it, and regulate it in such a way that it becomes tolerable and we thereby have the 'best of both worlds.' "[9] Now nothing, it would seem, could be further from the spirit and indeed the very letter of Michaels' work since the late 1970s, which has argued steadily, sometimes dismissively, and often controversially against the epistemological incoherence and political naivete of just that sort of concept of the subject, with its facile lucidity, reflexive judgment, and the freedom of choice supposed to express them. Michaels' essay "Is There a Politics of Interpretation?" (1983), for instance, makes the case with greater concision than the earlier and more famous "Against Theory" polemic:

> These claims [that "interpretations or ways of interpreting are the results of 'free'. . . political choices for which we should be held responsible . . . as we are for other political acts"] seem to me wrong, not so much in their emphasis on politics as in their account of interpretations as freely chosen and their consequent invocation of the ethical categories we think appropriate for describing choices.[10]

And *The Gold Standard and the Logic of Naturalism* (1987) extends the pointed institutional specificity of the "Against Theory" project in debunking the "political handwringing" of the "oppositional" wing of American Studies and its classically Liberal view of "important works of art as in some sense transcending or opposing the market."[11]

But the most challenging manifestation of anti-Liberalism in that book may be found in its theoretical, not polemical, claims, and specifically in three central points continually worked through the various readings of Gilman, Dreiser, Norris, and others that make up the book. The first of these is Michaels' theorization of an economic totality called "the market" which, in its all-constituting power, resists all attempts to ameliorate or temper it in the manner Jameson describes. In fact (as practiced readers of New Historicism will have already guessed) Michaels suggests that such attempts only serve to siphon off or neutralize potentially explosive (perhaps even revolutionary) desire and discontent, thereby further reinforcing the dominance of the market and extending its logic even more insidiously into incompletely colonized enclaves of social life. It is here that we may locate the book's second central claim in its characterization of the subject, or what Michaels more often prefers to call "the self." In Michaels' reading, the subject is not what makes the market and its fundamental structures (the exchange principle, for instance) possible, but is rather an *effect* and expression of the market. In fact, as we shall see, it is not too much to say, as one reviewer has, that for Michaels the self is always already the market.[12]

This leads us, in turn, to the third and, in many ways, most important dimension of Michaels' critique: its suggestion that we abandon the concept of ideology as a critical tool and replace it with what Michaels, after William James, calls "belief." This proposal has taken many forms, the most publicized (and, to my mind, increasingly tiresome) version of which is the "Against Theory" debate which began in the early 1980s and seems to have petered out at the end of the decade with the sequel, "Against Theory 2."[13] The critical terrain of "belief" is the crucial nexus in Michaels' work where the relations between self and market are conjugated, and it is there, at that site of social and economic reproduction, that the critical politics of Michaels' work must be confronted.

In "Saving the Text" (1978) Michaels offers a concise definition of belief

which will serve as well to characterize how the term is used in the later essays
and in *The Gold Standard*:

> These solutions [to the problems posed by our inability to achieve "disinterested-
> ness" in our criticism] are in many ways very different but the view that they have
> in common is that our beliefs are like filters through which we more or less accu-
> rately discern texts—the optimists imagine these filters growing ever more trans-
> parent, the pessimists ever more opaque. What I should like to suggest here is that
> both these views are mistaken because the model they hold in common is mistaken.
> Our beliefs are not obstacles between us and meaning, they are what make mean-
> ing possible in the first place. Meaning is not filtered through what we believe, it is
> constituted by what we believe (780).

Michaels' critique of "disinterestedness" is certainly salutary when taken
on its own. The problem, of course, is that we cannot take it that way, because
Michaels extends (and overextends) it with Knapp into a full-blown critique of
"Theory" in his later work. Let us leave aside for the moment Knapp and
Michaels' rather peevish (and, in Jameson's words, "reassuringly restricted")
characterization of "Theory" as "a special project in literary criticism."[14] Instead, we should notice what the polemical brouhaha over the "Against Theory" project obscures: that Michaels' critique of "distinterestedness" on behalf
of "belief" would seem to promise a pragmatist micro-political analysis of the
institutional production of belief on the model of Gerald Graff's *Professing
Literature*, Richard Ohmann's *English in America,* or Barbara Herrnstein
Smith's less historical *Contingencies of Value.* And this promise seems only extended in Michaels' contention later in "Saving the Text" that his position provides a way into "an objectivity that is limited but real," one "based not on the
attempt to match interpretations up to a text that exists independently of them,
but based instead on what readers believe" (787-788).

That promise, however, will remain unfulfilled. Instead, Michaels will focus
more and more on the general epistemological structure of "belief" as such,
and in extending the claims for its seamlessness and all-constituting power,
Michaels will undermine what initially seems most compelling about his sense
of "belief": that all interpretive choices, even when they seem "free," are reproductive of previously held beliefs that the subject cannot, through critical
reflection, fully master, even though she may now want to abandon them. In
"Is There a Politics of Interpretation?," for example, Michaels' aim is to demonstrate the quintessentially theoretical claim (and this hard on the heels of
"Against Theory") that "it does not make sense to say that you choose to believe anything at all" (336). This is so, he argues, because the epistemological
freedom required by the category of "choice" is fundamentally at odds with
the epistemolgical compulsion named by the category of "belief." Michaels'
version of the paradox goes like this: if you are free enough from assumptions
and beliefs to make a choice that is truly a *free* choice, then you are by the same
logic unable to make any choice at all because you will have no criteria upon
which to base that choice. Conversely, if you *do* possess the necessary criteria

to make such a choice, then it will no longer be a free choice at all, but rather an action compelled, shaped, and produced by (and, we should add, *reproductive of*) those beliefs and assumptions that provided the criteria for choosing in the first place (341, 343).[15]

This apparent frontal assault on ethical criticism (and therefore, of course, on the Liberal subject and his meliorative judgment) is not only sustained but in fact intensified in *The Gold Standard*'s contention that the identity of the subject of naturalism "consists *only* in the beliefs and desires made available by the naturalist logic—which is not produced by the naturalist subject but rather is the condition of his existence" (177, emphasis mine). At first glance, Michaels would seem to temper this unabashedly sweeping claim for the all-constituting power of "belief" (and, behind it, of this thing called "the naturalist logic") by introducing in this section what looks like an important distinction between "beliefs" and "desires." The latter—a term of considerable micro-political resonance in the context of post-structuralism[16]—might seem to hold out some promise to trouble and destabilize the seamless social totality, but in fact that possibility is immediately foreclosed in *The Gold Standard*. In Michaels' reading of "desire," the self is constituted as a fundamental instability, a "double identity" or "internal difference" (22) generated by the market and its fundamental logics of property and exchange. The subject of naturalism, in other words, can know no completion or self-identity because it is constituted by difference; as Sartre put it in a different critical register—in an attempt to characterize the unsolvable negation of the subject who is both consciousness and matter—it is "a being which is what it is not and which is not what it is."[17] (Sartre's point is an ontological one, but then, as we shall see, so is Michaels'—and this despite his apparent focus on economics, monetary debates among the Populists, and so on.)

It is this internal difference which sets going the "logic of naturalism" by which the self seeks to escape the market and the ceaselessly self-reproducing play of exchange by clinging "to definitions of texts, selves, or money," in Evan Carton's words, "as stable and essential quantities."[18] The fundamental instability of the market creates a self who therefore has, as Michaels puts it, "an insatiable appetite for representation" (19) which manifests itself in the belief that gold is the site of natural economic value, the text is the site of stable inherent meaning apprehended by the critic's adequated critique, and the subject is the site of inalienable self-possession and free self-proprietorship.

But in Michaels' view this unstable desire, far from destabilizing the system, only serves further to perpetuate it, because desire is "not subversive of the capitalist economy but constitutive of its power" (48). As Jameson points out, desire for Michaels is trapped in a logic of "infinite 'supplementarity' " (202-203); it is part of that ruse of the commodity which, in Frank Lentricchia's words, turns "the potentially revolutionary force of desire produced on capitalist terrain toward the work of conserving and perpetuating consumer capitalism."[19] To put it another way, "desire," like "belief," offers no means in Michaels' critique by which the self might be anything *other than* a purely reproductive agent of the market and its logic. It is clear from this vantage why the promise of a pragmatist micro-politics, more than hinted at in "Saving the Text," will remain unfulfilled in Michaels' later work: there is simply nothing for it to do.[20]

But if the lack that is desire is disarmed and recontained by Michaels' critique, the political efficacy of that plenitude known as critical distance and reflection is rejected as well, by definition, in Michaels' concept of "belief." Indeed, what makes Michaels' "belief" what it is—in contrast to the "interests" lucidly promoted and aligned by "ideological" critics or expunged, conversely, by "disinterested" formalist ones—is that you cannot have that sort of critical distance in relation to it at all. (If you could, you would be guilty of the for-Theory position opposed by Knapp and Michaels.) We can triangulate the relationship between "desire," "belief," and "ideology" in Michaels in this way: "belief" and "ideology" may exist, in Marx's famous phrase, "to reproduce the conditions of production," but because there is in Michaels' reading no Other to the market—no disruptive agent of negation (like "desire") to pose any real threat of fundamental change to the system—Michaels' concept of "belief" cannot tell us why we should *need* to secure the reproduction of a social and economic system which cannot be threatened in the first place. Another way of putting it is to say that Michaels' "belief," insofar as it exists, is superfluous.

Nevertheless, in *The Gold Standard*, Michaels argues that the critical concept of ideology must be abandoned on behalf of this notion of "belief." The concept of ideology, Michaels tells us, assumes

> the existence of subjects complete with interests and then imagines those subjects in more or less complicated (and more or less conscious) ways selecting their beliefs about the world in order to legitimate their interests. The subject of naturalism, however—at least as I have depicted him here—is typically unable to keep his beliefs lined up with his interests for more than two or three pages at a time, a failure that stems not from inadequate powers of concentration but from the fact that his identity as a subject consists only in the beliefs and desires made available by the naturalist logic—which is not produced by the naturalist subject but rather is the condition of his existence. (177)

For Michaels, in other words, the concept of ideology must be abandoned because it "refers," as Foucault puts it in a passage Michaels quotes approvingly, "necessarily to something of the order of a subject" (177). This is so for Michaels because to use the language of ideology is to immediately invoke the category of "interests," and "the effect of insisting on the primacy of interests," he argues in turn, "is to save the constituent subject" (178)—the subject who constitutes, as a metaphysical point of origin, the market and the logic of naturalism and not (what Michaels wants) the reverse.[21] This is not the place to mount an extensive review of the many debates over what ideology is and how it operates,[22] but two points should be raised here in response to Michaels' critique. It would be a mistake, I think, to assume that we have grounds here for abandoning the concept of ideology *tout court* as a critical tool. First, this Foucauldian critique of ideology and its "constituent subject" is perfectly correct as far as it goes, but it does not go far enough—which is to say that it goes as far as the vision of "expressive totality" of Lukács' *History and Class Consciousness* and not much farther. Foucault and Michaels after him are perfectly just, it seems to me, to reject the idealism of that position, which holds, as Martin Jay has characterized it, "that a totalizer, a genetic subject, creates the totality through self-objectification."[23] But that is far from saying (as Michaels' critique implies) that "ideology" is no longer a useful or powerful concept. What is really at issue in Foucault and in this passage in Michaels is only a limited, specific (and now largely discredited) concept of ideology and its attendant concept of the subject, one which is characteristic of a certain strain of Marxism (what Althusser called its "humanist" side) which, deriving from the Marx of the *Economic and Philosophical Manuscripts,* shares more than other varieties of Marxist critique with contemporaneous epistemological constructions of the Liberal subject.

In fact, the concept of ideology debunked by Michaels is considerably complicated by the later Marx himself, who conceives the subject not as unified and constituent of the social totality, but rather as a differential, conflicted, and above all relational—which is to say *social*—sort of creature whose identity is a product of what it is *not*.[24] And after Marx, the sort of ideology and its attendant subject characterized by Michaels has been rejected by many of the most influential later Marxist theorists themselves. To take only the most famous example, Althusser's enormously influential "Ideology and Ideological State Apparatuses"—which holds that "Ideology represents the imaginary relationship of individuals to their real conditions of existence"—conceives the relationship (as the Lacanian terminology implies) between ideology and the subject as anything but a facile alignment of self-interests by a lucid, rationalist subject.[25] Indeed, if ideology is, in Althusser's words, "a 'lived' relation to the real"[26] which exists and is reproduced in and only in material practices, then how could it be otherwise? These efforts tell us, I think, that Michaels' misgivings call not for an abandonment of the concept of ideology but rather for a continued investigation of it. But they also make it clear that what Michaels, with the help of Foucault, is rejecting is less the concept of "ideology" than a strategically narrow version of it. To put it another way, Michaels uses the categories of a more or less humanist subject to argue for the abandonment of the ideological subject *tout court*. But this move, I want to argue now, is itself quintessentially ideological.

Let me draw out in more detail what I've already hinted at: that Michaels' concept of "belief" is parasitical upon and remains trapped within the conceptual limits of the Liberal problematic. Perhaps the best way to get a fix on what we might call Michaels' "negative reproduction" of Liberalism is to return to the end of "Saving the Text," where Michaels criticizes Paul de Man for reinstating, even while seeming to reject, the desire for critical disinterestedness. In his claims that all interpretations and all readings are necessarily false, de Man, Michaels argues, has nevertheless reproduced the value of the text as a stable and unitary meaning (in this case, as a *lack* of meaning). What is disconcerting about de Man's position, according to Michaels, is that "it is very hard to see how any interpretation can be called false when no interpretation can be called true. It would seem that for any reading to be a misreading, there would have to be at least one reading which was not." Hence, he continues, "De Man wants to maintain the force of this false and he can do so only by insisting ultimately on an idealized (impossible) account of the true. . . . While giving up on the *possibility* of disinterested knowledge," he concludes, "De Man thus remains attached to the *ideal* of disinterestedness" (789).

It seems to me that this is exactly the dynamic at work in Michaels' putative rejection of the Liberal subject. To begin with, for Michaels' revisionary claims about the power of "belief" and the foreclosure of "choice" to have any force, his argument must continue to rely upon the values and the conceptual coordinates of the Liberal subject. Michaels concludes that de Man's critique "leaves him with a text whose meaning is not 'self-identical' or 'unchanging' but whose lack of meaning is" (790). But again, the same needs to be said for the subject-of-belief in Michaels, whose lack of stable self-identity (and therefore of Liberal freedom and volition) is unchanging in precisely this way. Time and again in Michaels—as in many another version of Liberalism—we find ourselves in the position of choosing either *that* sort of centered, self-reliant subject or no subject at all; either perfectly unfettered freedom of choice on the one hand, or totalizing and overstructuring "belief" on the other.

Michaels' rejection of the Liberal subject's freedom of choice, in short, is still rejection of a *Liberal* subject, not a reinvention or reimagining of what the subject might be. Such a reconception might pursue how the subject is constituted by race, or class, or gender, and might then seek to map the overlapping discursive zones and changing trajectories of a subject whose freedom is not all or nothing but rather complex and conflicted.[27] It is precisely this kind of investigation which is foreclosed, however, by the epistemological structure of Michaels' "belief" and the essentially Liberal limitations of his concept of the subject. (A symptom of this conceptual barrier, I think, is the rather anomalous texture of Michaels' critical writing, which is at once unmistakably deconstructive in spirit if not letter and at the same time heavily freighted with the vocabulary of "intentions," "belief," even "true belief.") All of which is to say that it would be harsh, but not unfair, to charge Michaels' treatment of the Liberal subject with what he himself writes of "oppositional" Americanist criticism: "As long as the best thing to do with consumer culture is renounce it, literary criticism will be happy" (*GS*, 15, n. 20).

But this is not all. Michaels doesn't merely accept the limits of Liberal subjectivity; in fact, he reinstates that subject on another, more powerful level—in this case, on the level of what *The Gold Standard* calls "the market." This might be difficult to see at first glance, particularly since *The Gold Standard* is often (understandably) criticized for promoting one version or another of "structural determinism."[28] Michaels' project requires a more sophisticated reading than this, however, because subject and structure—as Anthony Appiah has recently argued—operate at different levels of explanation; it would be a mistake, in his words, "to suppose an opposition between them in which they compete, so to speak, for the same causal space."[29] In *The Gold Standard*,

Michaels' procedure flies in the face of Appiah's distinction, because it collapses any constitutive difference between the subject of naturalism and the market structure—and it does so, moreover, asymmetrically. *The Gold Standard*, in other words, is constructed upon and limited by the categories and discourse of the subject, even when the economic and social structure are ostensibly under discussion. The universe of *The Gold Standard* can, perhaps, be called one of "structural determinism," but only if we first grant that social and economic structure has been curiously *subjectified* (as we'll see in a moment) through Michaels' exclusive focus on "exchange" and its homology with the "internal difference" of the self and the sign.[30]

By these lights, Michaels' position in "Is There a Politics of Interpretation?"—that the political responsibility of criticism depends upon the ethical possibility of free choice—is entirely symptomatic of his assimilation of the domain of structure (the realm of politics *per se*) to the domain of the subject (the realm of ethics).[31] All of which would be of little moment were it not for the fact, as Appiah's discussion makes clear, that any critique which wants to think the possibility of social change cannot *begin* with the category of the subject— even when, as in Michaels, that category looks to be all structure. As Appiah points out, we are—for obvious historical/intellectual reasons—much more expert at thinking the category of the subject than that of structure. For Appiah, however, this cuts both ways, because any discourse of the subject (even a putatively revolutionary type) is bound to be heavily freighted with logic and conceptual limits of "bourgeois humanism"—all of which we are quite adept at manipulating. But the political point of Appiah's argument is not that we should abandon the project of rethinking the category of the subject— something which, in any case, it is probably impossible to do. Instead, we need to redouble our attention to the political specificity and discursive difference of the category of structure—*particularly* if we want to think not social reproduction but social change.[32]

In Michaels, however, it is this specificity and difference which is effaced in his assimilation of structure to subject, "market" to "self." Michaels, in his way, admits this in *The Gold Standard*, where he defines the market in the title essay, with characteristically stubborn density, in this way: "It is, one might say, made up of people, and it acts like a person; but the person it acts like is not the people it is made up of" (179). What he means, I take it, is that the person the market acts like is the ideal, self-identical subject of Liberalism. And conversely, the people who make up the market are *not* this ideal Liberal subject, but rather the internally divided, incomplete, and unstable selves produced by the market. Michaels is right here, I think, but—as he might phrase it—what makes him right in this instance is also what makes him wrong. As Evan Carton correctly observes, in Michaels' deconstruction of the Liberal subject, "selfhood and writing are not so much implicated as equated with capitalism."[33] What makes this equation possible in Michaels' reading is a double reduction. First, capitalism is reduced to "the market" (rather than being treated, say, as a system of divided labor, increased Taylorization and de-skilling of the working class, and so on).[34] And second, the market is read in terms of exchange alone (rather than in terms of, say, distribution, whose class-specific dynamics would complicate and differentiate the social space in ways not readily accommodated by Michaels' paradigm). Michaels' privileging of exchange allows him to read in an impressively wide variety of textual materials the deconstructive undecidability which is for him synonymous with the market's effect.[35] At the same time, however, the price of Michaels' double reduction is that it immediately hypostatizes capitalism, in a very one-dimensional way, as an abstract logic which is self-identical because it is everywhere equally pervasive and structurally determinant[36] — in contrast, for example, to what Raymond Williams calls the productive unevenness of "dominant," "residual," and "emergent" economic modes and social logics.[37]

To put it another way, it is precisely *because* of Michaels' textualization and consequent homogenization of "the market" that he is able to provide his anatomy of the antinomies of the ideal Liberal subject. But it is that same textualization that prevents him from being able to theorize *either* the difference of those people who make up the market in the present, *or* any possibility of a different economic totality (and therefore, perhaps, a fundamentally different kind of subject) in the future. As Carton puts it, in Michaels' reading there is no politically charged or promising "positive term" — no possibility of "a contextualized — a socially produced, rather than a rhetorically projected — freedom" — because Michaels' analysis "restricts itself to the sphere of the terminological."[38] It may be true, in other words, that a materialist critique, as Fredric Jameson has argued, must be seen as a set of propositions not about matter but rather about language.[39] But what Michaels' textualization of the economic helps us to see is the danger of treating them as if they were *only* that. As a corrective to the too-rapid conflation of "selfhood," "writing," "capitalism," "the market," "exchange," "difference," and many another term in Michaels' scheme, we should be skeptical of what Perry Anderson has called "*the exorbitation of language.*"[40] As Anderson writes of Lévi-Strauss — in a passage pointedly applicable to Michaels' radical reduction of capitalism:

> No economy . . . can be primarily defined in terms of exchange at all: production and property are always prior. . . .
>
> For utterance has no *material* constraint whatever: words are free, in the double sense of the term. They cost nothing to produce, and can be multiplied and manipulated at will, within the laws of meaning. All other major social practices are subject to the laws of natural *scarcity*: persons, goods or powers cannot be generated *ad libitum* and *ad infinitum*.[41]

From this vantage, we can see that the fundamental theoretical shortcoming of Michaels' model is that it is finally too *simple*. To paraphrase Brecht's wonderful analogy between mapping the actions of the social subject and those of the fundamental particles of modern physics, their movements are difficult to predict not because there are no determinations, but because there are too many.[42] In Michaels, things are all too easy to predict, because the self-identical presence of the Liberal subject has been replaced by its self-identical absence.

CLAIMING THE SUBJECT; OR,
WHAT DOES WILLIAM JAMES MEAN?

Two inseparable problems in William James provide the critical locus for current struggles over his critical politics and his authority: the first is the meaning and, more difficultly, the political status of the term "belief" in James's lexicon. The second, in *The Principles of Psychology*, is central to the "Introduction" to *The Gold Standard*, where Michaels draws our attention to the fact that James's model of selfhood is essentially a model of ownership. James asks, what does consciousness "mean when it calls the present self the *same* with one of the past selves which it has in mind?" (quoted *GS*, 7). Our selves, James decides, must be joined by what Michaels calls "common ownership," but what or who, then, does the owning? Michaels sketches the problem for us:

> How, then, can we account for the way in which the present thought establishes ownership over past thoughts? Our mistake, James thinks, has been to imagine the thought as *establishing* ownership over past thoughts; instead, we should think of it as *already* owning them. The owner has "inherited his 'title.' " His own "birth" is always coincident with "the death of another owner"; indeed, the very existence of an owner must coincide with the coming into existence of the owned. "Each Thought is thus born an owner, and dies owned, transmitting whatever it realized as its Self to its own later proprietor." (9)

For Michaels, the Jamesian model of selfhood is a quintessential example of the totalizing power of the market, of the fact that the desires and beliefs of the self—in this case, the desire to understand precisely what is *other* than the social system and economic structure—always reproduce the logic of the market that constitutes them. James's account of the self is, in Michaels' words, a story of "the continual transformation of owner into owned" (22). In James, we learn a lesson which *The Gold Standard* aims to teach us again and again: that the logic of the market is not the effect of selfhood but its very condition. And consequently, the Jamesian self who might critically reflect on his beliefs can do so only within the purview of the market itself and the naturalist logic that constitutes the self who might engage in such reflection.

From this vantage, James's attempt to save the self from the brutalities of the early modern American variety of capitalism—with its Taylorization, its imperialist incursions in both Atlantic and Pacific, and its "abstraction" and "rationalization" (as James liked to call it) of cultural and intellectual life— turns out to be an unwitting repetition and indeed an insidious internalization of that very social and economic totality. Far from providing a stay against alienation and ruthless competitive individualism, James's Lockean property model of selfhood guarantees it, because freedom on this model is the right to dispose of and enjoy the property of the self—its capacities and potentialities (including, of course, its labor power)—as one wishes, a freedom which cannot help but be limited and threatened, however, by other self-proprietors who are trying to achieve the same sort of freedom. All of which is simply to grant the classic Marxist critique: that insofar as the self is conceived as a kind of private property, I will alienate and threaten your freedom insofar as I realize my own, and vice versa.[43]

To more fully understand the attractions and limitations of Michaels' reading of this problem in James,[44] it might be useful to compare it with Frank Lentricchia's powerful recent rereading of Jamesian "belief" in general and of this moment in *The Principles of Psychology* in particular. Lentricchia focuses on a different passage in James, but it is one which, if anything, makes the point even more emphatically than Michaels that James, as Lentricchia puts it, "finds (thinks he finds) truly inalienable private property located at (and *as*) the core of unique selfhood."[45] "It seems," James writes, "as if the elementary psychic fact were not *thought* or *this thought* or *that thought* but *my thought*, every thought being *owned*." "*In the widest possible sense*," James continues, "*a man's self is the sum total of all that he can call his . . .*" (quoted 814). Like Michaels—and, if it matters, before him[46]—Lentricchia recognizes that James's "overt commitment to the inalienable private property of selfhood . . . is an inscription of a contradiction at the very heart of capitalism"—namely, that property "can *be* property only if it *is* alienable," and that a self so concieved, therefore, is perforce an alienated self (816). Lentricchia and Michaels seem to agree, in other words, on the *fact* of James's reinscription of the central contradiction of capitalism at the center of the Liberal self.

What they do not agree on, however, is how that fact should be interpreted. Lentricchia's reading (in a moment that is perhaps overly generous to James) argues that

> James employs the language of private property in order to describe the spiritual nature of persons and in an effort to turn the discourse of private property against itself by making that discourse literal in just this one instance: so as to preserve a human space of freedom, however interiorized, from the vicissitudes and coercions of the marketplace. . . . (816)

But the critical sophistication of Lentricchia's reading of James must at the same time force us to ask: can you do that? Can James or anyone so turn the historically and politically freighted rhetoric of capitalism to advantage, even in an act of engagement as diligent as James's? Lentricchia's critique allows us, I think, to answer both "yes" and "no": "no" in the sense that James's property model of selfhood reproduces the logic of alienation which it would subvert; but "yes" because, in Lentricchia's reading, that is not the end of the story. For Lentricchia is at pains to situate this moment of discursive complicity with the system in James in the context of a larger, historically specific project of anti-imperialism which the later James undertook in earnest on many different sites (writing letters to the newspaper, giving talks to grade school teachers)—sometimes by seizing upon what Kenneth Burke would call the "ruling symbols" (like private property) of his day, and sometimes by doing precisely the reverse (as in his guerrilla warfare, within the institutions of academic philosophy, against what he called "rationalism"). For Lentricchia, James's discursive complicity with the system is only one component of a larger

project for social change, an undertaking which, being quintessentially pragmatist, is willing to use all that there is to use—including (especially) the politically powerful means of rhetorical identification.

Lentricchia's discussion in *Criticism and Social Change* of Kenneth Burke
will help to further underscore his differences with Michaels. Burke's concept
of "dialectical rhetoric" helps us to see that James's appropriation of the dominant discourse (always risky and, for Burke, often necessary) is driven by a
concept of political discourse as not "a simple negating language of rupture"—
or, what amounts to the same thing, the pure reproduction of the system in
Michaels' reading of James—"but a shrewd, self-conscious rhetoric that con-
serves as it negates."[47] Lentricchia's critique of theoretical idealism serves, for
my purposes, to underscore the paralyzing effects of Michaels' textualization
and consequent homogenization of the social space in general and of William
James's discursive complicity with the market in particular. "To attempt to
proceed in purity," Lentricchia writes,

> —to reject the rhetorical strategies of capitalism and Christianity, *as if such strat-
> egies were in themselves responsible for human oppression*—to proceed with the
> illusion of purity is to situate oneself on the margin of history. . . . It is to exclude
> oneself from having any chance of making a difference for better or for worse.
> (CSC , 36)

Ironically enough (it is ironic, at least, in light of Michaels' much-publicized
stand "against theory") a commitment to this idea of critical theory entails
both an attenuation of the primacy of language *and* a reduced claim for the
power of theory. And by these lights, Michaels' reading of James turns out to
be anything but the sort of interpretation forwarded in the "Against Theory"
project, since Michaels' position—that the self always reproduces the logic of
the market—maintains for itself the predictive power that theory in the high
classic mode has always wanted: a prediction, in this case, of the social as a site
of pure repetition.[48]

In this sense, Lentricchia's reading of James is perhaps as theoretical as
Michaels but is certainly less "theoreticist." Lentricchia insists on the unruly
materiality of the social, a materiality which is never wholly identical with the
languages which seek to produce and master it, and whose future status, therefore, is never predictable in advance. He would reclaim James not for his ability
to predict the future, but rather for the materialist imperative that resides in his
inability to do so. For Lentricchia, a pragmatist critique must attend not only
to the abstract, symbolic, or textual form of a concept but also to what Kenneth Burke (James's Pragmatist descendent in Lentricchia's criticism) calls its
"bureaucratization" in material, social form: "[P]ragmatism," Burke
writes—in a wonderful meditation on what he calls the "unintended by-prod-
ucts" of abstract concepts—"would note how the particular choice of materials and methods in which to embody the ideal gives rise to conditions somewhat at variance with the spirit of the ideal"[49]—a state of affairs, it probably
goes without saying, which cannot be foreseen in advance. Consequently, Lentricchia's version of Jamesian pragmatism "has no way of settling, once and for

all, the question it constantly asks: Does the world rise or fall in value when any particular belief is let loose in the world?" ("Philosophers of Modernism," 805). For Lentricchia, this is James's "most unsettling insight: that a rigorous philosophy of practice and consequences cannot in advance secure consequences without establishing precisely the sort of imperial authority . . . which that philosophy is dedicated to undermining."[50] In fact, though, Lentricchia's stronger point is that it could never do so anyway, even if it wanted to.

This open-endedness—this *unforeseeability*—of Jamesian pragmatism has been emphasized in other recent rereadings of James as well, most notably in Cornel West's construction of what he calls a "genealogy of pragmatism" in his recent study, *The American Evasion of Philosophy*. West's critique stresses above all the fact that for James we cannot know the status of a concept or figure (the Lockean property model of selfhood, for example) until it has been let loose in the world and *only later* returned to us. West would foreground for us James's first principle of pragmatism: "There can *be* no difference anywhere," as James phrased it in a late essay, "that doesn't *make* a difference elsewhere—no difference in abstract truth that doesn't express itself in a difference in concrete fact and in conduct consequent upon that fact, imposed on somebody, somehow, somewhere, and somewhen."[51] For West, the essence of Jamesian pragmatism is its *revisability*; its first principle is, in West's words, that "the universe is incomplete, the world is still 'in the making' owing to the impact of human powers on the universe and the world."[52] For West as for Lentricchia, Jamesian pragmatism insists upon an absolutely unbridgeable gap between concept construction on specific discursive sites and concept circulation in a broader set of contexts, and it is in that gap that the possibility of the social and the historical resides.

All of which seems to raise for a pragmatist critique two opposite problems which are nevertheless inextricably linked. On the one hand, this position seems to tell us that knowledge in the pragmatist sense is so deferred, dispersed, and contingent that it is hard to see how we can we reflect in any meaningful way not so much upon what we think, but rather (as Michaels might phrase it) upon what what we think does. On the other hand, this concept of pragmatist agency implies that we can know, in a fairly precise way, exactly what we are doing (hence we can, in Burkean good faith, rhetorically enlist support for it). In fact, James himself argues rather unabashedly that truth is "What would be better for us to believe"; it is *"the name of whatever proves itself to be good in the way of belief, and good, too, for definite, assignable reasons."*[53] From this vantage, the Jamesian self, *contra* Michaels, not only has a choice about what it believes, it also has sufficient critical distance on that belief to assign specific reasons for holding it.

West's critique nimbly approaches the second problem here by insisting upon a dimension of James's thought that tends to get lost in contemporary discussions, with their emphasis on action, power, and so on. For West, James's pragmatic theory of truth "preserves a realist ontology" and so avoids subjectivism even as it "rejects all forms of foundationalism" (67); in James's words, "with some such reality any statement, in order to be counted true, must agree" (quoted 64). At the same time, however, James stresses the constitutive and revisionist role of human action in the construction of that reality, and so rejects positivist accounts of truth as well. As West neatly puts it, "James retains a correspondence theory of truth, yet it is rather innocuous in that rational acceptability is the test for truth claims we accept" (67).

This does not exactly put to rest, however, the first problem we raised above: namely, how the pragmatist—who believes that critical ideas are really different only if their consequences in the world are different—can ever really assure, through critical reflection, that her ideas will turn out to be in practice what she thinks they are in theory. Lentricchia's response to this problem— again it entails a reduced claim for theory—is relatively straightforward: you can't assure that, but at the same time you can't do anything other than try to assure it. Just as Lentricchia agrees with Michaels on the *fact* but not the interpretation of the Jamesian property model of the self, so he similarly reads Jamesian belief as "a 'set of rules' for the action of changing-by-interpreting the world's various texts," as "instruments of desire" of wholly "temporal character," which are "born locally in crisis and have local consequences only."[54] But James's message for Lentricchia—and here is where he parts company with Michaels—is also that "theory" (critical reflection on "belief") is not something that one can be for or against because it is inescapable, not a matter of volition or intention but rather what James called "an appetite of the mind" and what Lentricchia calls "the need to generalize" and "to obliterate differences."[55] It is, to put it bluntly, a kind of conceptual imperialist within. In Lentricchia's reading of James, it is as if theory and practice are engaged in a battle on the terrain of belief, where their dialectical relationship constantly enacts a struggle of stabilization and destabilization, generalization and specificity, formalism and historicism, abstraction and concretion.

But it seems fairly obvious that to insist, as James does, that theoretical reflection is, *mutatis mutandis,* an "appetite of the mind" is to reinstate once again an essentialist concept of the subject which is twin to the ethical, Liberal self and its privileged qualities: reflexive self-consciousness, rationality, the instinct of higher reason, and so on. But here, it seems to me, is where Lentricchia's reading of James is both ingenious and forthright. Rather than attempting to solve or explain away the essential Liberalism of Jamesian pragmatism, Lentricchia takes it for granted. "The new pragmatists," Lentricchia writes in a passage worth quoting at length,

> flounder on one of James's strongest insights—that theory cannot be identified with agency and the self-conscious individual [and so cannot be rejected in the sense of "Against Theory"], that theory is the sort of force that tends to control individuals by speaking through them. And so does James. . . . The epistemological move to generalization may well be an "appetite of the mind" . . . [b]ut the economic and political move to generalize—the global generalization of labor known as capitalism—is not an unhistorical appetite; it is a locatable, historical phenomenon whose role tends to be blurred and repressed by James's liberal ideology of the autonomous self.[56]

What James *does* do, however, is all that a discourse of individual agency and practice can do: he pushes Liberalism to its absolute limits by "focusing the obsessive liberal vision of American literature at its extreme antinomian edge" where the subject dwells not as "variable expressive function of structure" but rather as "the antithesis of structure."[57] James's gamble is that he is too much within the dominant discourse of the Liberal subject; but his payoff is to unleash that discourse's anarchic tendencies against the private property side of Liberalism that threatens always to recontain them.

Like Emerson in his most radical moments—the Emerson who promotes a destabilizing politics of *"Whim"* in "Self-Reliance"—Lentricchia's James forces Liberalism toward desystematizing and detotalizing consequences that Liberalism in its milder, status quo forms would never tolerate, and in doing so he gives us a way of resisting the closure and objectification of the economic and social totality (in the form, say, of Michaels' "market"). Michaels' critique, on the other hand, falls prey in its textualization of the social to the theoretical idealism that plagues Emerson's concept of action: that once you have reflected upon the principles of right action, you no longer have any reason or need to act.[58] If we take Michaels at his word—that action and belief "are just two descriptions of the same thing" (and that belief, we know, is impervious to critical reflection) ["Politics?" 336]—then we are forced to conclude that for Michaels once you have acted, there is no need—and in fact no *way*—to reflect upon the principles of your actions. From this vantage, the difference between Lentricchia's James and Michaels' is the difference between a self-critical Liberalism and an uncritical one.

TOTAL SYSTEM AND THE PROBLEM OF HISTORICAL CHANGE

Lentricchia's reading of James confronts Michaels' on the terrain of the subject and agency. At the other end of the critical spectrum, so to speak—and, in Appiah's terms, at a different (which is to say *not competing*) level of explanation—Fredric Jameson has recently challenged Michaels' critique in *The Gold Standard* on the site of the social and economic totality—a site, Jameson points out, which is in Michaels shorn of "all of its (once inevitable) Marxist connotations" (193). For Jameson, the central challenge—and in some ways, I think, the signal interest—of Michaels' text is how powerfully it confronts us, from a critical vantage ostensibly "beyond ideology," with what Jameson calls "the dilemma of getting out of the total system" (204). *The Gold Standard* replicates this problem for us over and over again (nowhere more provocatively than in its reading of Dreiser's *Sister Carrie* and Norris' *McTeague*). "[D]o texts refer to social reality?" Michaels asks.

> If they do, do they merely reflect it, or do they imagine utopian alternatives to it? Like the question of whether Dreiser liked or disliked capitalism, these questions seem to me to posit a space outside the culture in order then to interrogate the relations between that space (here defined as literary) and the culture. But the spaces I have tried to explore are all very much within the culture, and so the project of interrogation makes no sense. . . . (27)

For those of us who subscribe, as Appiah puts it, to one form or another of "ontological reductionism"—to the belief that "social facts are composed out of human acts, intentions, beliefs, and their interactions with each other and with the nonhuman world"[59]—Michaels' presupposition here seems reasonable enough, and the conclusion that follows from it (much as we may resist it) would seem inevitable. Indeed, as Jameson points out, Michaels' position formally reproduces the double bind of the "Against Theory" critique: how can you imagine a utopian alternative to the existing social system (much less translate that imagining into effective practice) when the only epistemological tools that you have to undertake such a project are those provided by the system itself?

More forcefully than the "Against Theory" polemic,[60] *The Gold Standard,* then, presents us with what looks like an inescapable dilemma: either step outside the system (upon pain of indulging metaphysics or "theology") and imagine the possibility of a real alternative to it, or stay locked within the system and its logic (the only thing you can do, philosophically and theoretically, in good faith) and reproduce it, however much you may think you want to do otherwise. Here, as before, if we accept the terms of Michaels' characterization, then we are forced to accept his conclusions as well. But that, I think, is precisely what we need not do.

Michaels is persuasive, it seems to me, only if we conceive social change and political *praxis* in essentially ethical terms—which is to say in terms of voluntarism and "the taking of thought," as Jameson puts it (206)[61]—and only then if we accept Michaels' overly homogeneous characterization of the social and economic totality as reducible to an abstract logic of exchange and the market which pervades all aspects of social life equally (which is to say completely) and therefore at the same level (which is to say the only level, the level of textuality or representation). And if this is so, then I think we must agree with Jameson that Michaels' critique little touches the fundamental conceptual and political coordinates of the Marxist position, which does not conceive social change as a problem of ethical voluntarism and which focuses our attention in the economic sphere not exclusively on exchange and "the market" (which for Jameson, after Mandel's *Late Capitalism,* is in any case but a stage of capitalist development), but rather on the mode of *production.*[62]

In fact, in Marx himself it is hard to miss the repeated insistence in a variety of contexts that one need not be able to step outside of the social system into some metaphysical space to think the possibility of social and historical change. For Marx—this is the materialist point, I take it, of the critique of Hegel—the possibility of social change resides *within* the existing social system itself (where else would it be?), because the economic and social totality is never self-identical and uniformly dispersed but always internally differential and discontinuous—the prime example of this, of course, being the unequal relations of production at work in the fact of *class.*[63] And the same needs to be said, of course, for how Marxism produces the concept of the subject, and in doing so makes it possible to think the possibility of a kind of critical reflection on action which is not recontained by the Liberal problematic. Like the subject of Liberalism, the Marxist subject should and indeed *must* engage in critical reflection and intellectual *praxis*; unlike the Liberal problematic, however, the Marxist subject who engages in that reflection does *not* do so from a space of self-identical freedom and autonomy (or their self-identical negation, as in Michaels).

On a more empirical level, Marx will aim in *Capital* to demonstrate that the alternative to the capitalist totality is to be found precisely *within* the logics and dynamics of capitalism itself—not, in Jameson's words, "as an ideal or a Utopia but a tendential and emergent set of already existing structures" (206).[64] As Jameson points out, this is the "strong" form of what Marx means by the concept of "contradiction"—most centrally in the classical Marxist canon, the contradiction between the development of the forces and relations of production which is the very engine of class polarization and historical change itself.

It is this sense of the internally generative nature of contradiction which will later be accentuated in Althusser's theorization of the relationship between contradiction and "overdetermination." For Althusser, Marxist analysis "always studies economic structures dominated by *several* modes of production,"[65] and it is that "unevenness" or overdetermination which is "the motor of all development."[66] For Althusser as for Jameson (and to a large extent for all Marxists), however, the theoretical problem is how to retain this strong sense of contradiction without at the same time falling into the false assurance (and political danger) of some notion of teleological inevitability, and with it the naive historicism of what Althusser calls "the ideological model of a continuous time."[67] In a sense, of course, what is at issue here is nothing other than the status and politics of Marxism's base-superstructure model itself which, in the view of Lentricchia, harbors in its classic form a "latent totalitarianism" (*CSC*, 5). Lentricchia's admonition should be taken to heart—and it is increasingly shared by a number of contemporary critics, even "post-Marxist" ones like LaClau and Mouffe.[68] Indeed, it was shared by Althusser himself, who attempted to solve this problem by complicating it: by insisting on a reciprocal relationship between economic base and "semi-autonomous" superstructure, and by conceding the determination of superstructural forms by the economic mode of production only "in the last instance" (only to admit later that "the last instance never comes").[69] This was essentially the aim, whatever its problems, of Althusser's concept of "structural causality," which attempted to replace the crude economic determinism lurking in the base-superstructure model with a more syncretic model of totality in which, as Althusser famously defines it, *"the whole existence of the structure consists of its effects . . . is merely a specific combination of its peculiar elements, is nothing outside its effects."*[70] In a sense, then, Althusser's critique of "expressive causality"—of the view that, as James Kavanagh puts it, "all 'superstructural' contradictions in every social formation [are] indispensible 'expressions' or epiphenomena of a single, pure, *essential* [economic] contradiction"[71]—may be seen as a stay *against* the Stalinist temptation which is the extreme but quite logical political application of a belief in the teleological assurance held by an older kind of Marxism (or at least we hope it is older).[72]

This is not to say, of course, that we simply need to return in filial piety to our Althusser with renewed commitment—far from it. Several key components of the Althusserian project—the most well-known being, of course, his characterization of critical "science," over and against "ideology," as a "subjectless" procedure[73]—have rightly been criticized by E. P. Thompson, Sebastiano Timpanaro, and others within Marxism itself as harboring a dangerous "epistemological idealism."[74] It *is*, however, to agree with Fredric Jameson that the point to be made against Michaels' vision of the seamless, total system is simply "that systems, even total systems, change" (206). And if Anthony Appiah is correct in his assertion that all theories are in some sense mistaken because they are all partial, each one engaging specific "interests" and indulging specific "idealizations," then Jameson's point expresses something like the ultimate presupposition—what Appiah would call the "tolerable falsehood"—of historical materialism.[75] In theorizing the economic and social space as one of uneven development and disequilibrium—by positing contradiction *within* a discontinuous present totality—the Marxian critique allows us to see how it is that what can be confronted only textually always points to what textuality can never wholly contain or master: the world of the contingent, the material, and the historical. The text is always, to use Kenneth Burke's suitably inelegant phrase, a "would-be comprehending story"—partial, incomplete, and fissured, not self-identical and everywhere equally pervasive, as in Michaels' account— and it is in that "would-be" that both the necessity and the possibility of ideological reproduction and historical change reside.[76] It is in this sense that "It is the failure of imagination that is important," as Jameson puts it, "and not its achievement" (209). Recent Americanist critics like Walter Benn Michaels help us to read, in impressively nuanced detail, the daunting fact of that failure. To interpret that failure, however, we need to abandon our story of the Liberal subject, to realize that the story has already changed.

NOTES

1. I would like to thank Jonathan Elmer and Eva Cherniavsky for their helpful comments on an earlier draft of this essay.

2. Donald Pease's recent work on the formation of the field of American Studies is valuable (and sometimes entertaining) on this point. See in particular Pease's critique of Frederick Crews and Quentin Anderson in his editorial introduction to the special New Americanist issue of *boundary 2*: "New Americanists: Revisionist Interventions into the Canon," *boundary 2* 17 (1991): 1-37. For a longer discussion in something of a different register, see Russell Reising, *The Unusable Past: Theory and the Study of American Literature* (New York: Methuen, 1986).

3. An intelligent recent description of how this mechanism of Liberal freedom operates may be found in David Lloyd, "Kant's Examples," *Representations* 28 (Fall 1989): 34-54. I cannot do justice to the finely grained nuances of Lloyd's essay, but his critique of "liberal education" in the form of Kant's "exemplary pedagogy" (teaching by example) is directly pertinent to my concerns here. As Lloyd puts it, the contradiction of the liberal pedagogical project—the project that produces the liberal subject—is that "dependence upon examples remains a constant threat to what is to be produced, namely, a free relation of the subject to itself and to others, that is, a free conformity to

law" (38). The privileged form, as it were, of this contradiction is the Kantian concept of genius, which is "a productivity which is apparently at once rule-bound and free," and which "achieves what is elsewhere impossible, a following of examples combined with an independence from them" (41). In a similar way, the man in our joke needs to be confronted with evidence which contradicts his initial freedom of choice, so that the power of his more fundamental freedom may be demonstrated by its transcendence of that evidence.

4. Gregory S. Jay's discussion of "The Liberal Mind" will help make the point from a different vantage. As Jay's discussion of Lionel Trilling and others indicates, the dialectic of "difference" within the purview of Liberalism is not only not Marxist; it is not even, strictly speaking, Hegelian. As Jay puts it, in Liberalism "freedom turns into an indeterminate state rather than appearing as the concrete negation of particular historical conditions." The Liberal critic "cannot rejoin the history of ideas with the history of economics since he is committed to seeing ideas as the representations of willing subjects rather than as parts of an always already material signifying practice." See Jay, *America the Scrivener: Deconstruction and the Subject of Literary History* (Ithaca: Cornell UP, 1990), esp. 277-312.

5. The phrase belongs to Daniel Bell, who coined it in his books of the 1960s and 1970s, *The End of Ideology, The Coming of Post-Industrial Society* and *The Cultural Contradictions of Capitalism*. A helpful critique of the "end of ideology" mode of cultural criticism may be found in Gerald Graff's essay "American Criticism Left and Right," and particularly in his discussion of "consumerist pluralism," in *Ideology and Classic American Literature,* ed. Sacvan Bercovitch and Myra Jehlen (Cambridge: Cambridge UP, 1986), 91-121. In a recent essay, Giles Gunn makes what I take to be a similar point, but Gunn's argument turns out to be subject to the same problems as all "beyond ideology" critiques (which Gunn, in a way, concedes at the end of his essay by calling his position a "humanistic" pragmatism). In any case, his assimilation of Michaels' work to the sphere of "ideological" criticism is, given Michaels' explicit rejection of "ideology" as a critical concept, only half right. See his "Beyond Transcendence or Beyond Ideology: The New Problematics of Cultural Criticism in America," *American Literary History* 2 (1990): 1-18.

6. This point has been made more or less convincingly (to my mind at least) by Pease in the essay cited above and by others. See, for example, Geraldine Murphey, "Romancing the Center: Cold War Politics and Classic American Literature," *Poetics Today* 9 (1988): 737-47; and see, for an encyclopedic treatment of Americanism as a "substitute Marxism," Michael Denning, "The Special American Conditions: Marxism and American Studies," *American Quarterly* 38 (1986): 356-80.

7. Walter Benn Michaels, "Saving the Text: Reference and Belief," *MLN* 93 (1978): 771. Further references are in the text.

8. For the relevant documents, see *Aesthetics and Politics,* ed. and trans. Ronald Taylor et al., afterword by Fredric Jameson (London: New Left Books, 1980).

9. Fredric Jameson, *Postmodernism, or, The Cultural Logic of Late Capitalism* (Durham: Duke UP, 1990), 207. Jameson then goes on to offer Susan Sontag's book on photography as an example of just such a critique, with its "classically liberal recommendation of a kind of 'diet cure' for images." Further references to Jameson's book are in the text.

10. Walter Benn Michaels, "Is There a Politics of Interpretation?" *The Politics of Interpretation,* ed. W. J. T. Mitchell (Chicago: U of Chicago P, 1983), 335. Further references to Michaels' essay appear in abbreviated form in the text.

11. Walter Benn Michaels, *The Gold Standard and the Logic of Naturalism: American Literature at the Turn of the Century* (Berkeley: U of California P, 1987), 14, n.16. Further references to Michaels' book are given parenthetically in the text as *GS*.

12. See Evan Carton, "American Literary Histories as Social Practice," *Raritan* 8 (1989): 129-30.

13. This is the last essay of Knapp and Michaels in the series. It may be found in *Critical Inquiry* 14 (1987): 49-68.

14. Steven Knapp and Walter Benn Michaels, "Against Theory," *Against Theory: Literary Studies and the New Pragmatism,* ed. W. J. T. Mitchell (Chicago: U of Chicago P, 1985), 30. Further references are in the text. Jameson's description appears in *Postmodernism,* 181-82.

15. See also "Against Theory," 26-27, 29, which makes particularly clear the seamless and total character of "belief": "To imagine that we can see the beliefs we hold as no better than but 'merely different' from opposing beliefs held by others is to imagine a position from which we can see our beliefs without really believing them. To be in this position would be to see the truth about beliefs without actually having any—to know without believing" (27).

16. The most notable instance is perhaps to be found in the work of Deleuze and Guattari, and in particular in the "nomadology" of their later texts. The object of Michaels' critique, however, is the position of Leo Bersani in *A Future for Astyanax* (1976): "desire," Bersani writes, "disintegrates society, the self, and the novel"; that is why, in Bersani's words, "the containment of desire is a triumph for social stability" (quoted in Michaels, 47).

17. Jean-Paul Sartre, *Being and Nothingness,* trans. and intro. Hazel E. Barnes (New York: Philosophical Library, 1956), 100.

18. Carton, 129-30.

19. Frank Lentricchia, *Criticism and Social Change* (Chicago: U of Chicago P, 1983), 30. Many contemporary Marxist critics would agree with Michaels' critique of desire here; they would differ, however—for reasons we will investigate later in this essay—about how that fact should be *interpreted.* As Jameson points out, Michaels' critique of Bersani would hold for Kristeva and Deleuze as well—and would be shared by a contemporary Marxist critic like Franco Moretti—and reaches its "paranoiac-critical" terminus in the work of Baudrillard (*Postmodernism,* 202-3).

20. Stanley Fish has recently attempted, in effect, to address this very problem, and his theorization of "belief" only underscores for us the cloying self-identity of Michaels' use of the concept. Fish's position—in short, that our beliefs can change because the capacity for changing them is one of their built-in assumptions—is what we might characterize as the user-friendly or "soft" version of Michaels' concept of "belief." See Fish, "Change," *South Atlantic Quarterly* 86 (1987): 423-44.

21. The often quoted passage in question on the relation of subject and interest in the concept of ideology is from Marx and Engels, *The German Ideology,* Part One: "For each new class which puts itself in the place of one ruling before it, is compelled, merely in order to carry through its aim, to represent its interest as the common interest of all the members of society, that is, expressed in ideal form: it has to give its ideas the form universality and represent them as the only rational, universally valid ones" (65-66). Karl Marx and Friedrich Engels, *The German Ideology,* ed. and intro. C. J. Arthur (New York: International Publishers, 1970).

22. But for discussions of precisely that sort, see, among others, Terry Eagleton, *Ideology* (London: New Left Books, 1991); Göran Therborn, *The Power of Ideology and the Ideology of Power* (London: New Left Books, 1980); and, in a different register, *Ideology in Social Science,* ed. Robin Blackburn (New York: Pantheon, 1973). Excellent shorter introductions may be found in James H. Kavanagh, "Marxism's Althusser: Toward a Politics of Literary Theory," *diacritics* 12 (1982): 25-45, and in Myra Jehlen's introduction to *Ideology and Classic American Literature ,* 1-18.

23. Martin Jay, "The Concept of Totality in Lukács and Adorno," *Telos* 32 (Summer 1977): 130. For a more extended investigation of these matters, see Jay, *Marxism and Totality: The Adventures of a Concept from Lukács to Habermas* (Berkeley: U of California P, 1984).

24. See Perry Anderson, "Modernity and Revolution," *New Left Review* 144 (1984): 96-113, esp. 109-11. See also Norman Geras, *Marx and Human Nature: Ref-*

utation of a Legend (London: New Left Books, 1983). The paradigmatic instance of this fact in Marx, of course, is the economic and social class itself, which gets its identity only in *struggle* with other classes.

25. In fact, that sort of "interest-alignment" model of ideology which may be read in *The German Ideology* "is not Marxist" according to Althusser (and according, in his reading, to Marx's later work). See Louis Althusser, *Lenin and Philosophy and Other Essays,* trans. Ben Brewster (London: New Left Books, 1971), 127-86. This reconceptualization of the subject of ideology in light of Lacan's influence is already quite clear in Althusser's *For Marx* (1965), which—not coincidentally—mounts a sustained critique of Marxist "humanism."

26. Louis Althusser, *For Marx,* trans. Ben Brewster (London: New Left Books, 1977), 233-34.

27. This effort may take any of number of forms or models, one of the more famous of which is Pierre Bourdieu's concept of the *habitus.* See his *Distinction: A Social Critique of the Judgment of Taste,* trans. Richard Nice (Cambridge: Harvard UP, 1984), esp. 123, 170-73.

28. See, for example, Anthony Appiah's engaging discussion of this problem in Michaels and in others in "Tolerable Falsehoods: Agency and the Interests of Theory," *Consequences of Theory,* Selected Papers from the English Institute 1987-88, ed. Jonathan Arac and Barbara Johnson (Baltimore: Johns Hopkins UP, 1991), 63-90.

29. Appiah, 74.

30. All of which is to agree with Fredric Jameson's diagnosis, that in *The Gold Standard*—and this despite its plethora of historical materials and anti-Liberal polemic—"there remains the nagging feeling that all this does come down to the 'self' after all" (*Postmodernism,* 198).

31. See "Is There a Politics of Interpretation?" 335.

32. Appiah, 84.

33. Carton, 129.

34. Wilson's review underscores this asymmetry as well (473).

35. Wilson, 474.

36. See Carton, 129.

37. See Raymond Williams, *Marxism and Literature* (Oxford: Oxford UP, 1977), 121-27.

38. See Carton, 131.

39. Fredric Jameson, "Imaginary and Symbolic in Lacan: Marxism, Psychoanalytic Criticism, and the Problem of the Subject," *Yale French Studies* 55/56 (1977): 389-90.

40. Perry Anderson, *In the Tracks of Historical Materialism* (London: New Left Books, 1984), 40.

41. Anderson, *Tracks,* 43-44. Anderson's critique of the various appropriations of the Saussurian model of language, from Lévi-Strauss through poststructuralism, is particularly adept in situating these developments in the context of modern French intellectual history, and specifically in light of Sartre's failure to produce the second volume of the *Critique of Dialectical Reason,* and the consequent ascendency of the language/economics homology made possible by Lévi-Strauss's capitalization upon Sartre's failure.

42. Brecht is quoted in Sebastiano Timpanaro, *On Materialism* (London: New Left Books, 1975), 40, n.9.

43. The classic critique of the Lockean model of the subject is C. B. McPherson, *The Political Theory of Possessive Individualism: Hobbes to Locke* (Oxford: Oxford UP, 1962). As for the theorization which stands behind McPherson's own, it is readily available in Marx's "On the Jewish Question," where he argues that the practical application of Liberal "freedom" and "rights" is the right to private property. Hence, Marx tells us, the Liberal self sees "in other men not the *realization* but the *limitation* of his own freedom." Karl Marx, *Early Writings,* trans. Rodney Livingstone and Gregor Benton, intro. Lucio Colletti (New York: Vintage, 1975), 229-30. Marx's *The Eighteenth*

Brumaire of Louis Bonaparte will then be something like a reading of a historical example of this truth in action.

44. This is not to suggest that this passage in *The Gold Standard* constitutes Michaels' only use of James. In fact, Michaels has often written about James, and seizes on other passages from *The Principles of Psychology* in *The Gold Standard* itself.

45. Frank Lentricchia, "Philosophers of Modernism at Harvard, circa 1900," *South Atlantic Quarterly* 89, 4 (1990): 814. Further references are in the text.

46. I say this because Lentricchia's reading of this moment in James is first worked out in an essay which appeared in 1986, "On the Ideologies of Poetic Modernism, 1890-1913: The Example of William James," *Reconstructing American Literary History*, ed. Sacvan Bercovitch (Cambridge: Harvard UP, 1986). Michaels' reading of this specific problem in James, on the other hand, did not appear, so far as I know, until the publication of *The Gold Standard* in 1987.

47. Lentricchia, *Criticism and Social Change*, 33. The central example of this Burkean concept in action is to be found in Lentricchia's discussion of Burke's proposed substitution of "the people" for "the worker" at the first American Writers' Congress in 1935 (21ff.). Further references are in the text as *CSC*.

48. This is, I take it, the point made by Michaels' former student Howard Horwitz, who chides historicist "formalism" for its "idolatry of forms as essence and prescription, the notion that an idea or symbolic form has only one use or means the same thing in all contexts." See Horwitz, "The Standard Oil Trust as Emersonian Hero," *Raritan* 4 (1987): 118.

49. Kenneth Burke, *Permanence and Change*, 3rd ed. (Berkeley: U of California P, 1984), 282. On the "Bureaucratization of the Imaginative," see *Attitudes Toward History*, 3rd ed. (Berkeley: U of California P, 1984), 225-26.

50. Lentricchia, "Ideologies of Poetic Modernism," 245. This essay is an earlier version, different in some respects, of the treatment of James in *Ariel and the Police* and in the later "Philosophers of Modernism" essay.

51. William James, *Essays in Pragmatism*, ed. Albury Castell (New York: Hafner, 1948), 144.

52. Cornel West, *The American Evasion of Philosophy: A Genealogy of Pragmatism* (Madison: U of Wisconsin P, 1989), 65. Further references are in the text.

53. James, *Essays in Pragmatism*, 156, 155.

54. Frank Lentricchia, *Ariel and the Police: Michel Foucault, William James, Wallace Stevens* (Madison: U of Wisconsin P, 1988), 106-7.

55. Lentricchia, *Ariel*, 124-25.

56. Lentricchia, *Ariel*, 127.

57. "Ideologies of Poetic Modernism," 249.

58. Myra Jehlen, *American Incarnation: The Individual, the Nation, and the Continent* (Cambridge: Harvard UP, 1986), 84-85, 97-98. As Jehlen points out, for Emerson "willful intervention either to hasten the future's advent or, worse still, to redefine it can only distort the perfect order that already exists implicitly, and thus delay its explicit realization. Not only are deeds and revolutions not needed, they are forbidden" (85). Lentricchia's reading of Emersonian action stresses this contradiction as well, and both may be contrasted with Richard Grusin's interesting but, I think, mistaken discussion in his article "Revisionism and the Structure of Emersonian Action," *American Literary History* 1 (1989): 404-31.

59. Appiah, 77-78.

60. In "Against Theory," the unflaggingly abstract and formalistic quality of the examples used to clinch the argument provide the skeptical reader with an out, as it were, which appears to be foreclosed by the seeming historical density of the materials worked through in *The Gold Standard*.

61. On this point, see Jameson's brief illustrative discussion of the debate concerning the ethical nature of Second International socialism in *Postmodernism*, 205.

62. In this regard, it should be noted that a signal virtue of Jameson's brand of

Marxism for my discussion here is that it is capable of "out-totalizing" Michaels' critique, the better to help us to see that Liberalism is, in Jameson's terms, the "strategy of containment" at work in Michaels' project. See Jameson's *The Political Unconscious* (Ithaca: Cornell UP, 1981), esp. 53-54, 193-94, 210-19, and 266-70.

63. See Anderson, "Modernity and Revolution," 101.

64. Probably the most famous statement on this subject by Marx himself occurs at the end of the first section of *The Communist Manifesto,* where Marx tells us that "What the bourgeiosie, therefore, produces, above all, are its own grave-diggers."

65. Louis Althusser and Etienne Balibar, *Reading Capital,* trans. Ben Brewster (London: New Left Books, 1979), 300 n.24.

66. Althusser, *For Marx,* 217. The classic historical example of "overdetermination" in Althusser probably remains his discussion of Lenin and the relationship between the internal and international situation of Russia before the revolution (94ff.).

67. Althusser and Balibar, 104.

68. See their critique of the whole idea of "the social" in *Hegemony and Socialist Strategy* (London: New Left Books, 1985). For Marxist rejoinders, see Neil Larsen's introduction to his *Modernism and Hegemony* (Minneapolis: U of Minnesota P, 1990) and, for an extended critique, Ellen Meiksins Wood, *The Retreat from Class* (London: New Left Books, 1986).

69. The stakes in this recuperative move by Althusser would be underscored later by the work of Barry Hindess and Paul Hirst. See Kavanagh's discussion, 30ff.

70. Althusser and Balibar, 189. For a sophisticated and wide-ranging discussion of this concept and its moment in Marxist theory, see Jameson, *The Political Unconscious,* 24ff.

71. Kavanagh, 30.

72. For a useful overview of these issues within Structural Marxism, see Kavanagh. Jameson's discussion in *The Political Unconscious* (esp. 27-33) is of signal interest here as well. See also Lentricchia, *Criticism and Social Change,* 12-14.

73. Althusser, *Lenin and Philosophy,* 171. See also Kavanagh's discussion (27-28), which points out that Althusser's later *Essays in Self-Criticism* (1976) does not reject the science-ideology distinction, even as it admits to an earlier "theoreticism."

74. For representative critiques, see E. P. Thompson, *The Poverty of Theory* (New York: Monthly Review, 1980), and Sebastiano Timpanaro, *On Materialism,* trans. Lawrence Garner. For more sympathetic recent assessments of Althusser, see Michael Sprinker, *Imaginary Relations: Aesthetics and Ideology in the Theory of Historical Materialism* (London: New Left Books, 1987), and, in a different register, Ted Benton, *The Rise and Fall of Structural Marxism: Althusser and His Influence* (London: Routledge, 1984).

75. See Appiah, 77.

76. See Burke, *Attitudes Toward History,* 384-86.

The Great Mother Domesticated: Sexual Difference and Sexual Indifference in D. W. Griffith's *Intolerance*

Michael Rogin

A giant statue of the mother goddess, Ishtar, presides over *Intolerance* (1916), the movie D. W. Griffith made after his triumph with *The Birth of a Nation* (1915). Ishtar sits above Babylon's royal, interior court, but the court itself is constructed on so gigantic a scale that it diminishes the size of the goddess. Perhaps to establish Ishtar's larger-than-life proportions, Griffith's camera-man, Billy Bitzer, posed his nephew alongside her in a production still from the movie (fig. 1). Measuring "his six feet two inches against the towering height of Ishtar's goddess of love," Lou Bitzer is the same size as the sculpted grown man who sucks at Ishtar's breast; both males are dwarfed by the goddess' dimensions.*

Ishtar connects Griffith to the concern with originary female power current at the turn of the twentieth century. The appearance of the New Woman and

Elizabeth Abel, Ann Banfield, and Catherine Gallagher decisively influenced the argument of this paper and made invaluable comments on an earlier draft. Bertrand Augst showed Gary Wolf and me how to make the frame enlargements from *Intolerance* reproduced here, and, as always, Nancy Goldman and the Pacific Film Archive of the University Art Museum, University of California, Berkeley, were indispensable.

An earlier version of the article appeared in *Critical Inquiry* 15 (1989), 510-55; published by The University of Chicago. c 1989 by the University of Chicago.

*In the original version of this article, I mistakenly identified the man beneath Ishtar as Griffith himself, and I am extremely grateful to John Belton, Director of the Rutgers Program in Cinema Studies for the gentle way in which he corrected my error. The proper identification is in G. W. Bitzer, *Billy Bitzer, His Story* (New York: Farrar, Straus, Giroux, 1973), 155, from which the quote in the text is taken.

Suggestions in the original article, which took the photo as evidence for Griffith's (conscious and unconscious) intentions, are no longer tenable on their face, although Bitzer's autobiography contains no information concerning the circumstances under which the picture was taken, and whether or not it was at Griffith's behest. "The Great Mother Domesticated" was born from my seeing and puzzling over the meaning of this picture. In revising the first and last pages of the article, I have restored the image to its original place in the genesis of the text, using it to suggest an interpretation of *Intolerance* rather than as itself evidence either for that interpretation or for the director's intentions. I am grateful to Jim Breslin for helping me think about how to look at the picture with Griffith not in it.

Fig. 1: Ishtar, with Lou Bitzer. Courtesy of
the Museum of Modern Art/Film Stills Archive,
New York.

the attention to the matriarchal origins of culture were signs of a crisis in patriarchy. But the great mother could support masculine reassertion as well as
female power. Ishtar will help us see how.

Ishtar, the naked great mother, displays an unambiguous sexuality. But this
mother of stone shows no maternal interest either in the son at her breast or the
one at her feet, and the placement of the cameraman's nephew complicates her
sex even further. Far too small to be the goddess' lover, he more closely resembles her baby. The picture also suggests another possibility, however, by supplying the great mother with her missing phallus. Like Freud at about the same
time, the six-foot-two man between Ishtar's legs links the absent maternal
phallus to the baby.

This speculation may seem to have less to do with *Intolerance* than with
current critical fashion, and to deflect attention from Griffith's purposes and
from his movie. The director, however, had organized his two most important
previous films around the real and symbolic male organ. The castration of a

black rapist climaxes the original version of *The Birth of a Nation*. And a phallic mother dominates Griffith's first, feature-length movie, *Judith of Bethulia* (1913). The censorship controversy surrounding *Birth*, moreover, the controversy that produced *Intolerance*, posed Griffith (as he saw it) against emasculating female reformers. Attention to Griffith's film history will serve here to introduce *Intolerance* and clarify Ishtar's function in that movie. The subject of the phallic mother in *Intolerance*, far from being foreign to the founder of American film, emerges from Griffith's own preoccupations.

I.

Intolerance aside, Griffith made only one feature organized around a dominating female presence. In *Judith of Bethulia* he placed a sword in the widow's hand. The central scene of that movie, organized for a sexual climax between Judith and Holofernes, climaxes when she cuts off his head.

"To decapitate = to castrate," wrote Freud, and *Judith*, I have argued elsewhere, illustrates Freud's links between decapitation, castration, and fetishization. By cutting back and forth between Judith's body parts and the sword in the moments before the beheading, Griffith fetishized Judith's body. He substituted eroticized part-objects for the whole.[1] The fetish, according to Freud, reassured the male viewer that the woman had not lost her penis and that he, therefore, was not in danger of losing his. The fetish was a comforting substitute, wrote Freud, "not . . . for any chance penis, but for a particular quite special penis that had been extremely important in early childhood but was afterwards lost. . . . To put it plainly: the fetish is a substitute for the woman's (mother's) phallus which the little boy once believed in and does not wish to forego—we know why."[2]

The fetish defended against castration anxiety, according to Freud; decapitation evoked it. Freud himself used the Judith story to link decapitation to castration, and Griffith's camera made the same connection. Griffith cut from Judith's raised sword to Holofernes' head bouncing down a step to the king's headless body. The lone limp arm (one arm and not two) suggests at once the single phallic member and its absence. Holofernes is the headless body, Judith the woman with the penis.[3]

Film techniques—close-ups and cross-cutting—are peculiarly suited to display fetishization, since these techniques juxtapose part-objects. Film also depends on another mechanism central to Freud: scopophilia, the pleasure in looking. If fetishization denies sexual difference, however, according to writers in the Freudian tradition, voyeurism establishes it. The male viewer observes what the woman lacks; seeking woman as the bearer of the bleeding wound, his gaze subjugates female desire.[4] Holofernes, watching Judith and the other dancing girls, is the spectator's surrogate inside the film. But Holofernes is disempowered, not empowered, by his male gaze. As *Judith* illustrates the Freudian connections, it fails to reassure the male viewer. Judith relinquishes her sexual desire in order to dismember the man. Whether one sees the movie as denying sexual difference (through the fetish) or establishing it (through the gaze), Judith (contra Freud on the fetish) acquires the phallus from the king.

Judith also subverts Freud's account of female penis envy. The boy fears losing his penis, according to Freud, and the girl wants to acquire one. The boy must give up his mother to keep his penis; the girl must give up her wish for a penis and become a mother. Accepting the "fact" of her castration, the mature woman relinquishes her desire to take the man's penis; she wants it instead to give her a child. "The feminine situation is only established," wrote Freud, "if . . . a baby takes the place of a penis." That female acceptance of sexual difference inscribes heterosexuality and reproduces motherhood.[5]

The exchange of phallus for baby occurs in *Judith*, but it occurs in reverse, accentuating anxiety instead of dispelling it. Lillian Gish plays the domestic mother in *Judith*, as she would in *Intolerance*. Judith admires Gish's baby early in the film. The contrast between the two women points to a future foreclosed for the childless widow, and Judith replaces the baby with the sword. In addition to reversing Freud's normative, developmental direction, this substitution also supplies Judith with a baby of her own. That baby, issued forth from the hole in his torso, is Holofernes' head. A shawl covered Gish's baby so that only its head was visible. Judith wraps Holofernes' head in a shawl, places it in a basket, and carries it away. Like Freud's mature woman, Judith has given up her phallus for a baby. But she has first used Holofernes' sword to turn his phallus into her child.[6]

Links that established sexual difference for Freud are threats to male identity in *Judith*. Why do the founder of psychoanalysis and the founder of film share a symbolism of dismemberment and sexual difference and yet place the opposite valence on it? Why does Griffith ally himself with the black widow? Elsewhere I have located Griffith in the patriarchal crisis of the turn of the twentieth century. Judith, I argued, did not simply confirm male fears about female power; she turned them to rebellious advantage. Creating a modern art form against the conventions of the stage, Griffith made Judith his instrument for parricide. But the alliance of women and youth that was intended to liberate the sons threatened to empower the woman instead.

The New Woman—as figure of power or sexual desire—was taking over Griffith's screen in the films before *Birth*. *The Birth of a Nation*, I have argued, displaced female danger onto black men. The New Woman (from the book on which *Birth* was based and from Griffith's earlier films) is refeminized and made helpless. *Birth* took the sword from Judith and placed it in the hands of the Klan. Judith's sword saved the Jewish nation. The ritualized castration of a black rapist gave birth to America. Judith decapitated a patriarch. *Birth* returned the sword to the father's ghost, the white-sheeted shade who rode with the Klan.[7]

The Birth of a Nation established Griffith, in the words of *Photoplay* magazine, as "the founder of [the] modern motion picture."[8] Amidst anxieties about the power of movies to dissolve ethnic, class, and sexual boundaries, *Birth* created a respectable, mass audience for film. Transcending both the immigrant origins of the early one-reelers and the psychological disintegration threatening Griffith's films, *Birth* brought together in the motion picture palace northerners and southerners, immigrants and natives, cosmopolitans and provincials, workers and bosses, shopgirls and professional men and leisure-class women in a spectacle of national integration. *The Birth of a Nation,* Griffith claimed—in its unprecedented critical and mass audience appeal, in its unifying social content, and in its cinematic power to stand in for history—gave birth to the modern United States.[9]

But *The Birth of a Nation* also created a split in the forces of reform. Although most cultural guardians endorsed the movie, liberal humanitarians joined the NAACP in a campaign to stop the film from being shown. The conflict over *Birth* was not the only free speech fight being waged in the spring of 1915. "Films and Births and Censorship" ran a headline in the April issue of *Survey* magazine. The same people who believed *Birth* was not " 'objectionable from the standpoint of public morals' " supported the federal government's ban on Margaret Sanger's paper, *Woman Rebel,* and her indictment for sending obscene matter through the mail. The same vice crusaders who encouraged audiences to see *Birth* jailed Sanger's husband for disseminating information on birth control. *The Birth of a Nation,* concluded the National Board of (Film) Review, was historically accurate and educationally valuable. William Sanger, ruled the judge at his trial, was a " 'menace to society.' " As *Birth* swept the country in 1915 and 1916, advocates of birth control went to jail.[10]

Female reformers like Jane Addams who wanted *Birth* banned from the screen opposed censoring birth control information. *Survey* noticed this paradox without resolving it. But beneath the fights over free speech, in which players switched sides, lay a deeper consistency. Although Griffith published a pamphlet, *The Rise and Fall of Free Speech in America,* to attack the censorship of his movie, freedom of speech animated none of the adversaries in the battles over birth control and *Birth.* The two controversies turned, rather, on the control of female sexuality.[11]

Those opposing birth control and control of *Birth* wanted white men in charge of sex and procreation. *Birth of a Nation* warned against interracial sexuality, the alliance of white women and black men. Birth control, its opponents feared, substituted female pleasure for babies. And those who favored marriage for sexual gratification were compared " 'with the Negroes.' "[12] Birth control placed white women in charge of their own sexuality; it stood against the reproductive family and the paternal inheritance.

Birth raised the twin specters of the rapist and the mulatto to warn against interracial mixture. The eroticism generated by birth control, its opponents charged, would produce not mulatto babies but no babies at all. The mulatto and family limitation may thus seem like opposed dangers, the one implying proliferation and the other sterility, but they were united in racialist consciousness by the alleged infertility of the hybrid. They were united in the racial unconscious because both miscegenation and birth control broke the law that tied progeny to the legitimate father. Whether white women produced black chil-

The Three Fates

Fig. 2: Film censorship. From Griffith's *The Rise and Fall of Free Speech in America.*

dren, no children, or children only when they chose, they deprived the white man of his paternity.

Woman, according to Freud, needed to shift her desire from phallus to baby to accept her femininity. The controversies over birth control and *Birth,* by contrast, uncover the father's stake in sexual difference. Both supporters of birth control and critics of *Birth,* in their opponents' view, wanted to sever the connection between the paternal phallus and the baby. *Birth* and birth control, for those supporting the former and opposing the latter, offered alternative forms of castration. *Birth*'s castration restored power to white men. Birth control left the penis intact, but it performed a symbolic castration. Birth control advocates might defend their right to speak, but their speech, it was feared, destroyed the ground of the symbolic order itself in the words, laws, and conventions that sustained the name of the father.[13]

The very alliance of blacks and women imagined by opponents of birth control wanted to suppress *Birth.* In his cartoons for free speech, Griffith depicted the censor and female reformer as allies, who expropriate his control over castration and birth. The censor's scissors cut film in one cartoon (fig. 2) and attack a baby in another (fig. 3). Censors (who had already excised

INTOLERANCE

MARTYRED JOAN OF ARC

The development of the moving picture industry constitutes the birth of a new art.

The world-wide acceptance of moving pictures means the introduction of the most popular and far-reaching form of education the world has ever known.

In the future history will speak through the mouthpiece of the moving picture.

Fig. 3: Censorship as infanticide. From Griffith's
The Rise and Fall of Free Speech in America.

Birth's castration scene) threatened to take from the director his power to cut film. The threatened baby stood at once for the movie, *Birth*, for the "infant motion picture industry," and for the nation to which Griffith's movie had given birth.

Opponents of birth control shared Griffith's concern to save babies. They feared birth control would lead to a declining birth rate among Anglo-Saxons and to "race suicide." Germany had won "the warfare of the cradle" in the nineteenth century, complained Theodore Roosevelt; if Anglo-Saxon women did not produce more children, America would be swamped by the proliferating immigrants and blacks.[14] Castration, suggested the uncensored *Birth of a Nation*, was the alternative to race suicide. Whether they used birth control or the scissors of censorship, women must be prevented from either stopping or choosing the male seed. Censorship, like birth control, delivered over to women and blacks the power to make history and make life.

Intolerance resumes its time-honored mask.

Fig. 4: The mask of virtue. From Griffith's
*The Rise and Fall of Free Speech in
America.*

2.

The sexual politics of the two birth control controversies produced *Intolerance*. "Intolerance" appeared atop every page of Griffith's pamphlet defending free speech. Griffith was advertising his new film, whose enormous cost and length, and four parallel stories, made it the most grandiose project in the early decades of cinema.[15] The proclaimed subject of *Intolerance* was intolerance in world history, from ancient Babylon through the life of Christ and the Huguenot massacre to the modern metropolis. The actual subject of the movie was female sexuality. The theme of *Intolerance,* like the theme of the film about the Klan, was birth. As opponents of birth control were insisting on the political importance of producing children, Griffith shifted from political regeneration

Fig. 5: Babylon, the interior court.

to sexual reproduction. That shift in subject also entailed a shift in point of view, and both emerged from the controversies that generated the new movie. *Birth* wiped out female sexuality; its heroine, Lillian Gish, was an innocent, sexually menaced virgin. *Intolerance* celebrated the goddess of fertility and tied reproduction to heterosexual pleasure.

The Rise and Fall of Free Speech in America, Griffith's anticensorship pamphlet, made blacks into the sources rather than the victims of intolerance. "The malignant pygmy [of intolerance] has matured into a caliban," in Griffith's rhetoric, and behind the mask of virtue in one cartoon lurks the dark shadow of the censor (fig. 4).[16] *Intolerance* in no way retracted the racial politics of *Birth*. In the scenes of universal brotherhood that close both movies, no black faces appear. But *Intolerance* does depart, in a return of the repressed, from *Birth*'s aversion of female sexuality. Prince Belshazzar, an "apostle of tolerance and religious freedom," is introducing goddess worship into Babylon. He worships at "Ishtar's temple of love and laughter" (fig. 5). Intolerance is the hatred of heterosexual pleasure. *Intolerance* supports female desire.

In celebrating fertility, *Intolerance* stood with the opponents of birth control. Its sexual displays, however, not only reversed the direction of Griffith's previous movies but antagonized opponents of birth control as well. *Intolerance* undercut the oppositions in the birth control controversies in part, as we will shortly see, because Griffith was responding to the changing relationship of family life to urban public pleasures. He was also responding to the terms of *Birth*'s censorship struggle.

Radical supporters of birth control, like Margaret Sanger and Emma Goldman, placed birth control in the service of free love. No one attacked *Birth of a Nation*, however, by defending interracial sex, for the power of racial sexual taboos made such a position unthinkable. The white women and black men who favored censoring *Birth* did not demand the right to sleep together; they rather opposed those who discredited demands for racial equality by sexualizing them. Sanger led the fight for birth control in 1915, Addams the opposition to *Birth*. But women who opposed sexualizing racial issues were vulnerable to being labeled puritanical. The taboo on interracial sex, which Griffith exploited in *Birth,* now permitted him to depict female reformers as hostile not to racist hysteria but to sexual pleasure. He could present himself as repressing black sexual aggression, not female sexuality. Blacks, the promoters of intolerance in the free speech pamphlet, disappear from *Intolerance,* the movie. Their place is taken by sexually repressive American women, the NAACP's allies in the fight to censor *Birth.*

The Rise and Fall of Free Speech in America depicted censors as witch-burners, the filmmaker as their victim. The persecuted witches in *Intolerance* are women of the street in the modern story and supporters of the goddess cult in the ancient story. Juxtaposed against the female reformer — demanding control over sex in one of the battles behind *Intolerance* and over movies in the other — is the ancient goddess cult of love and fertility. And the effects of that cult subliminally reach into the modern city as well. By making female reformers rather than blacks its target, *Intolerance* opened up a space for urban, public, female-based pleasures. Attacking one negative stereotype of the feminist, the spinster, the movie sympathized with another, the libertine. Female sexual desire normally disturbed Griffith. Yet his deeper fear of female indifference to men, which, as we will see, *Intolerance* locates in lesbian alliances, opened up room for female heterosexuality. Faced with the withdrawal of women's interest in men, Griffith celebrated not simply women who satisfied male desire but women who needed men to satisfy themselves. The campaign against *Birth* had given Griffith back, and for the last time, the sympathy for modern urban women and workers that lay at the basis of his art.

3.

Although Ishtar rules Babylon, she appears in only one of the four stories that constitute *Intolerance*. Lillian Gish is supposed to preside over the movie as a whole. Echoing her brief appearance as mother in *Judith,* Gish rocks a cradle in *Intolerance*'s opening scene (fig. 6). "Out of the cradle endlessly rocking" reads the line from Whitman. Repeated to mark transitions between *Intolerance*'s four stories, the shot privileges motherhood as the source both of babies and of the movie. But the cradle actually serves to take Gish out of the body of the film. By marginalizing the domestic mother in the name of sanctifying her, Griffith made room for the love goddess and the spinster/lesbian.

The three female archetypes — Demeter, the great mother, Aphrodite, the love goddess, and Artemis, the celibate huntress and killer of men — appear in the concern with originary female power at the turn of the twentieth century. The first two are identified in J. J. Bachofen's *Mother Right*. Bachofen contrasted "the Aphroditean principle of carnal emancipation" to "the chaste, Demetrian character of a life grounded in strict order and morality." Artemis,

Fig. 6: Lillian Gish rocks the cradle.

so D. H. Lawrence believed, signaled the return of the woman under conditions of patriarchal repression. Griffith probably never heard of Bachofen or Lawrence, and *Intolerance*'s world history does not line up in every detail with theirs. But the similarities point to a shared male obsession with the feminine, a fascination that feared and celebrated women and wanted to make their powers available to men. The Aphroditean Ishtar, the Demetrian Gish, and Miss Jenkins the female reformer structure *Intolerance* and embed it in a larger cultural history.[17]

Ishtar is a fertility goddess, and she presides over marriage and reproduction. Love ends in marriage in Griffith's Babylon both in the shots of the marriage market and in the story of Belshazzar's wedding. Ishtar brings forth children, as the opponents of birth control wanted, and she is surely a mother on a pedestal. But she subverts Roosevelt's grounding of motherhood in male respect for " 'anything good and helpless.' "[18]

The goddess' size is not disjunctive with other representations of motherhood in turn-of-the-century America. Giant statues of women, most prominently the Statue of Liberty, are a feature of the period. Woman symbolizes the republic in the central building of the 1893 Chicago exposition. She holds aloft an upraised globe surmounted by an eagle and a staff with a liberty cap. Woman blesses the metropolis both in Chicago's White City and in Babylon. A ninety-foot suffragette graced the 1915 San Francisco World's Fair, and women with cornucopias symbolized female nurture throughout the country. Comparable maternal images would soon be produced to support American soldiers

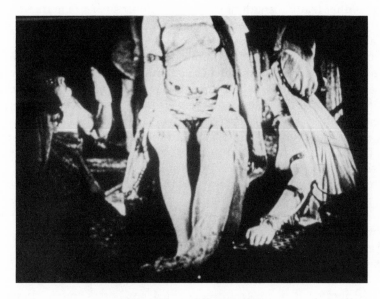

Fig. 7: The maternal matrix.

in World War I. A magazine advertisement for the Red Cross, for example, pictures a pietà demonstrating concern for suffering soldiers by "The Greatest Mother in the World," and in an advertisement for the YMCA the "great . . . mother love" of a *madonna della misericordia* enfolds her fighting sons.[19]

But these Christian icons, like the classical statues, contrast with the oriental Ishtar. Like Gish at the cradle, the classical and Christian representations desexualize motherhood. Ishtar resexualizes it. Ishtar was " 'the mother of mankind . . . who awakens passion,' " " 'the fruitful goddess of the earth,' " and " 'the patronness of love' " in the Bachofen-influenced sources on which Griffith drew for his portrait of Babylon.[20] Ishtar blesses marriage, to be sure, whereas Bachofen's Aphrodite presides over a promiscuous sexuality. But bacchanals and the marriage market insist on the sexual origins of motherhood. Ishtar also shatters the opposition between sex and female virginity. "Vestal virgins of love," nearly naked dancing girls, serve the goddess. Each virgin enters the temple of sacred fire (Gish reported in her autobiography)[21] and gives herself to a man who comes to worship there. Griffith shows viewers the sex of his vestal virgins, the source of their future motherhood. He moves his camera up the legs of one seated young woman, for example, to expose the blank, black space between her legs—the space Lou Bitzer will fill in the production still (compare figs. 1 and 7).

Babylon appeals to the prurient interest. By showing the fall of the city, Griffith may seem to disown responsibility for its revelry. According to that view, Griffith, counterposing the destruction of Babylon to the rescue of the endangered modern couple, stands with the family and against the city. The director's other feature-length films would support such an interpretation. But the cultural context for *Intolerance* and the images that dominate the film demand almost exactly the opposite reading.

Urban dangers threatened the family, in the Victorian view, and the home was a refuge from metropolitan life. Urban progressives, by contrast, promoted public activities to transform and strengthen private, conjugal existence. In creating Babylon, Griffith was responding to efforts to break down the opposition between the family and the modern metropolis. He intended a narrative not of binary opposition between the ancient and modern stories, the city and the home, but of incorporation and progress. But Griffith's images undercut the synthesis to which his narrative aspired. Unlike his progressive contemporaries, Griffith could not sublimate the city into the family. The city generated an excess of pleasure, weakening defenses and stimulating repression; pleasure gave way to impersonal, institutional control. Gish stands for the modern family, but Ishtar and the spinster/lesbian take over her movie. Ishtar is the archaic, whole mother. Instead of providing the ground for modern maternity, however, she is simply defeated. Her fall drains woman of heterosexuality and splits her in two. The domestic mother and the reformer supplant Ishtar. Although they battle one another they are also deeply allied, for both signify censorship not simply of male sexuality but of female desire for men as well. The good woman will take over Griffith's cinema in the decade after *Intolerance* and ultimately deprive him of his power to make films. *Intolerance*, Griffith's last stand for the modern metropolis and the New Woman, shows the sources and the limits of his modernism. We turn first to the progressive context for *Intolerance*, then to the interwoven four narratives, and look finally at the images themselves.

4.

The modern metropolis and the domestic mother were born together, as opposite sides of the same coin. The confined privacy of the home, in Laura Mulvey's formulation, protected against the chaotic crowd in the street. Severing reproduction from female sexual pleasure, as Thomas Laqueur has shown, Victorians separated biological and cultural maternity within the house from barren sexual excitement outside. But the urban world of entertainment and leisure posed threats to the middle-class family from below and from above. The lower-class city-by-night and the leisure-class, male homosocial tavern both threatened the ties that bound together the middle-class husband and wife.[22]

Popular entertainments such as the pre-Griffith one-reelers, originating on the margins of society, threatened the sanctuary of the home. But domestic melodrama domesticated the city-by-night, first in English theater and then in Griffith's one-reelers, by making the subject of popular entertainment into the danger to the home. Although the metropolis in domestic melodrama justified the family by threatening it, melodrama thereby maintained the family/city opposition. The places of popular, working-class entertainment, moreover, proved dangerously seductive to the middle class. The family triumphed in melodrama, but the city retained its subversive potential.

The middle-class family was under siege from upper-class forms of entertainment as well. Leisure-class culture separated the sexes, leaving women in charge of society and men seeking pleasure outside the home. Respectable men consorted with prostitutes; eating and drinking in taverns, they abandoned their children and wives.[23]

Babylonian prostitution and orgies of food and drink associate the ancient city with modern, leisure-class decadence. *Intolerance*'s modern story, in which the urban underworld threatens the family, had roots in domestic melodrama. But the movie was also part of the post-Victorian effort to bring the family and urban nightlife together. Babylon signified sensual excess and tyranny in the nineteenth-century imagination; it was the city as evil. The 1880s London campaign against child prostitution, for example, labeled the British capital the "modern Babylon." Vice crusaders were invoking "Babylon, the Great, the Mother of Harlots and of the Abominations of the Earth" from the Book of Revelation. The Jews were enslaved in Babylon, but though *Judith of Bethulia* took the side of the Jews against the invading Assyrians, *Intolerance* omits the Babylonian captivity. Griffith's invading Cyrus may "war on vice" like the purity crusaders, but he liberates no Jews, for *Intolerance* stands against the war on vice and with Babylonian pleasure. Griffith presented urban public entertainment not as a threat to conjugal happiness but as an alternative to the restrictive Victorian family.[24]

As progressives saw it, the repressive family generated its opposite, the disruptive city-by-night. Progressives in the new helping professions would mediate between the family and the city. They would organize leisure and drain it of its disruptive potential by sponsoring such institutions as urban parks and planned recreation, the school, the settlement house, the reform state, and the motion picture palace itself. *Intolerance* evoked one of these new institutions in particular: the urban cabaret. Ishtar, the ancient goddess of pleasure, blesses modern cabaret culture.[25]

Cabaret culture strengthened the family by bringing the sexes back together in arenas that offered a good time. The cabaret promised to end the opposition between children and the family on the one hand, and sexual gratification on the other, the opposition enshrined in the birth-control struggle. Lewis Erenberg writes,

> By permitting informal entertainments for respectable women, the cabaret marked a new departure in relations between the sexes and challenged the Victorian confinements that had limited the behavior of both men and women. In an open environment, good women could mix promiscuously with people of unspecified moral character from whom they formerly had been rigidly separated. By opening up an urban, public area, the café opened up respectable culture to a wider, more spontaneous world.[26]

The public dance craze of 1915-16, contemporaneous with the filming and release of *Intolerance*, insured the success of the cabaret. Dancing made cabarets profitable, transforming urban nightlife from all-male feats of drinking and eating to heterosexual performance. Public dancing offered a mixture of immediacy and distancing. Audiences observed a show whose dancing stars became celebrities; at the same time, members of the audience also danced, breaking down the audience/performer distinction. A comparable mixture of immediacy and observation characterized the progressive style in journalism, as genteel readers were made to feel present at behind-the-scenes revelations of real life. Movies also drew members of the mass audience into an immediate experience where they participated as observers. With its scenes of dancing and urban entertainment, *Intolerance* mirrored the audience participation in cabarets.[27]

Babylon may have been exotic in progressive America, but new styles of dress brought the foreign into restaurant, cabaret, and boudoir. "Back to Babylon for New Fashions" headlined *Photoplay* in April 1917. "When 'Intolerance' brought us Babylonian modes, straightway the designers took notice," announced the magazine. Fashion designers were making "the filmed ladies of Belshazzar's court" into "the real inspiration of the day."[28] *Intolerance* fed a trend that it did not originate. Already in 1914 the New York Follies Marigny had announced an Arabian Night in its series of special balls. "When I turn into Broadway by night and am bathed in its Babylonic radiance," wrote an anonymous contributor to *Atlantic,* "I want to shout with joy, it is so gay and beautiful."[29]

Two displacements made possible this celebration of urban pleasure: the extrusion of class conflict and the excision of the Negro origins of the cabaret. *Intolerance* registers them both, the first by what the screen displays and the second by what it hides. Working-class struggles disrupted urban America at the turn of the twentieth century. The metropolis threatened the middle-class family not only in pleasure-by-night but also in work-by-day. Class conflict at the point of production placed the middle class under siege, threatening the boundaries that insulated the home from the struggle for existence. (The 1894 Pullman strike, for example, kept Jane Addams' ailing sister from being reached by her husband and children before she died.)[30] Like urban nightlife, class conflict corrupted the work ethic and invaded the family.

The cabaret shifted value not only from the restrictive, moralistic family to scenes of public entertainment but also from the conflicted realm of work to what *Billboard* magazine called the leisure-time "eager pursuit of pleasure."[31] *Intolerance* domesticated leisure; and it removed class conflict from the open metropolitan present to the confined rural past.

A strike sets in motion *Intolerance*'s modern story. Although a title places us in a midwestern city, we are shown a pastoral scene. From a traditional perspective it was radical to allow class conflict into the American countryside. Such Griffith one-reelers as "The New York Hat" and "The Painted Lady," however, had already depicted a repressive, rural familial environment; the city (as in "The Musketeer of the Slums") was a liberating alternative. The strike in *Intolerance* perpetuates that opposition. The patriarchal factory owner, Jenkins, lines up with familial forces of repression. Although "the boy" (Bobby Harron) loses his father in the strike, that tragedy frees him to go to Chicago.

The most important industrial conflicts of the late nineteenth century, the Haymarket riot and the Pullman strike, took place in Chicago. Griffith, however, derived his industrial violence from the Ludlow massacre—the 1915 Colorado mining strike in which company militia killed strikers and their families—and not from an urban labor dispute. John D. Rockefeller, who controlled the Colorado Fuel and Iron Company, was the model for Jenkins. Ludlow was contemporary with *Intolerance;* the struggle and its investigation by the U.S. Commission on Industrial Relations dominated newspaper headlines in the months prior to the first filming of the modern story.[32] But by placing his strike in the rural past (the past symbolically, since the countryside stood for an older America, and the past in the movie's chronology), Griffith freed Chicago to stand for a progressive future.

The war between capital and labor threatened middle-class America. But Griffith's workers are bowed down even before their strike (see fig. 8), and the director sustained sympathy for the working class by depicting its defeat. He would apply that technique of threat containment, successful at the beginning of the film, to Babylonian sexuality. But Griffith wanted to shift from work to pleasure, to sublimate female sexuality and not simply displace it. As the conjunction of sympathy with defeat slid from working-class victims to the fall of Babylon, it would ultimately undo Griffith's project.

The strike, removed to the countryside, is shown, but the urban blacks who originated cabaret culture entirely disappear from the film. These black entertainers replaced the minstrel show, where whites in blackface had created the first form of American mass culture. The original cabarets retrieved the role of performer from whites playing blacks. But that returned sexual self-definition to black men and women, taking it from the white men who gained access to a fantasized black sexuality by putting it on. The urban New Negro in the first cabarets was a sexually explicit entertainer. *Birth of a Nation,* to be sure, had made its whites in blackface libidinal, but only to invent a black sexual menace. *Birth* climaxed and displaced minstrelsy by turning its blackface performers into New Negroes. The movie located the New Negro in the Reconstruction South, where he did not exist, demonized him as a rapist, and punished him. *Intolerance* eliminated New Negroes entirely from the culture they had brought into being.[33]

This excision followed the lead of the cabarets themselves. "Coon songs" featuring sexually active blacks peaked in the 1910s; by 1915 white performers like Sophie Tucker were replacing the blacks who had influenced them.[34] At the same time that whites took over the forms of cabaret entertainment developed by blacks, Griffith eliminated blacks from the modern city. He moved them to his ancient story instead, where "Ethiopians" briefly appear as members of Cyrus' invading army. The blacks play rural primitives, threatening the cosmopolitan culture that was actually being expropriated from them.

Urban nightlife links *Intolerance*'s modern and ancient stories, the two ep-

Fig. 8: Factory workers. Courtesy of the Museum of Modern Art/Film Stills Archive, New York.

isodes that dominate the film as a whole. Griffith conceived the modern story first and began filming it as a separate movie, "The Mother and the Law." The massive scale and success of *Birth,* however, and the attacks leveled against that film, made "The Mother and the Law" an anticlimax. The director reconceived the plot as one of four stories that would cover world history and that his theme and camera technique would unify.[35] The theme of "The Mother and the Law"—the husband faces execution for a crime he did not commit; the wife loses her baby—may seem to have nothing to do with Ishtar. But the metropolis spawns the romance between the young couple, and Ishtar's modern female antagonists generate the family tragedy.

"The dear one" (Mae Marsh) and the boy are both victims of the strike, but they only meet once the workers' defeat drives them into the city. The boy becomes an urban sophisticate under the tutelage of a gangster. The dear one attracts him by imitating the dress and walk of a woman of the streets. From one perspective Jenkins is the bad father, contrasted to the good but helpless fathers in the family. The strike Jenkins provokes kills the boy's father and sends the girl's to die in the city. But the movie also lines up all the fathers on one side of a generational conflict. The fathers stand for restriction, and the new urban family arises from the death of the old.

Prostrated by the first kiss between the boy and the dear one, her father dies soon after. He cannot adjust to the new conditions of urban life, a title announces, but his death offers opportunity as well as danger. The dear one goes out with the boy; when he tries to force his way into her apartment, she bars the door. Her resistance elicits a proposal of marriage, which replaces forced entry with domesticity. The marriage proposal, however, does not eradicate sex. In a shot sequence that deliberately eroticizes the break-in, the dear one opens her door just enough for the boy to place his head in the slit and kiss her (figs. 9-11).

The dear one and the boy bring street excitement into their room. But their new home will be menaced by the conflict between pleasure-seeking women and the forces of repression, the conflict that dominates both the ancient and modern stories. Griffith juxtaposes Babylon's "vestal virgins of love" to the "vestal virgins of uplift" in modern America. These menacing female reformers, the women who attacked *Birth,* close the public places of pleasure, the saloons and dance halls (and, by implication, the motion picture palace as well). A fine shot of ballroom dancing among the rich, with remarkable depth of field, introduces the modern story. The rich have their pleasures; workers dance in cafés. But working-class pleasure antagonizes the factory owner, Jenkins, and his "unmarried sister." Jenkins is a lonely, dried-up old man; he turns away from the working-class women who flirt with him in the street, retreats behind his desk, and gives his sister the money for reform.

Who are the women who tantalize Jenkins? Single working women in early twentieth-century New York (the city where Griffith made his one-reelers in the years before *Birth* and *Intolerance*) spent their evenings on the streets. They frequented public dance halls and other popular amusements. Seeking adventures with male companions, young women mixed easily with strangers. Their lan-

Figs. 9-11: The erotic source of
modern marriage.

guage and behavior broke down the traditional, rural distinction between the loose woman and the good girl. The exchange of sexual favors for gifts, meals, and entertainment was part of this working-class, urban night life; but although vice crusaders stigmatized working girls as loose women, and sought to raise the age of sexual consent to control female independence, the women of the streets depicted at the beginning of *Intolerance* are not professional prostitutes.[36]

The law creates prostitutes in *Intolerance* by stamping out public entertainment. The prohibition of public drinking and dancing drives pleasure underground. Instead of going to dances, men pick up prostitutes; instead of frequenting saloons for drinks, each person distills his own. While men look on, women are rounded up and taken off to jail. Prostitution, Griffith's contemporaries believed, originated with the sacred Babylonian fertility rites, and brothels in urban America contributed to the "Modern Babylon." But since Babylonian girls earned their dowries by prostitution, according to Charlotte Perkins Gilman, they were learning to be prostitutes and wives at the same time. Gilman deplored the Babylonian origins of modern marriage; Griffith celebrated it. The vestal virgins of love who display themselves for male pleasure are the ancestors of the modern women of the streets. Griffith in both the ancient and the modern stories places himself on the side of these women. Social purity reformers opposed birth control because, by separating sex from reproduction, it would make all women into prostitutes. *Intolerance,* by contrast, derived the modern family from female sexual availability.[37]

The high priest of Babylon opposes goddess worship. He secretly allies himself with Cyrus and the invading Persians. The bearded Cyrus resembles Holofernes. Like Holofernes and like Jenkins and the Babylonian high priest, Cyrus is a patriarchal villain. Since he is not weakened, as Holofernes is, by sexual ambiguity and desire, he is not in the power of women. And female power is even more menacing than patriarchy. The truly sinister figures in *Intolerance* are Miss Jenkins and her spinster allies. Instead of depicting sympathy for the Ludlow workers by such female reformers as Addams and Florence Harriman,[38] Griffith makes their hardheartedness cause the strike, as they raise the money to stamp out leisure-time pleasure by convincing Jenkins to cut wages at work.

"When women cease to attract men they often turn to reform," explains a title. The camera contrasts the misshapen "vestal virgins of uplift" to the pleasure-loving women of the streets. The Committee of Seven that orchestrates reform is composed entirely of women. Like the "Female Army" of suffragettes condemned in Walter Heape's *Sex Antagonism* (1913), Griffith's "spinsters" have "usurped" maternal authority.[39] But Griffith opposes his reformers not simply to Victorian mothers but to pleasure-seeking young women as well. He cuts from the virgins of uplift in the modern story to the woman taken in adultery in the movie's third story, the life of Christ. Christ protects the adulteress from those who want to stone her. Cut to the modern prostitutes being taken off to jail. Even in the schematic Christ episode, which contains but five brief scenes, Griffith celebrates domesticity (the marriage at Cana and "suffer the little children") and condemns intolerance of female desire.

Catherine de Medici orchestrates the Huguenot massacre in *Intolerance*'s fourth story, where the theme of religious intolerance also dissolves into sexual discontent. Although the Huguenot massacre supposedly has religious sources, religion is not visible on the screen. Catherine's hostility to romance between Protestant and Catholic derives from sexual perversion, not religious conviction; she opposes not Protestants but heterosexual love. Catherine, a large, mustachioed, masculine woman, is surrounded by effeminate courtiers. She controls "the heir to the throne, the effeminate Monsieur le France." At the massacre's climax Catherine's troops slaughter "bright eyes" and her betrothed.

Sexually punishing women — Catherine de Medici and Miss Jenkins — stand not just against pleasure but against the family as well. Urban nightlife made female sexual pleasure support the family. Catherine and Miss Jenkins, by contrast, embody a female invasiveness freed from masculine control. Female heterosexuality in *Intolerance,* as Bachofen had also argued, binds women to men. In the feminist debate of the early twentieth century, repeated today, over whether free (heterosexual) love liberates or entraps women, Griffith endorses entrapment.

Judith of Bethulia dismembered a king by feigning sexual desire, and flickers of genuine passion for Holofernes threatened her resolve. Ishtar, the mother goddess, blesses heterosexual love. Unlike Judith, moreover, Ishtar is not a human actor but a statue. The actual women with power in *Intolerance,* Catherine de Medici and Miss Jenkins, are demons. Two sympathetic women do take independent initiative in the film. One is the Babylonian mountain girl; the other is "the friendless one," the gangster's girlfriend in the modern story. Both are defeated. The mountain girl's ride to rescue Babylon fails to save the city and the friendless one will be incarcerated for shooting the gangster. Both women are allowed initiative not simply because they fail but also because their desire subordinates them to men. The mountain girl tells the priest's underling to "put away the garments of a female man. I shall love none but a soldier." She acts from her worship of Belshazzar, just as her modern counterpart is in thrall to the gangster. Alone in the city, the friendless one slips from working-class girl into kept woman. She gives herself to "the musketeer of the slums" and remains his sexual slave until she kills him. (A statue of a naked woman grasping a pillar appears on the screen after the friendless one and the gangster become lovers.)

Women without men threaten the family, the family to which the city has given birth. The underworld is part of the city, to be sure, and Griffith twins it with female reformers as opposing threats to the home. The musketeer frames the boy to punish him for leaving the gang, consigning him to the grid of prison and asylum that will also incarcerate his baby. But the threatened family, as we have seen, owes its existence to the underworld. Griffith counterposed the family to the city in his other features, virtue to sexuality. Instead of glorifying the family, however, that contrast made it claustrophobic and fragile. *Intolerance* derived the family from urban, sexual opportunities to give it a stronger foundation.

But Griffith did not believe in the synthesis of family, metropolis, and sexual pleasure to which his movie aspired; he could not imagine a sexually powerful man within the domesticated interior. Domestic melodrama, saving the family at the expense of its erotic urban roots, takes over the form and content of *Intolerance*. For when the boy relinquishes his gun to the musketeer, in order to marry the girl, he surrenders his manly power. Once in the family, the boy is innocent victim, not active protagonist. After the gangster assaults the dear one and is shot by the friendless one, police arrest the husband for murder. As he is feminized, the friendless one plays the role of Judith, the female avenger.[40]

Female reformers take the dear one's baby away, and the law condemns the boy to hang. Griffith has retreated to familiar thematic and technical ground. He cuts from preparations for the hanging to the ride of the friendless one to stop it. He intercuts a series of rides to the rescue in the modern story with the ride of the Persians against Babylon and with the mountain girl's ride to warn the city. The Huguenot massacre and the road to Calvary also appear. Babylon is destroyed, the modern family is reunited, and the friendless one faces prison for playing Judith. But *Birth* had already offered, in a more unified and powerful form, the climax through parallel montage. The four stories add grandiosity rather than cinematic or social complexity.

Melodrama subsumes the world in "an underlying manichaeanism," writes Peter Brooks, "putting us in touch with the conflict of good and evil played out under the surface of things."[41] Through "heightened dramatic utterance," melodrama supplies "grandiose moral terms" to everyday, domestic life.[42] Since melodrama relies on visual signs and intensified, dreamlike states, it is peculiarly suited to silent film. "The indulgence of strong emotionalism; moral polarization and schematization; extreme states of being, situations, actions; overt villainy, persecution of the good, and final reward of virtue; . . . high emotionalism and stark ethical conflict"[43] — these all characterize *Intolerance* and reach their height in the climax. But since melodrama relies on the "logic of the excluded middle," it can only counterpose opposites and not create something new. As in *Intolerance*'s climax, melodrama offers a return to innocence instead, "the misprision and recognition of virtue."[44] But Griffith's ride to rescue innocence defeats the director's project, for the failure to give birth to new authority leaves behind the splits — between family and city, virtue and pleasure, phallus and female body — that it was the movie's purpose to overcome.

Parallel montage, the juxtaposition of contrasting shots, is the film technique most appropriate to melodrama; Griffith falls back on it to bring his movie to an end. But against the melodrama that drives the narrative forward to its oedipal conclusion in the home stand the female icons Ishtar and Artemis. The two sets of opposed images over which they preside resist reduction to melodrama and give *Intolerance* its moments of power.[45]

One set of images — nightmare distortions, anticipating German expressionist cinema — depicts modern institutional space. The other set — crowd

Fig. 12: Jenkins at his desk.

scenes and dynamic montage—anticipate Soviet constructivism.[46] Griffith
brings fresh excitement to the populated crowd scenes of strikers, dancers, and
revellers. Like the nightmare, institutional visions that are their negative, these
scenes embody the movie's originality, for they are where Griffith brings something new into being. But the powerful filmic images undercut the narrative
progress that the movie's ideology intends. Griffith wanted to counterpose reform institutions to the family and to sublimate urban public pleasures into
domestic happiness. But reform and the family alike survive urban, public defeat. Since the family cannot contain, either thematically or visually, the forces
that pull against it, the visual power of *Intolerance* turns Griffith's domestic
melodrama upside down.

Postwar German filmmakers borrowed the moving camera from *Intolerance*
in the service of visual disorientation. They may have been influenced by the movie's spatial distortions and depersonalized figures as well. *Intolerance*'s expressionist scenes open up into large, empty, misshapen spaces that dwarf the humans
within. Like other modern artists, Griffith gives power in these shots not to the
figure but to the ground. A long shot shows Jenkins alone behind his desk (fig. 12),
a tiny figure stranded, as Robert Sklar puts it, in a sea of floor space.[47] Counterposed to this "positive negative space," in Stephen Kern's term,[48] are crowds of
multiplied, uniform figures. A shot of the blank, empty prison exterior when the
boy enters jail is followed by the sight of the milling mass of anonymous, replicated prisoners inside (fig. 13). The reproducibility of these figures is meant to con-
demn impersonal institutions. But the motion picture itself, with its reproducible
images, stands implicitly alongside them.

Fig. 13: The boy in prison.

Three vestal virgins of uplift, in the most terrifying expressionist scenes, invade the dear one's room. These women, who dress and move alike, constitute (in Henry Adams' words on the death of his sister) "a vision of pantomime with a mechanical motion" (figs. 14-16). They link the bad mother to the machine.[49] The three women examine the dear one's baby on their first invasion; on their second they knock down the mother, seize the baby, and take it away. (Judith turned Holofernes' head into a baby; the vestal virgins of virtue appropriate the mother's baby for themselves.) Griffith next shows "the Jenkins foundation," a modern, impersonal building. Deep corridors accentuate the large, empty anteroom in the foreground. Tiny, robotlike figures move through the halls (fig. 17). These miniaturized, mechanical women scurrying through empty space accentuate (by contrast) the nurturing function of Ishtar's size. The goddess fills the space left blank by the absent, negative, institutional mother.

The institutional spaces, however, are not completely empty. Barred cribs in which babies lie unattended line the wall of the nursery. Uniformed female attendants ignore the babies to dance with one another while a lone man looks on (fig. 18). The long-angled shot, which shrinks and depersonalizes the figures, accentuates the disturbing effect of women dancing with women. This scene contrasts to the female dancing done with and for men in lively, populated dance halls. Griffith links imprisoning institutional walls to women who neglect babies and men. The walled institutions define the bad mother. Cut from the dancing nurses to the Huguenot massacre, presided over by a gloating Catherine.

Catherine displays masculinity by dominating weak men in Griffith's de-

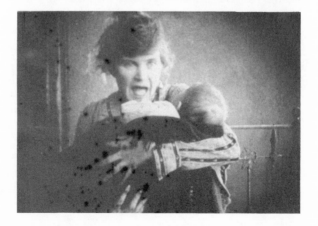

Figs. 14-16: The invasion of female reformers.

Fig. 17: The Jenkins foundation.

piction of degenerate court life. Griffith's court scenes are fantasy, but they accurately indicate that the male nightmare of female erotic bonding postdates the aristocratic age. Feudal sexual disarray implies male homosexuality. The director's modern lesbians form a community of women. Women also dance with women in Griffith's *True Heart Susie* (1919) to symbolize hostility to the family. But that scene lacks the cinematic and social interest of its counterpart in *Intolerance*. By linking lesbian sexuality to modern institutions, *Intolerance* displays a historically situated male nightmare. Artemis reappears in the modern city as a maiden in uniform.[50]

Just as Griffith's celebration of Ishtar responded to progressive hopes for the family, so his demonization of lesbians made visible contemporary fears. The concept of lesbian identity, Carroll Smith-Rosenberg and Ann Ferguson have argued, emerged in the early twentieth century partly as a response to a new medical discourse of deviance and partly as the self-definition of women in urban subcultures. By weakening the patriarchal power of fathers and husbands, industrial capitalism increased the life chances of women—in wage labor; in urban boarding houses where unmarried women lived without parental supervision; and on the streets and in public places of entertainment. The New Woman in these settings posed the threat not simply of free love and economic autonomy but also of erotic female bonding.[51]

The threat of the New Woman took different forms in progressive America—free, heterosexual or bisexual love in which Aphrodite was faithful to no one man; female independence, where women lived alone or with others of their sex; and self-proclaimed lesbian identity. Griffith was using the mannish lesbian to demonize all female autonomy.

On the one hand Griffith discredited female independence by (homo)sexualizing it. On the other hand, however, the fear of lesbianism expressed anxiety

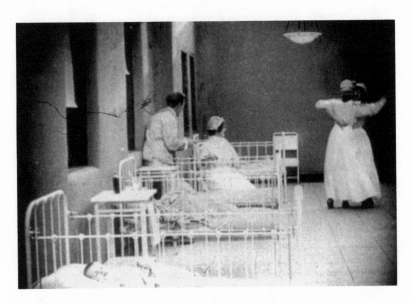

Fig. 18: Institutionalized child care.

about the sexual turn of women away from men. Late nineteenth-century men had attacked unnatural mothers, who favored birth control and abortion. By the progressive period the New Woman was demonized not just for rejecting motherhood but for rejecting men. Roosevelt had warned against race suicide in 1902 to attack the female college graduates who refused to marry and reproduce. Within a decade such women were labeled lesbians. First-generation New Women like Addams and Gilman had replaced personal with social mothering. The next generation, emerging as Griffith filmed *Intolerance*, made claims for homosexual and not just homosocial satisfaction. Women cross-dressed and danced together in the nineteenth-century homosocial female world before lesbianism was invented. By the progressive period such behavior was pathological from one point of view, a self-proclaimed statement of new sexual identity from another.[52]

The companionate family responded to the threat that women would abandon the home, the threat for which lesbianism stood. By contrast to the Victorian family, the ideology of companionate marriage joined sexuality to domesticity. But by defining the husband as breadwinner and the wife as nurturant and expressive, the companionate family reinscribed gender difference against the lesbian threat. A sexuality tied to fertility would recontain women inside the family.

Intolerance made visible the lesbian threat to the family. Worse yet, it located the danger in the very progressive institutions that were supposed to restore the family. The helping professions—teaching, social work, urban planning—provided careers for progressive women. Reformers saw the public sector and the family in relations of mutual superintendence and support. But the helping professions also provided space for communities of women, working and even (as in Addams' Hull House) living together. Describing such female institutions in turn-of-the-century England, Martha Vicinus writes, "The very idea of an effective women's community was frightening. It implied that women could be self-sufficient and that men were dispensable."[53] Griffith's modern city thus generated two prognoses: heterosexual libido domesticated by public institutions and recontained within the family, or a lesbian alliance of women and the state against the family. Progressive optimists looked forward to the first possibility. They imagined reform women in the helping professions using the state to foster domesticity. *Intolerance* denounced the helping professions for undermining the family; the director wanted to replace female reformers with motion pictures. But in spite of Griffith's wishes, *Intolerance* placed the sexual family not in the American future but in the destroyed, Babylonian past.[54]

Babylon is destroyed, in Griffith's narrative, as domestic melodrama reunites the family against the lesbian menace. The Babylonians celebrate their apparent victory over Cyrus with a bacchanal; it exposes them to Persian invasion. Revelers delay the mountain girl, and her ride to the rescue fails to save the city. The friendless one, by contrast, reaches the governor with her confession before the three hangmen cut the rope that would drop the boy to his death. (Their rehearsal is shown.) Griffith multiplies identical hangmen in his final image of murderous state power (figs. 19-21. Compare the cutting of the rope in this image with the cutting of film in Griffith's attack on state censorship, fig. 2). The three women barely visible in the background as Gish rocks the cradle (fig. 6) move forward to join her in the movie's final shot (fig. 22). The three vestal virgins of uplift who took the dear one's baby away are now domesticated; like Gish, they revolve around the cradle. A priest, helpless to save the boy from the state, was able only to hear his confession. The new institution for the urban masses, the motion picture, replaces the church as the agent of salvation. Film alone can rescue the family from the movies' progressive institutional competitors.

But Griffith's images undercut his domestic restoration. Only the populated, constructivist images have the power to counteract the expressionist ones. This side of *Intolerance*—the active crowds, short shots, and dynamic montage—gave birth to Soviet cinema. Sergey Eisenstein and V. I. Pudovkin were decisively influenced by the film, and the latter abandoned chemistry for moviemaking after he saw it. Lenin himself arranged to have *Intolerance* shown throughout Russia, where it was exhibited for a decade; the movie enjoyed its greatest success in the Soviet Union.[55] But Griffith's revolutionary film technique worked against his narrative intentions. Images that celebrated disorder inverted the cinematic values of *Birth of a Nation*. That reversal might merely have signified a shift in the sources of domesticity between the two movies, from cloistered female victimization to public female pleasure. The populated scenes are tied, however, not to apotheosis but to defeat.

Birth glorified the organized Klan mass and demonized the disorderly Ne-

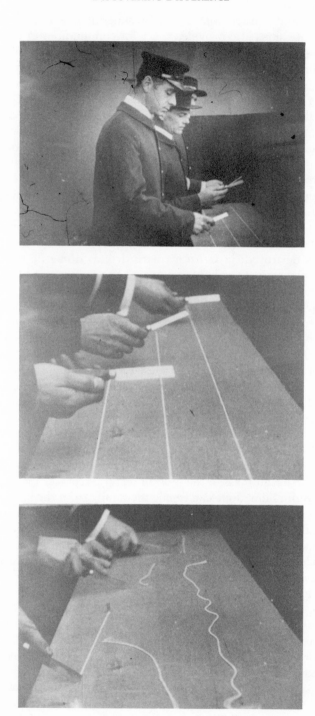

Figs. 19-21: Rehearsal for the execution.

Fig. 22: The domestication of the fates.

gro mob. *Intolerance* reverses that choice. It first does so in the strike scene early in the film. The mob of strikers resembles *Birth*'s Negroes and the militia lines up like the Klan, but Griffith has switched sides. His camera, instead of celebrating the line of force as in *Birth,* creates a classic example of dynamic montage. Griffith, as Sklar has said, cuts back and forth in shorter and shorter shots from the strikers (fig. 23), to their anxious families, to Jenkins isolated at his desk (fig. 12), to the militia (fig. 24). Jenkins, alone in empty space, gives the order to clear his property. The militia fires on the strikers, in the scene's culmination, and the camera pans over open space as the workers retreat.[56]

The heavily populated spaces in the shots of this scene, like the technique of montage itself, offer more than the eye can see. Griffith displays the industrial conflict in different pieces and from different angles, shattering the illusion of a single, all-encompassing, observer's perspective. Dynamic montage democratizes and pluralizes point of view, decapitating the classic omniscient narrator. At the same time, by throwing images on the screen, dynamic montage puts the director and not the democratic mass in charge. Disorder and multiplicity place the audience in the power of the man behind the camera, for he determines what viewers see. The method of the scene undercuts its message, locating viewers in the relation to the camera that strikers are to the factory owner.[57]

Just as dynamic montage overwhelms the individual viewer, so it does not encourage individual characters to develop and breathe. The technique creates sympathy for people as a mass rather than for individual, working-class lives. Joined with expressionist cinema, therefore, montage techniques place pressure on the traditional, autonomous subject, the individual that progressive reforms

Fig. 23: The strikers.

hoped to rescue. Expressionist images turn inward, arousing anxiety about a future for man alone; the strike scene celebrates the crowd.

Expressionist cinema dwelt on illness, according to Eisenstein; dynamic montage created something new. Eisenstein aligned the revolutionary film technique with social revolution. Dynamic montage signifies the director's power in *Intolerance,* but it registers the slaughter of the crowd.[58]

Griffith also used dynamic montage to display Babylon's interior court. He celebrated the city by moving his camera freely around it (mounting an elevator on a railroad car to sweep the camera up and over the city walls, the first crane shot in movie history), and by juxtaposing different parts of the urban landscape. *Intolerance* and *Judith,* the two films set in ancient cities and presided over by a woman, are the only two Griffith films to employ dynamic montage. The conjunction of woman and the city in these films freed Griffith from traditional, rural, patriarchal constraints. If the lesbian lies behind Griffith's expressionism, Ishtar presides over his dynamic montage. But the city that lies open before Griffith's camera (fig. 5) is equally vulnerable to Cyrus. We see Babylon from the inside only after the illusion of victory has relaxed the city's guard. The opening of the populated bacchanalian spaces foreshadows a city open to invasion.[59]

The Persian/Babylonian battle at the end of the film repeats the strike scene at the beginning. Massed Persians, shown in silhouette and head-on, echo the ride of the Klan. Griffith cuts from the Persians in directed, forceful movement to seminude, exhausted dancing girls. Babylonian revelry has left the city defenseless, but though there are traces of *Birth*'s black mob in the character of

Fig. 24: The militia.

the Babylonian crowd, our sympathies now lie with the city. Massed uniformed figures were heroic in *Birth*. Now, as the militia at the beginning of *Intolerance* or the Persians at the end, as the multiplied vestal virgins of uplift or the uniformed prisoners in jail, they are destructive of urban pleasure.

Birth celebrated the sword of castration that reestablished white male power. Cyrus repossesses that sword, " 'the most potent weapon forged in the flame of Intolerance.' " " 'Seize now the flaming sword,' " Ishtar's priests exhort her, but " ' "the warlike Ishtar" ' " (in one of Griffith's sources)[60] fails to follow in Judith's footsteps and decapitate the king. The most prominent sword in *Intolerance* is the one the camera dwells on as it runs through the Huguenot ingenue.

The intended moral of *Intolerance* is that Aphrodite the sexual matriarch, threatened by Artemis the cultural superego, must give way to Demeter the domestic mother. Griffith wants to contrast institutional reform to the family, Jenkins alone at his desk to Gish rocking the cradle. But the two shots of single figures behind single pieces of furniture, alone in empty space, echo rather than contradict each other (compare figs. 6 and 12). Both contrast to the populated, teeming, alive urban scenes. The opposition between claustrophobic, vulnerable family interior and empty, impersonal institutional space only emerges once the modern Aphrodite, the modern city, is reformed. After the prostitutes are taken away, Griffith depicts first the dear one threatened in her small room, then the empty institutional space of the orphanage. He cuts to the contrast with Belshazzar's feast, with its eating and sexual display. Other filmmakers would incorporate such scenes into the 1920s celebration of consumption. For Griffith they remained transgressive and forbidden. Cecil B. De Mille would make sexualized biblical epics for family entertainment. Birth control advocates, in a comparable domestication of the subversive, linked contraception to conjugal intimacy, not female sexual freedom. Griffith wanted to bring female sexuality, public pleasure, and the family together, but he could not do so. Griffith bade farewell in *Intolerance* to his embrace of the modern city and his flirtation with female sexuality.[61]

Griffith's failure to move forward into the culture of consumption is more instructive, nonetheless, than the accommodations that succeeded him. The alliance of women and the city retains its subversive potential in *Intolerance,* as the retribution of Belshazzar's feast, the fall of Ishtar, leaves behind only domesticity and the state. That denouement returns us to the production still of the young man between the great mother's legs, the visual with which this discussion began. What does the narrative of *Intolerance* as undercut by its images say about the fetish, the phallic mother, and Freud's narrative of female sexuality?

5.

Ishtar presides over *Intolerance* as the archaic mother attentive to her sons. The modern woman is split between lesbian and domestic; Ishtar is whole. But woman cannot be whole in male fantasy, according to Freud, because she lacks the phallus. The production still that comments on the movie gives her one. Supplying Ishtar with her phallus and baby, the picture endorses Freud's equation of the two. But Freud insisted women made that equation; *Intolerance* shows that the need for it is male. By what he shares with Freud, Griffith displaces the doctor from his privileged position as interpreter of sexual fantasies and makes him a patient, too. The production still from *Intolerance,* read as the conclusion of the movie, suggests the place of phallocentrism in establishing sexual difference.

Male gender identity, Nancy Chodorow has argued, is based on difference from the mother. The phallus is the sign of that difference; it signifies the separation of the male child from the original, maternal dual-unity and his entrance into language and culture. That separation, however, is fragile. At the same time that the penis signifies sexual difference and independence from the woman, it invokes the danger of its loss. To imagine a woman with a penis is to restore the originary unity and deny castration fear.[62]

The integrity of the separate male ego, symbolized by possession of a penis, succeeds and defends against an earlier psychic unity, that of the unseparated mother and baby. Freud, however, began not with the mother but with the penis. In analyzing fetishes as substitutes for the penis, he avoided the primary male substitution of a part for the whole, the substitution of the phallus for the union of mother and son. The fetish stands in for the phallus because the phallus is already a fetish.[63]

The original wholeness was the mother/baby symbiosis, the retrospectively imagined all-powerful dual-unity before consciousness of separation. The phallic mother restores that wholeness (Freud, sharing the male wish, had it exactly backwards) by substituting the penis for the baby. The phallus replaces the breast, in Geza Roheim's formulation, as the male identifies his own (fluid-producing) genital with the absent maternal source of pleasure. The pose before the nursing Ishtar points to the phallic mother's origins in the baby at the breast.[64] By restoring the missing penis to the mother, the son restores her connection to him.

Freud had proposed, like Griffith in *Intolerance,* to free women from sexual inhibition in order to save the conjugal family and to bind women to men. But the doctor lost faith in that enterprise as the early mother forced her way into his work. At that point, instead of analyzing the son's relations to his early mother, Freud turned to the girl's relationship to her missing penis. Insisting on sexual difference, the later Freud celebrated patriarchy. Griffith, unable to restore a credible patriarchy, exposes the mother repressed in Freud's project.[65]

Calling the mother-son bond "altogether the most perfect, the most free from ambivalence of all human relationships" in his writings on female sexuality, and attributing preoedipal conflicts to daughters and not sons, Freud voiced a male wish. Griffith displays the trouble with the early mother against which that wish defends. Freud continued, "A mother can transfer to her son the ambition which she has been obliged to suppress in herself, and she can expect from him the satisfaction of all that has been left over in her of her masculinity complex."[66] Claiming the mother wanted to make the son her extension, Freud voiced the son's wish to complete the mother by becoming her phallus. Griffith creating *Judith,* Lou Bitzer posing before Ishtar, represented that desire.

Griffith imagined, with Judith and Ishtar, different versions of the archaic mother. The early mother who is whole by acquiring a sword threatens to turn on the son. Both Freud's and Griffith's Judith placed the phallus/baby equation in the service of female revenge, woman's resistance to sexual difference. Ishtar, the mother goddess, sanctified sexual difference. The phallus turned into baby restores the mother to the son.

On the one hand, then, Ishtar is the great mother who takes care of her sons. But giving Ishtar back a phallus also reveals the failure of *Intolerance* to dissolve the early mother into the companionate family. The phallus stands for the move from identification with to desire for the woman. But in that shift there is a loss. Griffith wanted the family union—father, sexual mother, and baby—to replace the original dual-unity. The progression that began with Judith, the woman with the penis, was to end in the modern home. The failure of the family to include sexuality and empower the father left the early mother as unsublimated excess. And the sexuality she sanctioned prevented her subjects from seizing the sword in self-defense. Restoring the maternal phallus to Ishtar points to the fact that the baby cannot do that organ's work.[67]

Women, according to Freud, had to accept the "fact" of their castration. That fact is a male wish to derive female from male development, turn women into lesser men, and make motherhood their fulfillment. Turning women into castrated men, however, destabilizes the sexual difference it is intended to guarantee. The male oscillates between reassurance that woman lacks a phallus and is therefore different and inferior, and the wish that she have a penis so as not to remind him of castration. Phallocentrism, therefore, does not simply establish sexual difference; it enforces sexual hierarchy against the threat of castration, of men becoming women, of the end of the difference between women and men.

Lesbian reformers are the bearers of that threat in *Intolerance*. "What does a woman want?" Freud asked.[68] Ishtar signified what Griffith wanted women to want; the lesbian scenes are the nightmare against which Ishtar as whole mother defends. Lesbian fiction, Sandra Gilbert and Catharine Stimpson have suggested, replaces the binary structure of sexual difference with multiple, fluid relations—like those caricatured in Griffith's communities of mechanical women. Griffith makes those women masculine to claim they want to be men; what he fears (the dancing scene shows) is that they do not want men.[69]

Birth control, its opponents charged, allowed women to behave like men, for it severed sex from reproduction. Lesbianism, a more perfect form of nonreproductive sexuality, allegedly completed the phallicization of women. But the mannish lesbian, as depicted in *Intolerance* and contemporary cultural documents, defended against a still deeper fear that the object of female sexual desire was not the male at all.

In denying female sexuality, the culture that produced Freud and Griffith identified sex with the phallus. When the sexual woman returned, she brought with her in the production still that same identification.[70] Making Ishtar the woman with the penis/baby insists on her orientation to men. But the impassivity in the face and bearing of the statue undercuts the wish for the maternal look. Disowning the male need for the woman with the penis, *Intolerance* attributed that need to lesbians. But lesbian sexuality, its proponents began to argue in the progressive period, emancipated the woman from desire for the phallus. Lesbianism aimed to establish woman as genuine difference, not as a castrated man who needs penis and baby to complete her. Since the lesbian—she claimed and Griffith feared—required neither the male organ nor his child, she would make the man insignificant. The oedipal mother chooses another man, but the son who has relinquished her can become a father himself. The lesbian lives in a world absolutely closed off to the man. She chooses a love object so different from the son, that he cannot replace the object of her desire. The lesbian is the woman fatally and finally lost to the male-child.

"We should be . . . indifferent," says Luce Irigaray, naming Griffith's nightmare. Irigaray gives female indifference the three meanings it has in *Intolerance*: women no longer defined by their difference from men; women indifferent to men, leaving the mirror empty by refusing to reflect them; and women undifferentiated from one another, forming a female community.[71] The distorted, empty spaces in *Intolerance*'s expressionist scenes depict the anxiety of female indifference.

Lou Bitzer fills the empty space between Ishtar's legs. Griffith fills the empty space in the movie with urban crowds and with the intercutting of dynamic montage. But the family restoration, I have argued, failed to incorporate these alternatives to the bad mother. Lou Bitzer's position between Ishtar's legs alludes thematically to Cyrus' invasion and dismemberment of the city, formally to Griffith's moving camera and dynamic montage. Unable to locate masculine reinsertion within the family, however, Griffith failed to lay the archaic mother to rest. The progressive cultural synthesis between the companionate family, regulatory institutions, and the city-by-night flourished in the urban 1920s. *Intolerance,* conceived as the foundation of that synthesis, could not support it. The movie's disintegration exposes the warring forces — regulatory family and surveillance state, subversive city and independent woman, female sexual self-definition and lesbian identity — that modern American political culture is still trying and failing to contain.

NOTES

1. Sigmund Freud, "Medusa's Head," *Collected Papers,* ed. and trans. James Strachey, Joan Riviere, and Alix Strachey, vol. 5 (New York: Basic Books, 1959), 105. See also Michael Paul Rogin, " 'The Sword Became a Flashing Vision': D. W. Griffith's *The Birth of a Nation"* in *"Ronald Reagan," the Movie and Other Episodes in Political Demonology* (Berkeley: U of California P, 1987), 201-3.

2. Freud, "Fetishism," *Collected Papers,* vol. 5, 199. See also Neil Hertz, "Medusa's Head: Male Hysteria under Pressure," *Representations* 4 (1983): 27-54.

3. See Freud, "The Taboo of Virginity," *The Standard Edition of the Complete Psychological Works of Sigmund Freud,* ed. and trans. James Strachey, vol. 11 (London: Hogarth Press, 1953-74), 205-8. On the woman with a penis, see Geza Roheim, "Aphrodite, or the Woman with a Penis," *The Panic of the Gods and Other Essays,* ed. Werner Muensterberger (New York: Harper, 1972), 169-205; and Sandra M. Gilbert, "Costumes of the Mind: Transvestism as Metaphor in Modern Literature," *Writing and Sexual Difference,* ed. Elizabeth Abel (Chicago: U of Chicago P, 1982), 199-201. On the phallic fetish and the woman in recent Lacanian feminist film criticism, see Kaja Silverman, *The Subject of Semiotics* (New York: Oxford UP, 1983), 122-29, and *The Acoustic Mirror* (Bloomington: Indiana UP, 1988), 5-26; and Teresa de Lauretis, *Technologies of Gender: Essays on Theory, Film, and Fiction* (Bloomington: Indiana UP, 1988), 99-108.

4. See Laura Mulvey, "Visual Pleasure and Narrative Cinema," *Women and the Cinema: A Critical Anthology,* ed. Karyn Kay and Gerald Peary (New York: Dutton, 1977), 412-28; and Stephen Heath, "Difference," *Screen* 19 (1978): 51-112.

5. Freud, "Femininity," *New Introductory Lectures on Psycho-Analysis, Standard Edition,* vol. 22, 128. Freud asserts "the fact of her castration" in "Female Sexuality," *Collected Papers,* vol. 5, 257. See also "Some Psychological Consequences of the Anatomical Distinction between the Sexes," *Collected Papers,* vol. 5, 186-97; "the fact of being castrated" is on p. 191.

Griffith imagined Freud's progression from penis to baby the year he made *Judith,* in *The Battle of Elderbush Gulch.* Mae Marsh (I use the actress' name to underline the continuity of her appearances in *Gulch, Birth,* and *Intolerance*) comes to stay with the Cameron brothers, who refuse to allow her puppies to enter the house. The dogs run off; by following them into the woods, Marsh places herself in danger. Griffith borrowed this scene (and the Cameron name) for *The Birth of a Nation,* where a black rapist kills Marsh and is punished by castration. In *Gulch* Indians kill one of the puppies instead and are killed in return, precipitating an Indian attack. Marsh's refusal to give up her puppies and accept domestic confinement has placed the frontier in danger. During the Indian attack, however, she atones for her independence. A baby crawls into danger during the attack and Marsh risks her life to save it; she has replaced the puppy that took her out of the house with the baby that takes her inside. At the movie's end the Cameron brothers allow her to bring her remaining puppy in with her.

6. I am indebted to Ann Banfield for seeing the beheading as a birth, and to Michael Fried for the understanding of Gish's significance in *Judith*.

7. See Rogin, " 'The Sword Became a Flashing Vision,' " 190-223. On the patriarchal crisis and the New Woman, see Nina Auerbach, *Woman and the Demon: The Life of a Victorian Myth* (Cambridge: Harvard UP, 1982); Rosalind Coward, *Patriarchal Precedents: Sexuality and Social Relations* (London: Routledge, 1983); Carl Schorske, *Fin-de-Siècle Vienna: Politics and Culture* (New York: Knopf, 1980); Gilbert, "Costumes of the Mind," 209-17; and other sources cited in Rogin, " 'The Sword Became a Flashing Vision,' " 342-43 n.28. For a recent linking of phobias about blacks and female sexuality, using European materials contemporary with *Birth* and *Intolerance*, see Sander L. Gilman, *Difference and Pathology: Stereotypes of Sexuality, Race, and Madness* (Ithaca: Cornell UP, 1985).

8. Selwyn A. Stanhope, "The World's Master Picture Producer," *Photoplay* 7 (1915): 57.

9. See Rogin, " 'The Sword Became a Flashing Vision' "; and Lary May, *Screening out the Past: The Birth of Mass Culture and the Motion Picture Industry* (New York: Oxford UP, 1980), 19-71.

10. "Films and Births and Censorship," *Survey* 34 (3 April 1915): 4. See also David M. Kennedy, *Birth Control in America: The Career of Margaret Sanger* (New Haven: Yale UP, 1970), 32-34, 72-87; and Charles H. Parkhurst, "The Birth of a Nation," *Focus on "The Birth of a Nation,"* ed. Fred Silva (Englewood Cliffs: Prentice-Hall, 1971), 102-3.

11. See "Films and Births and Censorship," 4-5; and D. W. Griffith, *The Rise and Fall of Free Speech in America* (Los Angeles, 1916).

12. May, *Screening out the Past*, 19.

13. See Jane Gallop, *The Daughter's Seduction: Feminism and Psychoanalysis* (Ithaca: Cornell UP, 1982), 19-21. I follow Gallop, who follows Jacques Lacan in distinguishing the male organ—penis—from its function as signifier, as carrier of meaning, phallus. But since the latter refers to the former, and the former's human significance does not exist apart from symbolizations, it is not always possible to maintain the distinction in language. See Lacan, "The Signification of the Phallus," *Écrits*, trans. Alan Sheridan (New York: Norton, 1977), 281-91.

14. See Kennedy, *Birth Control in America*, 42-47.

15. On the making of *Intolerance*, see Richard Schickel, *D. W. Griffith: An American Life* (New York: Simon, 1984), 309-31.

16. Griffith, *The Rise and Fall*, 1, 5.

17. J. J. Bachofen, *Myth, Religion, and Mother Right: Selected Writings of J. J. Bachofen*, trans. Ralph Manheim, Bollingen Series, no. 84 (1861; Princeton: Princeton UP, 1967), 103. See also D. H. Lawrence, *Women in Love* (New York, 1920), 8-9; Christa Wolf, *Cassandra: A Novel and Four Essays*, trans. Jan van Heurck (New York: Farrar, 1984), 145; Sandra M. Gilbert, "Potent Griselda: 'The Ladybird' and the Great Mother," *D. H. Lawrence: A Centenary Consideration*, ed. Peter Balbert and Phillip L. Marcus (Ithaca: Cornell UP, 1985), 130-61; and the sources cited in note 7 above. Catherine Gallagher first suggested to me the bearing of Bachofen and Lawrence on *Intolerance*.

18. Kennedy, *Birth Control in America*, 52.

19. See Burton Benedict, *The Anthropology of World's Fairs: San Francisco's Panama Pacific International Exposition of 1915* (Berkeley: Scolar's Press, 1983), 13-17. I am indebted to Debora L. Silverman for this source and to Michael Meranze for the World War I images.

20. William M. Drew, *D. W. Griffith's "Intolerance": Its Genesis and Its Vision* (Jefferson, N.C.: McFarland, 1986), 52. Griffith's sources were Morris Jastrow, Jr., *The Civilization of Babylonia and Assyria: Its Remains, Language, History, Religion, Com-*

merce, Law, Art, and Literature (Philadelphia: Lippincott, 1915), and Archibald Henry Sayce, *Lectures on the Origin and Growth of Religion as Illustrated by the Religion of the Ancient Babylonians* (London: Williams and Norgate, 1888). These authors' endorsements of the movie were printed on souvenir programs. See Drew, *D. W. Griffith's "Intolerance,"* 61.

21. See Lillian Gish, *The Movies, Mr. Griffith, and Me* (Englewood Cliffs: Prentice-Hall, 1969), 170-71; and Karl Brown, *Adventures with D. W. Griffith* (New York: Da Capo Press, 1973), 169.

22. For this and the following paragraph, see Mulvey, "Melodrama in and out of the Home," *High Theory/Low Culture: Analysing Popular Television and Film,* ed. Colin MacCabe (Manchester: Manchester UP, 1986), 80-100; Thomas Laqueur, "Orgasm, Generation, and the Politics of Reproductive Biology," *The Making of the Modern Body: Sexuality and Society in the Nineteenth Century,* ed. Catherine Gallagher and Thomas Laqueur (Berkeley: U of California P, 1987), 1-41; Richard Sennett, *Families Against the City: Middle-Class Homes of Industrial Chicago, 1872-1890* (Cambridge: Harvard UP, 1970); and Barbara J. Berg, *The Remembered Gate: Origins of American Feminism: The Woman and the City 1800-1860* (New York: Oxford UP, 1978).

23. See Lewis A. Erenberg, *Steppin' Out: New York Nightlife and the Transformation of American Culture, 1890-1930* (Chicago: U of Chicago P, 1984), 5-55. See also Deborah Gorham, "The 'Maiden Tribute of Modern Babylon' Re-examined: Child Prostitution and the Idea of Childhood in Late Victorian England," *Victorian Studies* 21 (1978): 365-66.

24. See Gorham, "The 'Maiden Tribute of Modern Babylon' Re-examined," 353-54; Judith Walkowitz, "Male Vice and Feminist Virtue: Feminism and the Politics of Prostitution in Nineteenth-Century Britain," *History Workshop* 13 (1982): 83-84; and Drew, *D. W. Griffith's "Intolerance,"* 53, 61. Edwin Long's 1882 "Babylonian Marriage Market," a piece of respectable pornography depicting sexually available girls for sale, commanded the highest price of any nineteenth-century painting on the London art market. It illustrates the decadence associated with Babylon by sympathizers and enemies alike that *Intolerance* was trying to overcome. See Gilman, *Difference and Pathology,* 91-93.

25. See *The Culture of Consumption: Critical Essays in American History 1880-1980,* ed. Richard Wightman Fox and T. J. Jackson Lears (New York: Pantheon Books, 1983); Erenberg, *Steppin' Out;* Christopher Lasch, *Haven in a Heartless World: The Family Besieged* (New York: Basic Books, 1977); May, *Screening Out the Past;* Warren I. Susman, *Culture as History: The Transformation of American Society in the Twentieth Century* (New York: Pantheon Books, 1984), xix-xxx, 271-86; Robert H. Wiebe, *The Search for Order 1877-1920* (New York: Hill and Wang, 1967); and Jane Addams, *The Spirit of Youth and the City Streets* (New York: Macmillan, 1909).

26. Erenberg, *Steppin' Out,* 114. See Christina Simmons, "Companionate Marriage and the Lesbian Threat," *Frontiers* 4 (1979): 54-55.

27. See *Steppin' Out,* 123, 146-71; and Christopher P. Wilson, "The Rhetoric of Consumption: Mass-Market Magazines and the Demise of the Gentle Reader, 1880-1920," *The Culture of Consumption,* 39-64.

28. Lillian Howard, "Back to Babylon for New Fashions," *Photoplay* 11 (April 1917): 39-40.

29. Erenberg, *Steppin' Out,* 118-19; see also 129.

30. See Addams, *Twenty Years at Hull-House* (1910; New York: Macmillan, 1960), 160.

31. Erenberg, *Steppin' Out,* 114.

32. See Drew, *D. W. Griffith's "Intolerance,"* 32, 111; Zeese Papanikolas, *Buried Unsung: Louis Tikas and the Ludlow Massacre* (Salt Lake City: U of Utah P, 1982); and Graham Adams, Jr., *Age of Industrial Violence, 1910-1915: The Activities and Findings of the United States Commission on Industrial Relations* (New York: Columbia UP, 1966), 161-73.

33. See Erenberg, *Steppin' Out*, 151-53; Robert C. Toll, *Blacking Up: The Minstrel Show in Nineteenth-Century America* (New York: Oxford UP, 1974); and Rogin, " 'The Sword Became a Flashing Vision,' " 223-25.

34. See Erenberg, *Steppin' Out*, 176-202.

35. See Schickel, *D. W. Griffith*, 303, 306.

36. See Kathy Peiss, " 'Charity Girls,' and City Pleasures: Historical Notes on Working Class Sexuality, 1880-1920," *Powers of Desire: The Politics of Sexuality*, ed. Ann Snitow, Christine Stansell, and Sharon Thompson (New York: Monthly Review Press, 1983), 74-87; and Gorham, "The 'Maiden Tribute of Modern Babylon' Re-examined," 362-67.

37. See Ruth Rosen, *The Lost Sisterhood: Prostitution in America, 1900-1918* (Baltimore: Johns Hopkins UP, 1982), xv, 116; Walkowitz, "Male Vice and Feminist Virtue," 92 n.44; and Charlotte Perkins Gilman, *Women and Economics: A Study of the Economic Relations between Men and Women as a Factor in Social Evolution* (1898; New York: Harper, 1966), 97. For a recent, feminist interpretation of Ishtar, prostitution, and marriage in Babylon, see Gerda Lerner, *The Creation of Patriarchy* (New York: Oxford UP, 1986), 126-57.

38. See Adams, *Age of Industrial Violence*, 146-47.

39. See Martha Vicinus, *Independent Women: Work and Community for Single Women, 1850-1920* (Chicago: U of Chicago P, 1985), 262.

40. On the connections among the boy, the friendless one, and Judith, I have benefited from the remarks of Gregg Jay.

41. Peter Brooks, *The Melodramatic Imagination: Balzac, Henry James, Melodrama, and the Mode of Excess* (New Haven: Yale UP, 1976), 4. The melodramatic sources of silent film are indicated on pp. 47 and 79.

42. Brooks, *Melodramatic Imagination*, 14, 8.

43. Brooks, *Melodramatic Imagination*, 11-12.

44. Brooks, *Melodramatic Imagination*, 18, 28.

45. *Intolerance* thus supports the claim in recent Lacanian feminist film criticism that, in Mary Ann Doane's words, "The figure of the woman is aligned with spectacle, space, or the image, often in opposition to the linear flow of the plot. . . . The transfixing or immobilizing aspects of the spectacle constituted by the woman work against the forward pull of narrative" (Mary Ann Doane, *The Desire to Desire: The Woman's Film of the 1940s* [Bloomington: Indiana UP, 1987], 5). See also Teresa de Lauretis, *Alice Doesn't: Feminism, Semiotics, Cinema* (Bloomington: Indiana UP, 1984), 79-82, 117-20, 142-43; and Dana P. Polan, *Power and Paranoia: History, Narrative, and the American Cinema, 1940-1950* (New York: Columbia UP, 1986), 251-308. On melodrama and parallel montage, see Sergey Eisenstein, *Film Form: Essays in Film Theory*, ed. and trans. Jay Leyda (New York: Harcourt, 1949), 205, 223, 227-30, 234-37, 243-45, and 253; and Rogin, " 'The Sword Became a Flashing Vision,' " 203.

46. Griffith's dynamic montage is constructivist in its assemblage. However, as Donald Wayne pointed out to me, the images themselves are often orientalist in a way foreign to constructivist painting. Eisenstein did use orientalist images, but only to depict the old, corrupt order, not to celebrate revolution. On German expressionist distortion of images and montage's juxtaposition of them, as the two contrasting forms of antirealist cinema, see André Bazin, "The Evolution of the Language of Cinema," *What Is Cinema?*, trans. Hugh Gray, vol. 1 (Berkeley: U of California P, 1967), 23-40.

47. See Robert Sklar, *Movie-Made America: A Cultural History of American Movies* (New York: Random, 1975), 63.

48. Stephen Kern, *The Culture of Time and Space, 1880-1918* (Cambridge: Harvard UP, 1983), 153; see also 142-43.

49. Henry Adams, *The Education of Henry Adams: An Autobiography* (1918; Boston: Houghton, 1973), 288; see also 379-90, 427-35, 441-47, and 459-61. Griffith's phalanx of identical women looks like a hostile response to the "vigilance committee of women," the "colonels" depicted in Charlotte Perkins Gilman's female utopia, *Her-*

land, just as Ishtar is the counterpart to the "Great Over Mother" who presides over *Herland*'s "Altar of Motherhood." *Herland* was being serialized in Gilman's monthly magazine *The Forerunner* as Griffith worked on *Intolerance.* It is extremely unlikely that Griffith knew of *Herland;* the concurrence is evidence of shared images of female community in the progressive period, not of direct influence. See Gilman, *Herland* (1915; New York: Pantheon Books, 1979), 20, 120.

50. The reference is to the German expressionist film *Mädchen in Uniform* (1931).

51. See Simmons, "Companionate Marriage and the Lesbian Threat," 54-59; Carroll Smith-Rosenberg, *Disorderly Conduct: Visions of Gender in Victorian America* (New York: Knopf, 1986), 119-49, 176-81, 254-83; and Ann Ferguson, "Patriarchy, Sexual Identity, and the Sexual Revolution," *Feminist Theory: A Critique of Ideology,* ed. Nannerl O. Keohane et al. (Chicago: U of Chicago P, 1982), 149-58.

52. This paragraph and the next rely on the sources cited in the previous note. See also Carl Degler's introduction to Gilman, *Women and Economics,* xxvi; and Vicinus, *Independent Women,* 31-36, 207-8, 285-91. Clemence Dane's novel, *Regiment of Women* (1917), was the most famous British warning against the lesbian threat contemporary with *Intolerance.* Like *Herland* and *Intolerance,* Dane's *Regiment* characterizes female solidarity in military terms. See Vicinus, *Independent Women,* 207-8.

53. Vicinus, *Independent Women,* 31.

54. The fissures exposed by *Intolerance* foreshadow the sexual politics of the 1980s because that politics has its origins in the progressive period. The 1980s new right (plus male cultural conservatives on the political left) claim that female emancipation allied with the state is destroying the family; that was also Griffith's fear. A progressive alliance of reform women wants to use the state to support new family forms; for these women childcare centers, maternity leaves (and, in some cases, antipornography ordinances) are the child-labor laws and settlement houses of the 1980s. The new family was companionate in the progressive period; now it encompasses two heterosexual wage-earners; gay and lesbian couples; single mothers; and various forms of female community. Some radical feminists, finally, the heirs of Emma Goldman and (the pre-1920s) Margaret Sanger, endorse the domestic breakdown and sexual liberation that *Intolerance* was trying to contain.

55. See Drew, *D. W. Griffith's "Intolerance,"* 137-39, 144.

56. See Sklar, *Movie-Made America,* 63.

57. My understanding of dynamic montage has benefited from the comments of Jack Boozer. See Bazin, "The Evolution of the Language of Cinema," and "The Virtues and Limitations of Montage," *What Is Cinema?* 1:24-25, 41-52.

58. See Eisenstein, *Film Forum,* 201-3, on expressionism; 205, 223-53 on Griffith; and 241-45 for a discussion of *Intolerance.*

59. See Schickel, *D. W. Griffith,* 319-20, 327; and Rogin, " 'The Sword Became a Flashing Vision,' " 203.

60. Drew, *D. W. Griffith's "Intolerance,"* 44, 52.

61. See Kennedy, *Birth Control in America,* and Simmons, "Companionate Marriage and the Lesbian Threat," 55. As he embraced a Victorian sensibility on screen, his desire for young actresses repeated itself in his private life instead of leading to companionate stability. See Schickel, *D. W. Griffith,* 416-564, and Rogin, " 'The Sword Became a Flashing Vision,' " 207-8, 233-35.

62. See Nancy Chodorow, *The Reproduction of Mothering: Psychoanalysis and the Sociology of Gender* (Berkeley: U of California P, 1978), 104-7, and Dorothy Dinnerstein, *The Mermaid and the Minotaur* (New York: Harper, 1976).

63. See Gallop, *The Daughter's Seduction,* 22; Silverman, *The Acoustic Mirror,* 5-23; and Jessica Benjamin, "A Desire of One's Own: Psychoanalytic Feminism and Intersubjective Space," *Feminist Studies, Critical Studies,* ed. Teresa de Lauretis (Bloomington: Indiana UP, 1986), 78-101.

64. Roheim, "Aphrodite, or the Woman with a Penis," 189, 194-96.

65. See Freud, " 'Civilized' Sexual Morality and Modern Nervous Illness," *Standard*

Edition, vol. 9, 177-204; and Rogin, "On the Jewish Question," *democracy* 3 (1983): 101-14. My thinking on these matters is heavily indebted to conversations with Elizabeth Abel and to her book, *Virginia Woolf and the Fictions of Psychoanalysis* (Chicago: U of Chicago P, 1989).

66. Freud, "Femininity," *Standard Edition*, vol. 22, 133. The editor's footnote lists other instances of Freud's remarks on the mother-son bond.

67. Ishtar's descendant, Aphrodite, is born in Greek myth from the castrated genitals of Ouranous, castrated by Kronos, his son. Aphrodite is a bisexual goddess, Roheim's woman with a penis. Her Babylonian ancestry points to Griffith's Ishtar and her birth from castration to his Judith. See Roheim, "Aphrodite, or the Woman with a Penis," 169-71.

68. Freud is quoted in Ernest Jones, *The Life and Work of Sigmund Freud*, ed. and abr. Lionel Trilling and Steven Marcus (New York: Basic Books, 1961), 377.

69. See the following three essays in *Writing and Sexual Difference*: Abel, "Introduction," 5-6; Gilbert, "Costumes of the Mind," 193-220; and Catharine R. Stimpson, "Zero Degree Deviancy: The Lesbian Novel in English," 243-60.

70. See Roheim, "Aphrodite, or the Woman with a Penis," 174-76.

71. Luce Irigaray, "When Our Lips Speak Together," trans. Carolyn Burke, *Signs* 6 (1980): 71.

Choicelessness as Choice: The Conflation of Racism and Sexism

Carolyn A. Mitchell

> She is new world black and new world woman extracting choice from choiceless-ness, responding inventively to found things. Improvisational. Daring, disruptive, imaginative, modern, out-of-the-house, out-lawed, unpolicing, uncontained, and un-containable. And dangerously female.
> —Toni Morrison,
> "Unspeakable Things Unspoken"

On Saturday, October 12, 1991, the second day of the Clarence Thomas con-firmation hearing, we expected to see the witnesses who were to testify on behalf of Anita Hill, the woman who charged Thomas with sexual harassment. Instead, Clarence Thomas returned to the stand. The television cameras were angled so that he was constantly foregrounded. Virginia Thomas, his wife, sat in the background; John Danforth, the Republican Senator from Missouri, sat at her side during the entire day. This arrangement seemed innocent enough: Senator Danforth, friend and mentor to Clarence Thomas, having advised the maligned nominee to the Supreme Court, now sits in public sup-port of his beleaguered wife. The television cameras, mostly aimed at Thomas' face and upper torso, but consistently showing frames that included the Sena-tor, the wife, and Judge Thomas, also seemed innocent enough. The steadiness of the camera's gaze on this configuration was not new, given the contempo-rary format of televised Congressional hearings, yet this "tableau" was deeply disturbing.[1]

Senator Danforth and Mrs. Thomas were silent and static; Clarence Tho-mas spoke steadily in response to his interrogators, but his verbal and body language seemed frozen, confirming the stillness of the tableau. The television camera not only framed these three people but also reduced them to apparent

This essay is an extended version of the first Ida B. Wells Lecture, presented on February 7, 1992, under the auspices of the Women's Studies Program at Indiana University.

stasis in order to maintain the integrity of the arrangement. The audience rec-
ognized the participants according to its understanding of the configuration
representing husband, wife, and prominent supporter. However, the camera's
control is intrusive and belies the apparent innocence of the scene. The coer-
civeness of the camera's control of the image problematizes the "message" rendered. Susan Sontag's critical work, *On Photography,* and Teresa de Lauretis'
text, *Technologies of Gender,* are useful here, insofar as they raise critical questions about this use of the camera.

Sontag suggests that there "is an aggression implicit in every use of the camera," an observation that is even more applicable to the television camera. She
continues,

> There can be no evidence, photographic or otherwise, of an event until the event
> itself has been named and characterized. And it is never photographic evidence
> which can construct—more properly, identify—events; the contribution of photog-
> raphy always follows the naming of the event. What determines the possibility of
> being affected morally by photographs is the existence of a relevant political con-
> sciousness. Without a politics, photographs of the slaughter-bench of history will
> most likely be experienced as, simply, unreal or as a demoralizing emotional blow.[2]

Sontag's analysis provides a context for a more rigorous consideration of contemporary photography since the television camera (particularly the live mini-
cam) changes the "contribution of photography" by both creating (filming)
and "naming" the event. This dual function obstructs the development of a
"relevant political consciousness." In so doing, those in control of the television camera are capable of manipulating public knowledge of an event, and,
ultimately, shaping public opinion.[3]

A "relevant political consciousness" cannot be formed in a vacuum; one
must know something about history. Responsibility for providing historical
knowledge is the crucial issue here, since television is theoretically conceived of
and commonly perceived as a value-free medium. Therefore, what is presented
might inform (like the evening news), but is not intended to teach. Issues about
objectivity, on the one hand, and entertainment, on the other, surface once
more in a context over which a viewer has little control beyond shutting off the
TV.

What disturbed me about the choreography of Senator Danforth and of
Clarence and Virginia Thomas is that it in fact called up a page from American
history that has been unread by most of the viewers tuned in that day. In this
instance, the television camera, "acting" consciously and "objectively," recre-
ated a historical "space-off," which Teresa de Lauretis describes as

> borrowed from film theory: the space not visible in the frame but inferable from
> what the frame makes visible. In classical and commercial cinema, the space-off is,
> in fact, erased, or better, recontained and sealed into the image by the cinematic
> rules of narrativization. . . . But avant-garde cinema has shown the space-off to ex-
> ist concurrently and alongside the represented space, has made it visible by remark-
> ing its absence in the frame or in the succession of frames, and has shown it to
> include not only the camera (the point of articulation and perspective from which

the image is constructed) but also the spectator (the point where the image is received, re-constructed, and re-produced in/as subjectivity).[4]

In the "space-off," as I will use the term in my analysis, is the subliminal history to which I referred above, invoked *and* made visible by its obvious absence. The "represented space" is the deft arrangement of Clarence and Virginia Thomas and Senator Danforth. The "space-off" in this context can also be interpreted in literary terms as Toni Morrison's "unspeakable things unspoken" or, as she puts it more wryly, "the ghost in the machine."[5] Occupying the "space-off" is the convergence of African American history and American history and Anita Hill, whose glaring absence during this day of Thomas testimony cannot go unremarked.

Sontag and de Lauretis both make it clear that the camera is not an innocent conduit through which objective and neutral information is conveyed. The camera, particularly the TV camera, manipulates and shapes public opinion today in much the way that the "press, the pulpit, and the parlor"[6] shaped public opinion in the nineteenth century. However, the ubiquity of the television camera makes the shaping seem more "natural," more spontaneous, and, therefore, is more insidious. The press, the pulpit, and the parlor, however, remain the unmentioned but accepted source for what the camera reveals about "traditional" American values. This observation is the basis for my critique that the message implicit in the "space-off" vies with the represented space of the Danforth/Thomas configuration.

In order to understand the historical implications of this configuration and of Clarence Thomas' avowal that he was the victim of a "high-tech lynching," it is necessary to see the parallels between the last decades of the nineteenth and twentieth centuries. Ida B. Wells, the journalist and political activist, born a slave in Holly Springs, Mississippi, in 1862, provides the connecting link with her anti-lynching campaign which she began in 1892. On one hand, women and people of color have made tremendous progress; on the other hand, that progress is always contained by hegemonic forces that dictate the nature and extent of change. Hence, hegemony manipulates public consciousness by providing apparent elements of progress while circumscribing truly systemic change. As we all know too well, people of color and women are most often pawns in this process.

To begin with the Danforth/Thomas configuration. The scene is first of all a reinscription of patriarchal power. Danforth is the authority figure present to remind both the black man and the white woman of their place. Danforth is the symbolic father of Virginia Thomas and the symbolic master of Clarence Thomas. His presence insures the appropriate reading of Mrs. Thomas as a dutiful daughter and a proper lady and empowers Clarence Thomas to speak, invoking the historical memory that the African American man from slavery to the present has had no authority to speak on his own behalf. Danforth's relationship to Clarence Thomas is reminiscent of nineteenth-century African American slave and personal narratives which were legitimate only if a foreword by a white person validated their authenticity. Danforth's presence is a reminder that slaves had mobility only if they carried passes written by the master. He, therefore, is representative of the master class which has written a pass allowing Thomas to "journey" to the Supreme Court. Thomas has no inherent credibility; he neither could nor would be a player in this high-stakes political game if the conservatives did not have a specific agenda in nominating him.[7] I don't think it is "over-interpreting" to suggest these analogies. In fact, it is primarily by expanding the "frame" that one sees what is hidden in the "space-off." The use of "represented space" is deeply disturbing as the camera pans from the troubled and troubling image of Thomas to that of the serenely confident Danforth, who is backgrounded so that his presence visually overshadows Thomas, though as I mentioned earlier, Thomas is in the foreground, the literal position of prominence and the traditional position of power.[8]

Next to Senator Danforth is the equally troubled and troubling image of Virginia Thomas, whose position is as vexed as her husband's. I believe the cameras were positioned to play with the public's subliminal perceptions about the laws against interracial marriage. In the context of the Thomas marriage, Clarence Thomas' comment about being the victim of a "high-tech lynching" is highly charged, and race and gender are inseparable here.[9] Thomas is quoted by Ernest Allen in a special edition of *The Black Scholar* as saying:

> And if you want to track through this country in the 19th and 20th century the lynchings of black men, you will see that there is . . . a relationship with sex, and an accusation that that person cannot shake off. That is the point that I am trying to make . . . that this is a high tech lynching. I cannot shake off these accusations, because they play to the worst stereotypes we have about black men in this country.[10]

Clarence Thomas is situated as black and male; Virginia Thomas as white and female. Anita Hill's position as black and female is that which forces us to reckon with the conflation of race and gender. She is the bridge to the "space-off." Put simply, these images represent the taboos associated with miscegenation.

Allen then sums up the history contained in the charge of lynching:

> First, it served to justify the ritual murders of African American political leaders as well as other black individuals who stood up to economic exploitation and disfranchisement. Second, the "pedestaling" of the white female, in turn, resulted in her being stripped of her own self-determination, for protection by white males also implied dependency. Third, by invoking the alleged hypersexuality of African American females, it tended to cloak the very real acts of rape of black females by white males. And lastly, it served to obscure the fact that, historically speaking, so-called racial miscegenation in American society was infinitely more the result of liaisons forced upon black women by white men, than white women by black men.[11]

The erased history of African Americans described above by Allen and contained in the "space-off" is first written by Ida B. Wells in her crusade against lynching. Trudier Harris writes in the introduction to the Schomburg Library edition of Wells's *Selected Works* that she set out to show that the causes of lynching were rooted in the economic and social repression of the race, not in the emotionally charged accusations of rape that usually led to the deaths of black men. In the volatile post-Reconstruction climate of Ku Klux Klan activity and increasing Jim Crow laws, Wells [Barnett] made herself a target of threatened violence by refusing to be silent in the face of intensified lynching. . . .[12]

Ida B. Wells's crusade begins with the mob murder of "three young black businessmen, deemed too prosperous by white competitors, [who] were summarily lynched" in Memphis, Tennessee, on March 9, 1892.[13] One of the young men, Thomas Moss, had encouraged blacks to leave Memphis because of the injustices they experienced. Wells continued to encourage the exodus started by Moss before his death. Her crusade, therefore, began on an economic note which had important ramifications. Wells writes in *Crusade for Justice*, her autobiography:

> The city of Memphis has demonstrated that neither character nor standing avails the Negro if he dares to protect himself against the white man or become his rival. There is nothing we can do about the lynching now, as we are outnumbered and without arms. The white mob could help itself to ammunition without pay, but the order was rigidly enforced against the selling of guns to Negroes. There is therefore only one thing left that we can do; save our money and leave a town which will neither protect our lives and property, nor give us a fair trial in the courts, but takes us out and murders us in cold blood when accused by white persons.[14]

Black people, supported financially and morally by Wells and other African Americans, left Memphis in droves. The loss of their buying power prompted whites to appeal to Wells to stop the emigration. She refused. This incident underscores the degree to which African Americans recently freed from slavery posed an economic threat by competing with white businessmen and merchants, while paradoxically sustaining these same people financially. This incident is the beginning of Ida B. Wells's anti-lynching campaign, which became more extraordinary as Wells became increasingly more political and militant.

Overt and covert allusions to political and sexual anarchy on the part of black men are directly linked to the spurious justifications condoning lynching after Reconstruction. Ida B. Wells was quick to point out that the ploy of accusing black men of raping white women was politically motivated. She uses statistics about lynching tallied in the white press—both to document the frequency of the crime and to emphasize the times that rape is the charge. In so doing, she disproves the charges against black men by using evidence from the white press itself. Wells's findings are fascinating, as the following information from her pamphlet *Mob Rule in New Orleans* illustrates:

> Of these thousands of men and women who have been put to death without judge or jury, less than one-third of them have been even accused of criminal assault. The world at large has accepted unquestionably the statement that Negroes are lynched only for assaults upon white women. . . .
> During the past five years the record is as follows:
> Of the 171 persons lynched in 1895 only 34 were charged with this crime. In 1896, out of 131 persons who were lynched, only 34 were said to have assaulted

women. Of the 155 in 1897, only 32. In 1898, out of 127 persons lynched, 24 were charged with the alleged "usual crime." In 1899, of the 107 lynchings, 16 were said to be for crimes against women. These figures, of course, speak for themselves, and to the unprejudiced, fair-minded person it is only necessary to read and study them in order to show that the charge that the Negro is a moral outlaw is a false one, made for the purpose of injuring the Negro's good name and to create public sentiment against him.[15]

Wells continues, "Individual Negroes commit crimes the same as do white men, but that the Negro race is peculiarly given to assault upon women, is a falsehood of the deepest dye. The tables given above show that the Negro who is saucy to white men is lynched as well as the Negro who is charged with assault upon women. Less than one-sixth of the lynchings last year, 1899, were charged with rape."[16]

Ida B. Wells believed that raising the cry of black male assault on white, Southern womanhood signaled collusion between the political and economic infrastructure determined to maintain the balance of power that would be upset by giving black men the right to vote. The refiguration of African American male aspiration for political, economic, and social parity into sexual terrorism is the unspoken and unwritten agenda which still shapes the public perception of black males and accounts for the success of the Willie Horton ploy in the 1988 Republican presidential campaign. Clarence Thomas' marriage, the accusation of sexual harassment against him, his bid for the Supreme Court seat resurrect the hidden history which I maintain is concealed in the television "space-off." Thomas' comment on "high-tech lynching" is even more problematic, given the history of Ida B. Wells's crusade. His manipulative choice of terminology is distorted and dishonest, given the unfortunate history of lynching in America.

Angela Davis in *Women, Race & Class* suggests that by the turn of the twentieth century

a serious ideological marriage had linked racism and sexism in a new way. White supremacy and male supremacy, which had always had an easy courtship, openly embraced and consolidated the affair. During the first years of the twentieth century the influence of racist ideas was stronger than ever. The intellectual climate — even in progressive circles — seemed to be fatally infected with irrational notions about the superiority of the Anglo-Saxon race. This escalated promotion of racist propaganda was accompanied by a similarly accelerated promotion of ideas implying female inferiority. If people of color — at home and abroad — were portrayed as incompetent barbarians, women — white women, that is — were more rigorously depicted as mother-figures, whose fundamental raison d'etre was the nurturing of the male of the species. White women were learning that as mothers, they bore a very special responsibility in the struggle to safeguard white supremacy. After all, they were the "mothers of the race." Although the term *race* allegedly referred to the "human race," in practice — especially as the eugenics movement grew in popularity — little distinction was made between "the race" and "the Anglo-Saxon race."[17]

Clarence Thomas opened a very complex discourse in characterizing his hearing on sexual harassment as a "high-tech lynching." If rape and lynching were not inscribed together in the public mind, then we might say that Thomas was highly ironic in suggesting that he was being lynched as an "uppity nigger," meaning that he was an audacious, conservative black man, daring to seek a position on the highest court in the land. But with either interpretation, Anita Hill figures as the accuser and we cannot ignore the implication of Clarence Thomas' words that Anita Hill, totally erased from "represented space" at Saturday's hearing, "cried rape" in accusing him of sexual harassment. Just as race and sex cannot be ignored in considering Thomas' position, so they cannot be ignored in considering the positions of Anita Hill and Virginia Thomas.

Anita Hill is the victim of revisionist history in which she (not the white woman) accuses a black man of rape. Ernest Allen writes:

> the connection between the lynching of black males and racial stereotypes had to do with the alleged rape of white females, not the sexual harassment of black ones. I know of no historically recorded instance of a black man's being lynched for sexually harassing or even raping a black female.[18]

Thomas' accusation is a devious attempt to divert attention from the charge of sexual harassment and is all the more troublesome given that sexual harassment and rape are factors in a dangerous continuum. Virginia Thomas' position is a cruel reminder that she occupies the privileged place vis-à-vis Hill in the unfolding dynamics of the male/female, white/black configuration. True to history, Anita Hill is erased.

Race and sex are inextricably linked here, but to critique the "conflation of racism and sexism" is to understand that the history which I have summarized is located in the occluded area of the "space-off," where the camera insinuatingly alludes to a little-known and imperfectly understood historical dynamic existing in the "space-off" of public memory. It calls to mind the reality that the coalitions between white and black women remain vexed. The presence of Senator Danforth in the tableau discussed above implies the value of the white woman over the absent Anita Hill. Virginia Thomas is a pawn in a power struggle that instantly separates her from solidarity with women of color. Danforth is the social/psychological father-figure maintaining domestic order, "domestic" here meaning national order. Virginia Thomas is located between Danforth and Thomas; Thomas, at this point, is chosen to protect patriarchal authority against the barbarians — that is, others like himself, the *unchosen* hordes.

Henry Vance Davis, also writing in the special edition of *The Black Scholar,* subverts the intent of Thomas' controversial term, "high-tech lynching," with his own more controversial, destabilizing image of Thomas as a "high-tech overseer." He argues that whites who "seek to derail development of the pluralistic multicultural community will continue to throw a twentieth century, high-tech overseer into the breech."[19] Vance intersects Thomas' presentation of himself as a victim by covertly alluding to the fact that the overseer in slavery was often another slave, chosen expressly for his ability "to keep law and order" among his peers in oppression. He is strategically placed to control his own people, while keeping the master apprised of possible insurgency.[20]

Clarence Thomas is the "high-tech overseer" chosen to guard the corridors of power against insurgency from within and without. Virginia Thomas is the white woman who reinscribes both national and personal domesticity, using domesticity as a tool in the political service of conservative Republicans. She is both the wife of a conservative nominee for the Supreme Court position and a highly successful middle-class woman. Her presence serves to highlight her vested interests, which are also the interests of John Danforth and his cohorts. My point, however, is that Danforth's presence "vests" her, as well as Thomas.

At issue for Virginia Thomas, as a white woman, is reinterpretation of her "virtue." As Ida B. Wells put it, protection of white women's virtue was the ostensible reason given for lynching black men. Danforth's presence reminds the observer of the political agenda supported by the "protection" of white women, while also reminding us that white men objectified white women, even as they protected them. (Remember Ernest Allen's point that "the 'pedestaling' of the white female . . . resulted in her being stripped of her own self-determination, for protection by white males also implied dependency.") But more complicated is the fact that Danforth, in the context of the public hearing, also protects Virginia Thomas from being perceived as "poor white trash," since her marriage to a black man (regardless of his status) automatically de-classes her. Her virtue, as it is used in support of family values and domesticity and to civilize the barbarian (in other words, her "virtue" civilizes Thomas), is also re-encoded here to insure her upper middle-class status, as well as to endorse her husband, Clarence Thomas. John Danforth's positioning beside Virginia Thomas is about the nuanced workings of hegemony: next to him, she is simultaneously rendered powerful and powerless.

Robyn Wiegman suggests the way in which this collusion can work to the benefit of a man like Danforth in her essay on "Black Bodies/American Commodities":

> a rethinking of feminism's ideological and theoretical basis is particularly important in the early moments of the 1990s when the broad conservative retrenchment instigated by the Reagan administration and legally secured under George Bush makes it imperative that feminism confront its own complicity with dominant power structures. This is most urgent in the arena of racial relations where, as civil rights advancements of the 1960s have been steadily eroded, dominant cultural discourses can proclaim the victimization and discrimination of white men and, as restrictions on reproductive freedom are enacted, a poor female population disproportionately composed of women of color is positioned for its most devastating impact.[21]

Clarence Thomas, as a black man, is not only objectified by Danforth's presence but also separated figuratively from other blacks—especially, in this case, from Anita Hill. Thomas' lone positioning in the foreground of "represented space" is even more problematic if we now consider that the action in the "space-off" speaks to a profound psychological/ethical split between Thomas and the African American community, a split which amounts to betrayal. In turning his back on affirmative action (the twentieth-century offering of "forty acres and a mule"), Thomas positions himself as the overseer for white men claiming reverse discrimination.

Sontag's *On Photography* and de Lauretis' *Technologies of Gender* are central texts in understanding Clarence Thomas' use of the term "high-tech lynching." The innovative technologies that brought America the hearings on all the major television channels also brought the most private aspects of Thomas' life to the viewing public; his private life is now inextricably bound to the subliminal history in the "space-off." His trope certainly captured the historical indifference to truth which is implicit in lynching as instant "justice." The politics of the camera as seen in represented space and the "space-off" manipulated the public's perception of Thomas for good or ill.

And what about Anita Hill? Rosemary Bray in the *New York Times Magazine* for November 17, 1991, anticipates my thoughts about the conflation between racism and sexism. She writes in her article, "Taking Sides Against Ourselves," that Anita Hill, "caught between conflicting loyalties to race and gender . . . faced a predicament that has tormented black women for more than a century."[22] The treatment of Anita Hill by Arlen Specter and Orrin Hatch brackets the progress of black women. Anita Hill's intellectual and professional stature was accepted until she challenged the hegemonic structure with her charges of sexual harassment against Clarence Thomas. Though Hill is a loyal and conservative Republican, she in fact was the one lynched—by Thomas, Specter, and Hatch. Their treatment of Hill was the beginning of retaliations which could ultimately mean the loss of her job. For standing up to the political power structure, her segment was excised from the University of Oklahoma Law School publicity video. There is, in my opinion, a correlation between this effort to silence her and the words of Chris Wilson, New Hampshire youth coordinator for the short-lived Patrick Buchanan presidential campaign. Wilson, who was enrolled at the University of Oklahoma law school (fall semester 1991), says in *Newsweek*: "Basically, we went about the business of making Anita Hill's life a living hell."[23]

My title is a variation on the words of Toni Morrison, writing about Sula, the title character from the novel of the same name. Morrison writes,

> She is new world black and new world woman extracting choice from choicelessness, responding inventively to found things. Improvisational. Daring, disruptive, imaginative, modern, out-of-the-house, outlawed, unpolicing, uncontained, and uncontainable. And dangerously female.[24]

Anita Hill, her politics notwithstanding, is all of the above. She stands in the tradition of black women such as Harriet Jacobs, Sojourner Truth, Ida B. Wells, Rosa Parks, women who have "extracted choice from choicelessness." She is the ongoing site where race and gender merge/conflate, the place where race and gender are exploited by hegemonic interests.

Nevertheless, Hill is lauded by feminists who focus on sexual harassment as the full measure of her dilemma, making her an icon in their single-minded, reductive adulation of her. As an icon, she is embraced by liberal and conservative women who elevate gender above race, since race for them is a variable that can be used or not. Race is simply not a pressing issue for them. They have used Hill's situation (and rightly so) to politicize sexual harassment in this election year, but their fervor mutes the complexity of her situation as black *and* female. Not surprisingly, she is rejected for equally complex reasons by black and white women who remind us of the paradox of "choicelessness as choice" in the politics of either vocalizing instances of sexual harassment, or of remaining silent. Anita Hill's treatment by the senators is the embodiment of male perception which, to date, has not, without condition, accepted a woman speaking about her experiences of sexual harassment or abuse. Hill's situation is addressed by Trinh T. Minh-ha, who writes, "You who understand the dehumanization of forced removal-relocation-reeducation-redefinition, the humiliation of having to falsify your own reality, your voice—you know. And often cannot *say* it. You try and keep on trying to unsay it, for if you don't, they will not fail to fill in the blanks on your behalf, and you will be said."[25] You will be named/said whore, liar, jealous/spurned woman.

The black woman is consistently silenced, most glaringly in the hearing and in history by her utter erasure from the site of discourse. Yet, given the placing of the "space-off," she is ever present. As Clarence Thomas sat, framed with his wife and Danforth, the absent Anita Hill loomed as the confrontation between the black man and black woman forcing questions about a common black voice into the public arena. Lastly, and implicitly, Anita Hill emerges as a challenger to Virginia Thomas. The public confrontation between a black woman and a white woman is the quintessential "no-win" situation, since both are powerless, but Anita Hill more so. Race and gender are of exceptional importance here and Anita Hill is obliterated twice again, erased by Thomas and his cohorts *and* by Virginia Thomas. Anita Hill's position as black and female is doubly vexed because it represents the conflation of race and gender.

The title of this essay, though intended to speak most completely of Anita Hill's situation, paradoxically addresses the complexities of Clarence Thomas' position as he seeks what is arguably the most coveted position in America. And, "choicelessness as choice" also reflects the dilemma of a viewing public without a "relevant political consciousness"—a public which is ignorant of the camera's politics. How does the viewing public cope with the "unspeakable things unspoken" embedded in its residual memory of the proceedings televised on October 12, 1991? The issues of editing, sequencing, scheduling are all determined at a site which traps and manipulates "the spectator (the point where the image is re-constructed, and re-produced in/as subjectivity."[26] What does the spectator re-construct or re-produce "in/as subjectivity" of African American history? Thus, Clarence Thomas and Anita Hill and the viewing public are marginalized in the visual erasure of the "space-off." Only Senator John Danforth and Mrs. Virginia Thomas (however compromised and tenuous her place may be) occupy "known" history.

NOTES

1. The use of the term "tableau" here is meant to suggest a *tableau vivant*, or "living

picture," an arrangement of motionless and silent participants in the reproduction of a known work of art (especially a painting), which an audience would recognize without undue difficulty. I am thinking specifically of the "tableau vivant" in Edith Wharton's novel *The House of Mirth* (New York: Signet, 1964), 138-43, primarily because the scene foregrounds Lily Bart in exquisitely revealing drapery, while backgrounding but making perfectly obvious the issues swirling around her sexuality, sexual and social behavior, and social status. Conscious use/manipulation of the tableau to suggest a hidden agenda is the point here.

2. Susan Sontag, *On Photography* (New York: Delta, 1977), 7, 19.

3. Susan Sontag's book, though problematic, is an excellent commentary on photography and on the complex uses of the camera as the technology evolves. Sontag is prescient in her observations about the implications of photography on our lives. Her text was the first to suggest to me that use of the camera is not always innocent or benign. Therefore, the development of the docudrama with its mix of fact and fiction and the presentation of television shows like "911," "Unsolved Mysteries," and "48 Hours" came as no surprise. Such shows both create and sustain an element of paranoia in the viewing public by playing on issues of "law and order," which are foregrounded in the public's mind. The manipulation of audience is made possible by the ubiquity of the camera in the hands of producers who then control the message. In my opinion, the camera was used in this way on October 12, 1991, the second day of the Thomas-Hill hearings.

4. Teresa de Lauretis, *Technologies of Gender: Essays on Theory, Film, and Fiction* (Bloomington: Indiana UP, 1987), 26.

5. Toni Morrison, "Unspeakable Things Unspoken: The Afro-American Presence in American Literature," *Michigan Quarterly Review* 28 (1989): 1-34. The full context of the quoted phrase is this: "Another [focus] is the examination and re-interpretation of the American canon, the founding nineteenth-century works, for the 'unspeakable things unspoken'; for the ways in which the presence of Afro-Americans has shaped the choices, the language, the structure—the meaning of so much American literature. A search, in other words, for the ghost in the machine" (11). Morrison's thoughts about the ways in which the presence of Afro-Americans has shaped American literature has equal relevance to the ways in which this presence has shaped American history. The choice of Clarence Thomas to replace Justice Thurgood Marshall on the Supreme Court of the United States is a good illustration of the need to explore the "unspeakable things unspoken." It is in this context that the "space-off" and "unspeakable things unspoken" might be seen as synonymous.

6. See Angela Davis, *Women, Race & Class* (New York: Vintage, 1983), 52, n.19.

7. The conservatives clearly needed a person of color to replace Justice Thurgood Marshall; and they needed a conservative person of color. Clarence Thomas, given his position against affirmative action, etc., was the black candidate qualified to help modify and/or abolish civil rights legislation. In addition, the need to steer Thomas through the Senate hearings was determined by the drubbing the conservatives had taken in their unsuccessful attempt to appoint Robert Bork to the Supreme Court. This is the context in which I perceive Thomas being coached and endorsed by Danforth.

8. Danforth's position vis-à-vis Thomas reinforces the historical fact that a black man can be used by the white power structure to suit whatever agenda is immediately expedient. In my opinion, Thomas is used positively to advance the conservative agenda in much the same way that Willie Horton was used negatively to get George Bush elected. Preservation of political and financial power is still the crucial factor in this scenario. Using, but circumscribing, is the pattern; it is applied most visibly and consistently against the black man, who, prior to universal suffrage, was the major threat to patriarchal hegemony. According to my colleague Linda Charnes, it is not far-fetched to mention Mike Tyson in this context—especially in relation to Donald Trump's suggestion that Tyson be freed and allowed to donate millions and millions of dollars to rape victims. What is missing from Trump's "plan" is information about the financial stake

he has in Tyson's freedom and Tyson's continued presence in the ring (especially at the Taj Mahal, Trump's casino in Atlantic City). I would argue that the implementation of universal suffrage has not radically altered this fact, since the women's vote, with rare exceptions, has simply supported the status quo. Hence, the black man is still the major political threat to the patriarchal power base and his presence is manipulated to suit the need of the moment, keeping him powerless. The dilemma facing black men is when and how to play the game—and how to assess the stakes.

9. A. Leon Higginbotham, Jr., Chief Judge Emeritus, U.S. Court of Appeals for the Third Circuit, reminds Clarence Thomas of the Racial Integrity Act passed in the state of Virginia in 1924 and upheld by the Virginia Supreme Court as late as 1966. The Racial Integrity Act cites the fact that Almighty God "separated the races [because] he did not intend for [them] to mix"; thus, interracial marriages were illegal in Virginia. See Higginbotham, "An Open Letter to Justice Clarence Thomas from a Federal Judicial Colleague," *University of Pennsylvania Law Review* 140 (1991), 1005-1028.

10. Ernest Allen, Jr., "Race and Gender Stereotyping in the Thomas Confirmation Hearings," *The Black Scholar* 22 (1991-92), 13-15 (the quoted passage is on p. 14).

11. Allen, 14.

12. *Selected Works of Ida B. Wells-Barnett*, intro. Trudier Harris (New York: Oxford UP, 1991), 3.

13. Wells, *Selected Works*, 5.

14. Ida B. Wells-Barnett, *Crusade for Justice: The Autobiography of Ida B. Wells*, ed. Alfreda M. Duster (Chicago: U of Chicago P, 1970), 52.

15. Ida B. Wells-Barnett, *On Lynchings* (New York: Arno Press, 1969), 47.

16. According to a special report entitled *The Ku Klux Klan: A History of Racism and Violence*, published by Klanwatch in 1982, "It was the boredom of small-town life that led six young Confederate veterans to gather around a fireplace one December evening in 1865 and to form a social club. The place was Pulaski, Tennessee, near the Alabama border" (8). This was the beginning of the Ku Klux Klan. The novel *The Clansman* (1905) by Thomas Dixon romanticized the group. However, according to Michael Rogin, D. W. Griffith's film *The Birth of a Nation*, based on *The Clansman*, popularized the group and brought its racist ethic to the nation. See Rogin, " 'The Sword Became a Flashing Vision': D. W. Griffith's *The Birth of a Nation*," *Representations* 9 (1985), 150-95, and Thomas Dixon, *The Clansman: An Historical Romance of the Ku Klux Klan* (1905; Lexington: U of Kentucky P, 1970). Pertinent to my essay is the fact that this motion picture reveals in stark images the ability of the camera to manipulate "represented space" and "space-off." Even more important is that the film, considered a classic, traffics in the worst stereotypes about African Americans. Rogin reminds the reader that "Celebrants of *Birth*'s formal achievement, with few exceptions, either minimize the film's racialist content or separate its aesthetic power from its negrophobia" (150). The film depicts in graphic detail the beast-like black man lustfully chasing the innocent white woman, who commits suicide by jumping from a cliff. That the black man is played by a white actor in "blackface" is very important.

17. Davis, *Women, Race & Class*, 121.

18. Allen, 15.

19. Henry Vance Davis, "The High-tech Lynching and the High-tech Overseer: Thoughts from the Anita Hill/Clarence Thomas Affair," *The Black Scholar* 22 (1991-92), 27-29 (the quoted passage is on p. 29).

20. See Chapter 32, "Dark Places," *Uncle Tom's Cabin* (1852; New York: Washington Square Press, 1962), for Harriet Beecher Stowe's treatment of the "Negro overseer." One could read Stowe's words as a parable of Thomas' positioning vis-à-vis the political power structure and black people, the problematics of Stowe's own agenda notwithstanding. She writes:

> Legree had trained them [Quimbo and Sambo] in savageness and brutality as systematically as he had his bulldogs; and, by long practice in hardness and cruelty,

brought their whole nature to about the same range of capacities. It is a common remark . . . that the Negro overseer is always more tyrannical and cruel than the white one. . . . The slave is always a tyrant, if he can get a chance to be one. (353)

21. Robyn Wiegman, "Black Bodies/American Commodities," *Unspeakable Images: Ethnicity and the American Cinema,* ed. Lester D. Friedman (Urbana: U of Illinois P, 1991), 311-12.

22. Rosemary L. Bray, "Taking Sides Against Ourselves," *New York Times Magazine* (17 November 1991): 56, 94-95, 101 (the quoted passage is on p. 94). See also the little known but excellent essay, Frances Beale, "Double Jeopardy: To Be Black and Female," *The Black Woman: An Anthology,* ed. Toni Cade [Bambara] (New York: Signet, 1970), 90-100. Beale's essay is as relevant in 1992 as it was in 1970.

23. *Newsweek* (10 February 1992): 19.

24. Morrison, 25.

25. Trinh T. Minh-ha, "Difference: A Special Third World Women Issue," *Discourse* 8 (1986-87): 11-37 (the quoted passage is on p. 12).

26. de Lauretis, 26.

Contributors

EVA CHERNIAVSKY is Assistant Professor of English and Adjunct Assistant Professor of Women's Studies at Indiana University. She has published on Puritan confessional narrative, nineteenth-century sentimental fiction, and sentimentalism in postmodern science fiction. She is currently completing a book-length project, *"That Pale Mother Rising": Sentimental Discourses in Nineteenth-Century America.*

JONATHAN ELMER is Assistant Professor of English at Indiana University. He has published articles on the rhetoric of the pornography controversy, Roland Barthes, and aspects of Poe's work. He is completing a book-length manuscript titled *Poe and the Imagination of Mass Culture.*

MICHAEL T. GILMORE is Professor of English at Brandeis University. He is the author of *American Romanticism and the Marketplace* and a contributor to the forthcoming *Cambridge History of American Literature.* His essays have appeared in numerous journals and collections, including, most recently, *The Columbia History of the American Novel.*

MYRA JEHLEN teaches English at Rugers University. She is the author of *American Incarnation: The Individual, the Nation and the Continent.* Her essay in the present volume grew out of the preparation for a contribution to the first volume of the forthcoming Cambridge Literary History of the United States, *New Worlds, New Words: The Literature of Discovery and Colonization.*

JAMES H. JUSTUS, Distinguished Professor of English at Indiana University, is completing a study of the antebellum writing of the Old Southwest, from which "The Underheard Reader in the Writing of the Old Southwest" is drawn. He has published essays on Brown, Hawthorne, Poe, Melville, Chopin, Hemingway, and Faulkner and other figures of the Southern Renascence. His *The Achievement of Robert Penn Warren* received the Landry award for 1981, and his edition of Joseph G. Baldwin's *The Flush Times of Alabama and Mississippi* (LSU Press) appeared in 1987.

CHRISTOPH K. LOHMANN is Professor and Associate Chair of English at Indiana University. He teaches American literature and culture, has published essays on Hawthorne, James, and E. L. Doctorow and has served as one of the series editors of *W. D. Howells: Selected Letters* (1979-83) and *W. D. Howells: Selected Criticism* (1993).

TERENCE MARTIN is Distinguished Professor of English at Indiana University. He has held fellowships from the American Council of Learned Societies, the Guggenheim Foundation, and the Huntington Library, and has published numerous studies of nineteenth-and twentieth-century American writers, among them *The Instructed Vision, Nathaniel Hawthorne,* essays on Cooper, Poe, and Cather, and a chapter on forms of revenge in the American Romance in *The Columbia History of the American Novel.* He is an associate editor of *The Columbia Literary History of the United States* and of *American National Biography.*

CAROLYN A. MITCHELL is Associate Professor of English at Indiana University. She is writing on African American women writers and spirituality, a project which includes an essay, " 'A Laying on of Hands': Transcending the City in Ntozake Shange's *for colored girls who have considered suicide/when the rainbow is enuf* " in Susan Squire's anthology, *Women Writers and the City* and an essay, " 'I Love to Tell the Story': Biblical Revisions in *Beloved*" in the Autumn 1991 issue of *Religion &*

Literature. Her teaching interests are in twentieth-century American fiction, African American and women's literatures.

MICHAEL ROGIN is professor of political science at the University of California, Berkeley. His most recent books are *Subversive Genealogy: The Politics and Art of Herman Melville* (1983), and *"Ronald Reagan," the Movie and Other Episodes in Political Demonology* (1987). An earlier version of his essay in the present volume appeared in *Critical Inquiry* 15 (1989): 510-55.

CARY WOLFE is Assistant Professor of English at Indiana University in Bloomington. He has published on nineteenth- and twentieth-century American literature and culture and on critical theory in such journals as *diacritics*, *Cultural Critique*, and *American Literature*. His first book, *Pound and/or Emerson: The Limits of American Literary Ideology*, is forthcoming from Cambridge University Press.

CYNTHIA GRIFFIN WOLFF currently holds the Class of 1922 Chair of Humanities at the Massachusetts Institute of Technology. She has published widely on American literature, feminist criticism, and cultural studies. Her books include: *A Feast of Words: The Triumph of Edith Wharton* (Oxford, 1976), and *Emily Dickinson* (Knopf, 1986). Currently she is working on a biography of Harriet Beecher Stowe and a book on mid-nineteenth-century multicultural American narrative: *The American Renaissance Rag.*